MOVEMENT IS LIFE

MOVEMENT IS LIFE

The Autobiography of
PRUNELLA STACK

To

Best wishes

from

Prunella

COLLINS AND HARVILL PRESS
LONDON 1973

The author wishes to express her gratitude to:

G. Bell & Sons Ltd for permission to quote from *Movement is Life* by Mrs A. J. Cruickshank and Prunella Stack (London 1937);

Wm Blackwood & Sons Ltd for permission to quote from 'With a Fighter Squadron in Malta' by Squadron-Leader Lord David Douglas-Hamilton, published in *Blackwood's Magazine* in April and May 1944;

Gerald Duckworth & Co. Ltd for permission to quote from *Fire of Youth* by Eric Muspratt (London 1948);

The Bodley Head Ltd for permission to quote from John Pudney's poem 'When Bullets Prove', published in *Air Force Poetry* (London 1944);

Faber and Faber Ltd for permission to quote from Vernon Watkins's poem 'Song', published in *The Lady with the Unicorn* (London 1948);

H. E. Bates for permission to quote an extract from his poem 'Give them their life' which appeared in *Air Force Poetry* published by The Bodley Head Ltd in 1944.

ISBN 0 00 262502 4

Set in Monotype Garamond

Made and Printed in Great Britain by
William Collins Sons & Co. Ltd, Glasgow,
for Collins, St James's Place and
Harvill Press, 30A Pavilion Road,
London SW1

To my Mother

My grateful thanks to:

My son Iain, for giving me the idea of this book, and his wife Oria, for help in selecting pictures;

Denis Richards, for reading the manuscript and for providing invaluable criticism and advice;

Vicki Barter, for typing the manuscript and for her continual enthusiastic support.

Contents

Illustrations

Illustrations continued

Thanks are due to the following for the use of their
photographs: Janet Jevons at Anthony Buckley, Fayer,
Bassano, Studio Briggs, J. Campbell Harper, A.C.K.
Ware, Central Press Photos, Photo-Hausmann, Marian
Rietveld, Cape Argus, Sunday Telegraph, Oria
Douglas-Hamilton.

Foreword

I have to tell three stories: my own story, my mother's story, and the story of the movement which she founded – the Women's League of Health and Beauty.

These stories are intermingled – each affects the other – and yet they are also distinct. If I were to try to tell my own story without the other two I should be leaving out a major portion of my experience and inheritance, yet at the same time there are important areas of my life which neither the League nor my mother entered.

'Although the word is common to all, most men live as if they had each a private wisdom of their own.'

I know that deeply felt experience appears unique to the recipient, but in fact it cannot be of much interest to anyone else unless it reveals some pattern or synthesis, or depicts a way of life and thought of a particular era.

For my generation, the Second World War was a catalyst; for my mother the First World War fulfilled the same rôle. We both suffered the same loss at almost the same age; we overcame it in different ways. The League was born in her mind out of her longing to preserve peace. It was her creative answer to the pain of war. Mine was the upbringing of my two sons, and the continuation of her work. This, as I see it, is the pattern that draws together the threads of our experience, and that unites the three stories. I have tried to tell them as truly as I can, but I do not forget that one person's truth can never be the whole truth. I can only write what I have been told, or what I saw and felt, not all that happened.

CHAPTER I

Early Days and a Love Story

♣

WE lived in London, so my earliest memories are of London towards the end of the First World War.

My child's London was a city of double-decker open-air buses, of horse-drawn milk-carts, of searchlights in the parks where I played, and of muffin men who rang a bell through the streets at tea-time to sell their wares. The London squares were not yet ruined by parked cars, and no aeroplanes roared overhead. Street-lamps were lit at twilight, and in many areas of the city a quiet village life could be lived.

Zeppelin raids, however, did occur, and one day a bomb fell at the end of our street, shattering the windows of all the houses. Walking past them next day, on my ritual afternoon outing, I was amazed by their blank stare and upset by the knowledge that something was badly wrong; what, I did not know. I was curious to look into the rooms and yet disconcerted by the intimacies the broken windows exposed. The war had suddenly invaded my childish world, and extended it to a mysterious grown-up one, where disquieting things could happen which people would not explain. I remember this sense of anxious unease much more clearly than the actual danger of the moment when glass fell on the end of my bed.

Khaki figures came and went through our house. My mother and her sister Nan entertained soldiers from the Dominions, giving evening parties for them, and offering them hospitality. I and my cousin, Drella, who lived with us, and with whom I shared my childhood, were sometimes lifted from our beds and carried downstairs to be propped up on the piano where we sang 'Tipperary' and 'Pack up your Troubles' to the assembled company.

I was rewarded by the gift from two of the New Zealand soldiers of a large toy monkey. He was called 'Pritch' – an amalgam of their names – and I loved him more than any doll. He went everywhere with me, and slept in my bed at night.

The love I lavished on Pritch was a pointer to a capacity for strong emotional relationships which was to remain with me throughout my life, often bringing heartache as well as happiness. My conception of love was a purely romantic one: the union of twin souls. Only recently have I realised that space as well as intimacy is a necessary ingredient for the success of any close relationship.

Life has taught me that love must include respect for another's freedom, and this entails a measure of privacy and independence which both sides must observe. People, like trees, need space into which they can branch out if they are to achieve their fullest growth. It is an act of real love to help to provide such space, when often it would be easier to remain in the cosy security of a guarded intimacy.

However, at the age of three or four, I knew none of this. Like most small children, I wanted an immediate response to my emotional demands. This Pritch supplied, for, as I invented his reaction myself, it could be as fervent as I chose. Pritch was always there and never failed me.

My mother never failed me either, but was not always there. She had responsibilities and duties which took her away. The greatest delight was to share discoveries or experiences with her. She possessed a child's capacity to create a magic aura round commonplace things, so that everything one did with her became unique. I remember expeditions through the grimy bushes in the big garden behind our house which were metamorphosed into safaris through an African jungle. She kindled my imagination and shared with me her sense of beauty. She also had strong views and a swift Irish temper, so that often quarrels blazed between her and her sister Nan. But her personality was too out-going to nurse grievances or bear malice, and both sisters had a sense of humour which generally rescued them, and restored harmony. My mother drew people to her with her gaiety and sympathy, and was a natural centre and confidante for her family and friends.

She was the second daughter in an Irish family of two boys and four girls. Born and brought up in Ireland, she knew the Dublin of Yeats and Synge during the turn of the century. The family lived for a while in one of the tall Georgian houses in Merrion Square. My grandfather, Theodore Stack, was a doctor, until his hearing failed him, and then a dentist who founded the Royal Dental Hospital in Dublin. A man of vision and energy, he was capable of decisive action. When deafness overtook him and he could no longer practise as a doctor, he crossed the Atlantic and enrolled at the Harvard Dentistry School, where he obtained the highest degree in dentistry. In his late forties, a premature stroke reduced him to a state of paralysis. He was unable to speak for many months and had to communicate with his family by writing down his demands. With characteristic determination he refused to be defeated. Starting with grunts and indistinct utterances he gradually regained the power of speech, and, although always thereafter an invalid, resumed his place as the fountain-head of the family's ideas.

Not long ago, I visited the Royal Dental Hospital in Dublin, in order to see his portrait, which for many years hung in the board-room there. A typically Irish face gazed at me from the heavy Victorian frame: deep-set green eyes, jutting greying brows, high cheek-bones, a straight nose, ruddy cheeks, and a strong jaw with only a hint of middle-aged thickening of flesh. His hair was still dark; the portrait must have been painted at the height of his powers, just before his stroke. How much of himsel. he had bequeathed to his second daughter, I thought. My mother also possessed the same direct gaze, the same humorous mouth, and gave the same impression of vital well-being.

She inherited many of his traits, including his generosity and extravagance, and was his favourite daughter. After his stroke she was constantly at his side (living in Blackrock, a suburb of Dublin, on very little money, instead of in fashionable Merrion Square). She and 'Pappy', as she called him, would sit together looking over the sea to the far distant Mountains of Mourne, visible on a clear day, or watching for the sails of the yacht which her two brothers manœuvred in the windy waters of Dublin Bay. She would read and talk to her father for long periods, and she must have been much influenced by his views, and by his courageous outlook on life.

My grandfather's parents came respectively from the North and the South of Ireland, although both were Protestant. His father was George Hall Stack, a QC and Fellow of Trinity College, Dublin, who lived at Mullaghmore, Omagh, County Tyrone, and his mother was Mary Orpen (aunt of the painter Sir William Orpen) whose home was Artully Castle, Kenmare, County Kerry.

If my mother's decisive character came from her father, her good looks were inherited from her mother's mother, one of the six beautiful Miss Blakes of Castlegrove, County Galway. (I still possess the eighteenth-century harp which this great-grandmother played.) Like many Irish county families, the Blakes were very poor, and Nannie, my great-grandmother (after whom my mother's sister Nan was called) must have been thankful to marry my great-grandfather, Dr Edward Thompson, and to move from the decrepit splendour of Castlegrove to the cosy county town of Omagh in County Tyrone. She settled into her new home and produced a family of four boys and one girl, Charlotte, my grandmother. Her husband, Edward, was Medical Superintendent at the Omagh Infirmary for forty years, their eldest son, also Edward, following him for another forty years: eighty years' service in all by the two Edwards, father and son.

The Blakes were Protestants, so Castlegrove was burned down during the Troubles. The huge stables still exist, but the family graveyard is in a state of sad disrepair.

In spite of her life as a country doctor's wife my great-grandmother remained conscious of her inheritance. When her only daughter announced that she wanted to marry their neighbour, the doctor Theodore Stack, she objected. His family connections were not aristocratic enough, in spite of the intellect of his father, and the artistic talents of his Orpen mother. The young couple were forced to wait for several years before they could marry.

After my mother's death, I found a packet of closely-written letters which my grandmother had sent to my grandfather at this time. In them she counselled him to have patience, and a belief in God's goodness and providence. Evidently the scientifically trained young Theodore wanted more tangible evidence that all would eventually be well. It was difficult to decipher the crabbed Victorian handwriting (the lines written first horizontally, and then crossed vertically on the paper), and to understand how much those letters had meant at that time. They were moving to read, and they reinforced earlier impressions of my grandmother's faith.

Sometimes as a child I used to drive to church with her. We travelled in an outside car, where the passengers sat back to back on long seats, gazing at the sides of the road, while a small pony driven by a coachman with a whip, trotted along at a leisurely pace. During this journey we would pass several tin-roofed revivalist meeting-houses, but our goal was the Church of Ireland to which my grandmother belonged, and where we eventually ended, sitting in a shiny brown pew. During the service I remember stealing glances at my grandmother's serene face, with its milkmaid complexion ('never put anything but soap and water on my face all my life') and wondering if she knew that she must soon die, and if that was what she was praying about.

During my early childhood I spent most summer and Easter holidays with my grandmother. She was living then at Portrush in the north of Ireland. Her house was built on a headland jutting out into the wild Atlantic, and days there were filled with wind and intermittent sunshine. The wide stretches of yellow sand ended in cliffs of grey limestone, topped with close-cropped grass where sheep grazed. The pools resting in the rocks at the cliffs' base were a happy hunting-ground for children; my cousin Drella and I would return at the end of the day clasping jam-jars containing anemones, starfish and other treasures of the deep, and carrying bedraggled bunches of sea-pinks and harebells picked on the cliffs' summit and from among the grey stones.

I remember one incident very clearly. I must have been six or seven years old at the time.

I was sitting on the beach with Nelly, our nurse, surveying a complicated network of fortresses and moats which I had constructed to be filled by the incoming tide. Nelly drowsed in the afternoon sun, and over both of us sea-gulls wove their changing pattern of flight against a high blue sky. I was suddenly acutely conscious of their swiftness, strength and grace. I imagined acutely the joy and freedom of their flight. The murmur of the waves breaking and withdrawing mingled with the gulls' cries, and these voices of the beach lulled me into a dream.

Suddenly it was violently broken. The sound of a shot rang out from the sand-dunes above the beach, followed by a wild flurry of gulls' wings and raucous cries of alarm. Something white dropped out of the sky on to the beach and at the same moment I saw a group of boys emerge from the sand-dunes. One of them carried a gun.

A hot, slow anger mounted from my heart to my head, accompanied by a conviction that an outrage had been committed which must be stopped. I had no idea how to stop it, but I turned away from Nelly and started to plod slowly along the beach to where the white object lay. I bent down and picked it up. It was dead, surprisingly heavy and bereft of all beauty and freedom. I clasped it in both arms and felt its weight against my chest, and the dampness of the blood which ran over my hands. Nelly ran after me. 'What are you doing, Prunella?' she said. 'Put down that smelly bird at once! You mustn't interfere with the boys' games.' I turned from her without answering, and made for the sand-dunes. The coarse whins whipped against my bare legs and the deep soft sand engulfed my feet. The boys were silent, watching me come. The sun beat down and I was out of breath from the climb and from the weight of my burden. I held out the bird which was stiffening in my arms.

'You must not shoot the gulls,' I said.

The boys were surprised and nonplussed. They jeered, and then fell silent.

'You must not shoot the gulls,' I repeated. To me it seemed so obvious that there was nothing more to say. Suddenly my conviction disarmed the boys. They smiled and glanced at one another, half-shamefaced, half-amused. They hesitated, and then they turned away. I had won!

I felt no sense of triumph over this episode, only surprise that grown-ups considered it eccentric. The sequel to the story was that Drella and I buried the bird, and then dug it up two weeks later to see how it was getting on. We were appalled at its macabre dissolution, and the procession of white maggots which crawled purposefully over the decaying body.

My mother and her sisters went to Alexandra School in Dublin, and then to Alexandra College. Their brothers were at Trinity College, studying engineering and medicine, and the girls, too, were given training for a career. The eldest sister, Nan, was sent to Paris to study singing, and the younger girls, Charlotte and

Norah, took degrees in Mathematics and English. They were a hard-working family (my mother won the Jellicoe Memorial Latin Prize at school, after having learned Latin for only a year), and had gifts of concentration and self-discipline. But these could be thrown to the winds on occasion, in typical Irish fashion – by no one better than by my mother – and the mood of the moment indulged in. This mood might be to dream, to laugh, to love, or to quarrel. Whatever it was, it was surrendered to completely, and quite often it led to impulsive action.

At eighteen, my mother had a severe attack of rheumatic fever, and after her recovery remained at home, looking after her father. She had learned the violin, and she now practised it for hours every day, losing herself in her music, as later she would lose herself in dance and movement. With her warmth, gaiety and beauty she was a focal point for the student friends her brothers brought home from Trinity; and when she was twenty-two, the inevitable happened, and she became engaged to one of them. Her fiancé was young, impecunious, and had some time to go before he could take his medical degree, so marriage was not an im- immediate possibility. A year or so later, her chance came to study abroad and she went to London to take a course in remedial health exercises at the Conn Institute.

Mrs Josef Conn was a pioneer in physical training who believed that the scientific system of health building which she had learned from Sir Frederick McCoy, M.D., K.C.M.G., of Melbourne University, was the answer to all the 'ills that flesh is heir to'. She was dramatic as well as far-seeing. When she gave a lecture-demonstration on her methods she would produce from the bosom of her immaculate evening dress a knife, which she would brandish at the audience, saying: 'Do not allow a surgeon to subject you to this!' A woman of decision and originality, she inspired my mother, who wrote later about this training:

The more steadily I worked, the more fascinated I became, and the more astonishing the results, probably because the system was so perfectly suited to women ... Suddenly, one day, I had an awakening. If this body-training was solving for me most of my physical problems, surely *in the trained body must lie the solution for many other women as well*. Surely the trained body can supply one secret of a simple happy life, for the body trained becomes independent of outside help. It is its 'own best doctor', masseur, pharmacopoeia . . . it automatically accumulates within itself a power of resistance to disease with each disease resisted, and a glorious sense of daily well-being that colours the whole personality, and creates atmosphere in every woman's home. Thus my health sense was developed, and I was conscious of an inner feeling of freedom and power that must be experienced to be understood.

The foundations of my mother's life work had been laid. She became Mrs Conn's best pupil, and when her training was over, she was given a post on the staff of the Conn Institute.

My mother had a fund of vitality and idealism which she would have given to any work that she undertook. It was fortunate for her that the career which she chose was such a suitable vehicle for her enthusiasm. She could heal and inspire as much by her presence as by her professional skill, and had a genuine interest in the problem of each pupil. But this generosity of heart was to lead her into grave personal difficulties.

Her fiancé was now studying for his final medical degree. Alone in Dublin, he found the strain intolerable, and perhaps also he was anxious about his fiancée's charms blossoming without him in the wider environment of London. He pressed for an immediate marriage, saying he would never pass his examinations without it. My mother was absorbed in her new work; she had already met my father, though only as a distant cousin and friend; but possibly that meeting accounted for some of her reluctance to marry hurriedly. However, her fiancé pressed harder, even threatened suicide. Caught in this dilemma, her impulsive nature responded. She agreed. The couple were married hastily in London in a register office; he returned immediately to Dublin, and she continued her work.

'Why did Molly do it?' her younger sister Charlotte, said to me years later. 'She didn't love her fiancé. I suppose she thought his life would be ruined if she didn't marry him. But later she had to think of three lives being ruined: his, your father's and her own. She was always impulsive and headstrong. She knew nothing of the facts of life, as they are called to-day. They were never spoken of in our time. I remember Nan, my elder sister, asking our mother one day about them. All she replied was, "Your husband will tell you." But my sister Molly didn't find out from that husband. She signed her name in a register office, that was all. They never lived together, or set up house or anything. He went back to Dublin and she went on with her work.'

A few months later her family travelled from Dublin to Portrush for the long summer holiday, and my father and his sister came to stay.

My father, Hugh Bagot Stack, was a third cousin of my mother's. They shared a great-great-grandfather, William Stack. His son Edward married Tempe Bagot, daughter of Walter Bagot of Fontstown, and so Bagot blood, traceable to John Bagud, who came to Ireland with Strongbow in 1172, began to run in Stack veins.

My father's grandfather was George Bagot Stack, who joined the East India Company, married Elizabeth Whitehead, served as an attaché under Sir Charles Napier at the conquest of Sindh, and died in India at the age of forty-two.

His son Edward, my father's father, continued the tradition by entering the Indian Civil Service. Soon after, he married Rosalie Oldham from Adelaide, taking her with him to India. Two children were born to them, my father Hugh and his sister May. The whole family were returning to Australia for a spell of leave, when Edward was taken suddenly ill, and died at sea. This tragedy cut short what promised to be a brilliant career in the Indian Civil Service, and left his young widow alone with two small children. She re-married after a few years, and went to live in England with her new husband, Henry Luttman-Johnson, taking with her my father and his sister, who were then brought up in England with their step-father, and two step-brothers. The family led a conventional English life, living in Sussex and London; all three boys were educated at Winchester College.

I never knew my father, but my mother made him live for me. In her eyes, and those of his sister and step-brothers, he was a person of great charm – gentle, strong and brave. When he went to Ireland for his fateful summer holiday in 1909, he was a young lieutenant in the Indian Army, home on leave from his regiment, the 2nd/8th Gurkha Rifles.

How hard it is to reconstruct feelings and passions of long ago! As I write the bare facts of my mother's and father's story, their figures emerge from an Edwardian past overlaid by a patina of nostalgia, and so dated that it is now impossible to see it truly.

And yet my mother and father were people of real flesh and blood; a young man and a young woman on the threshold of life – vital, charming, gay. They fell violently and irrevocably in love. I suppose my mother, already married, tried to resist. I suppose my father foresaw his family's disapproval, if he should introduce this wild Irish girl into their conventional midst. Or perhaps they thought of nothing but each other and their own overwhelming feelings. At any rate, on the last evening of my father's visit, on a high headland over the Atlantic, while waves thundered against the cliffs and a moon rode the sky, they sealed their future with a promise to marry, come what may.

Divorce in those days – particularly in old-fashioned Ireland – was not only rare, it was scandalous. It says much for my mother's family that they supported her completely in the course of action she now proposed. Her father died shortly after the summer family holiday, so she was bereft of his advice. The only way to get a divorce was to produce evidence of adultery, and although it was customary for the man to be accused as the guilty party, even if not actually so, my mother insisted on taking all the blame herself. This uncompromising attitude wounded a number of people besides herself, but it was typical of her to demand the truth. My father, back in India with his regiment, asked his colonel for compassionate leave, came home, and together they produced the evidence. My mother's letter to her husband, enclosing the evidence, was published in the *Irish Times*, the divorce received maximum publicity, and shame and scandal descended upon my mother's and my father's families. It is almost impossible to-day to realise how disgraceful a divorce was then considered, and what courage was necessary to go through with it.

Although so personal and intimate, I have recounted this episode in my mother's life because to me it contains the seeds of much of her future development. It shows her impulsive and headstrong nature, her capacity for passionate feeling, her lack of concern with the results of her actions, her pertinacity, and her determination to live in truth and for truth rather than for convention.

My father's mother, Rosalie, was deeply upset, and made the couple promise to part for a year. This they loyally did – tragically, when you consider the shortness of their subsequent married life. At last, in 1912, they were married in London, and left together for India. They settled in the hill-station where my father's regiment was quartered, and my mother soon won all hearts. Not, however, before she had caused some misgiving in this masculine stronghold of Empire, by growing 'Votes for Women' in her flower bed.

I was born at Lansdown, in India, on the 28th of July 1914. Austria declared war on Serbia on the same day. My mother and father had eight days of combined parenthood, and then on the 5th of August his regiment was ordered into action overseas, leaving for an unknown destination. War, which was to engulf the whole world, had cut an irreparable swathe across their lives.

The moment came when the regiment must depart. My mother stood in the garden of her bungalow, shading her eyes with her hand, watching the procession pass. The officers rode at the head of their men: tough little Gurkha soldiers, mountain people of legendary courage whom she had already grown to know and love. She saw my father. He turned his horse up the hill to say goodbye to her; he had promised that their farewell should be in their own home. She watched him as he rode back to rejoin his men, and gazed until his white horse was lost to view. There was then nothing to see but the high wide sky, empty in the early morning sunshine. Slowly, as she stared, a huge arch appeared across it. It was made of wispy wreaths of cloud, like vapour trails, which formed themselves into letters. She read their message: *Riding to his death*. As gradually as they had appeared, the clouds vanished again. Once more the sky was empty, while the letters burned their message into her mind.

The Gurkha soldiers were marching to disaster. They were up against impossible odds in those early days of the war in France. Their small stature was dwarfed in the high trenches; the cold climate, with mud and incessant rain, sapped their health; their officers, wearing different uniforms from the men, were picked off by snipers, one by one. Nevertheless, they fought magnificently. The Indian Army Corps, under General Willocks, held nine miles of front line, without reserves, from mid-September to mid-November 1914. The heroism and fighting qualities of the Indian troops repeatedly threw back very strong numerically superior German attacks. My father's 2nd/8th Gurkhas were outstanding in their defence, their qualities of loyalty and courage binding them to one another and to their officers.

Years later, I experienced an instance of their devotion, when the son of my father's *subadar,* visiting London for the first time, came to see me in my London flat. He rang the doorbell early in the morning before breakfast, and when I appeared told me that he had come to pay his respects to me, the daughter of his father's well-loved Sahib: a charge laid on him by his father if ever he should visit England. Seeing my father's curved Gurkha knife hanging on the wall he said: 'Keep that always. It is a Gurkha's best possession. It will protect you.'

The regiment gone, my mother embarked for England on the first possible ship. I was two months old. The long slow dangerous voyage, unbearably hot in the Red Sea, required all her powers of endurance. The troop-ship in which she sailed was crowded; all the children on board contracted 'prickly heat' and suffered a loss of weight.

Throughout the journey anxiety for my father consumed her. The war news which filtered through the ship was scrappy and incomplete. She knew nothing of my father's posting to France, or of the Gurkhas' ordeal there. Her psychic vision remained, but her ingrained optimism and hope fought its message every day. She arrived at Plymouth after two months at sea. Cut off from news, from family, from friends, this was a very different home-coming from the one which she and my father had often imagined.

The ship berthed, and an hour or so before passengers could land, newspapers were brought on board. There was no one to protect my mother from reading the casualty lists. She turned at once to the lines of names. One stared up at her:

Stack. Edward Hugh Bagot. Lieutenant, 2nd/8th Gurkha Rifles. Killed in action, November 1st.

He died on All Saints' Day, 1914 – fighting against an overwhelming attack. Right up to the end, since the day he landed in France with his Gurkhas, he had been an inspiration to his fellow-officers and his little Gurkhas, with his twinkling eyes, his kindness, his staunchness, and his capacity to inspire and lead.

So my uncle, his step-brother, described my father's death to me in a letter years later.

Two of my mother's sisters met the ship and took my mother back to their flat in London. The family home in Ireland had broken up with their father's death and the family was scattered. The days of peace seemed like a fast-fading dream, a vanished era which was already unreal and unrepeatable. Then, my mother had fought for and won two years of married happiness. Now, nothing remained, except her memories and her child.

CHAPTER 2

Growing up

IT was the evening before my mother's first lecture-demonstration in London. I was lying in bed beside my cousin Drella watching the glow of the gas fire, before which stood a clothes-horse covered with our garments. Two small white blouses, two pairs of black shorts, and two green tunics were hanging there, carefully washed and pressed for tomorrow. Everything had been prepared, so that there was time for us 'to rest and relax and become artists', as my mother had said. She was always adamant that an artistic quality should be contained and preserved in her work, and that tiresome details necessary to achieve this should be attended to well in advance. I was excited, yet confident. I had practised her exercises ever since I could remember, and had learned dancing since I was four years old. I was only afraid that I might forget to bring something vital. It was difficult for me to remember practical details – I had no common sense, and was liable to retreat into a dream, oblivious of everything except my own imaginings. These were usually concerned with whatever book I happened to be reading, in which I became completely absorbed. The characters lived on when the pages of the book closed, and were often more real to me than the people around me.

My world was a feminine one. My mother's two sisters, Nan, the eldest and Norah, the youngest, were living with us, and her third sister, Charlotte, a school-teacher, often came for the school holidays. My cousin Drella, six months younger than I, was also part of the household.

She was the daughter of my mother's brother, whose own mother had died at her birth. Thereafter, she had come to live with us. She called my mother 'Mummy', and she and I were brought up together, and were like sisters. Drella's real name was Cinderella (she had been born on Christmas Day) and her nick-name was 'Me, too'. As the youngest she had constantly to assert her rights. In temperament, we were at opposite poles, for Drella was practical where I was dreamy, realistic where I was romantic, and much more clear-seeing about people's motives and behaviour. We quarrelled, as all children do, but by and large we were very fond of one another. Our closest friends were Peggy and Joan St Lo, sisters a few years older than ourselves, whose mother was a friend of my mother, and who attended her children's class. Together we four children learned my mother's exercises, and demonstrated her methods, becoming indoctrinated with her ideas from an early age.

When the war ended, my mother resumed her teaching of health exercises, and built up a small clientèle of private patients, mostly sent to her by doctors for remedial treatment. Apart from her genuine interest in her work, it was essential for her to supplement her very small income and inadequate Army pension. Money was a constant worry, and we were brought up to count the pence. (I remember when I first took over the housekeeping at the age of thirteen, I was given only £2 a week to cover it.) But my mother never let lack of means cramp her style. She was capable of wildly generous gestures on occasions, and as far as her work was concerned, she was determined it should always be produced to meet the highest standards. For her first London lecture-demonstration she had hired the Aeolian Hall in Wigmore Street, and secured Lord Dawson of Penn, the King's physician, to take the chair.

I was now nine years old, so my mother must have been just forty. Like Mrs Josef Conn before her, she lectured in evening dress (without, however, producing a knife from her bosom). She still possessed her radiant charm, and a figure which was an excellent advertisement for her methods, but now she wore a chiffon scarf across her throat, to hide a slight swelling there, the result of an enlarged thyroid gland which had appeared the day after my father's departure for the war. She never bothered to seek medical advice about this danger signal to her health, but ignored it except for an occasion such as this, when she must make a professional appearance.

I cannot remember much about this demonstration except the suppressed excitement beforehand – four children chattering back-stage – the applause after my mother's speech, and my own appearance in a dance called 'Caprice'. For this I took the stage alone, and experienced for the first time the thrilling contact between an audience and a performer when things go right. After my final bow, as I ran off, I heard someone say 'Isn't she sweet?' I thought and hoped they meant me, and though I was pleased at this appreciation I accepted it as a natural right. This was partly my mother's fault – she brought me up to feel myself someone special – and partly my own innate egoism. Peggy and Joan were much more talented at dancing than I, but I was always given the best parts. It says much for their natures that they were not filled with lasting resentment. To give my mother her due, I think she starred me chiefly because I was the most marketable product in her entourage – her own daughter, brought up from birth on her methods – and the most likely vehicle to secure the publicity she needed, and for which she had an unerring instinct.

This lecture-demonstration widened my mother's scope, brought her new pupils, and gave her the opportunity to write for the press. She knew how she wanted her work to develop and expand, but she was much hampered by lack of space and funds. Her sisters shared her frustration. Nan, in particular, longed to do something about it. Afterwards, she wrote of this time:

My sister Molly was essentially a visionary, and it would have been a tragedy if anything material had ever been allowed to swamp her, or cramp her style. But big ideas are hard to reconcile with a very slender purse, and sometimes it was well nigh impossible to make both ends meet . . . I felt convinced that if Molly could get a little more scope, just a tiny chink, she would push open the door to success and forge ahead with her work. If she had a studio where she could give bigger classes, instead of a much too small drawing-room in our house! . . . But how could such a place be found and paid for? All my worldly wealth consisted of a legacy of £250. Still – great schemes have been started before now with less than this . . . I put my name and my needs on the books of the nearest house-agent.

Some time later the house-agent telephoned to say he had the perfect proposition – a house with an eighty-foot drawing-room, and possibly permission to convert. The sisters leapt into a taxi, to view it. Nan wrote later:

It was a lovely room, in a regular mansion of a house, with a beautiful garden at the back. I can still see Molly's radiant expression as she looked around. 'What classes I could hold in a room like this!' 'Molly, it shall be your studio, *coûte que coûte*,' I said.

The place was heavenly, roses were blooming in our garden (it was already ours) and the sun was just setting over the trees in the estate behind. I had a triumphant feeling as I looked out of the drawing-room window and realised that at last I could do something tangible to help. I'd take the house and sign the lease, and then Molly could forge ahead. She could start her school for teachers, and thus give permanence to her work. She could educate the children, develop her schemes, expand and grow in such surroundings, and not be hampered any longer by lack of space.

£250 was a tiny sum for such a venture, and little did I realise the debt and difficulties I was in for . . .

Nan went on to describe the entry into the house:

The furniture arrived late in the afternoon and was engulfed in huge, empty spaces. Carpets looked like mats, and curtains like window-blinds in those big, lofty rooms . . . I was beginning to get cold feet, as I sat waiting for Molly in the big drawing-room. Why was she so late? I turned on the lights to cheer me up. Would she never come? Why could she not keep an appointment? Suddenly she appeared with a bottle of champagne under her arm. We were shaking with excitement. Molly looked round the room and said, 'My lovely studio, doesn't it look grand all lit up?'

Her enthusiasm was infectious. At last, at last. Here was scope; here was happiness. We sat there together in the middle of that big room . . . We drank to her schemes, to her visions of the future.

We moved into this lovely house in Holland Park when I was ten. Until then, the only garden we had known was the large communal one which stretched along the back of the terrace of houses in Maida Vale where we had lived. The garden at Holland Park was a revelation. I can still remember sitting in hot sunshine below a syringa tree in full bloom, its heady scent and velvet petals filling me with delight. There were other new shrubs to discover, and Holland Park itself – the Ilchester estate which stretched beyond our garden railings a mile or so through to Kensington High Street – to explore. This area of private park – now tamed and administered by the Greater London Council –

was then a tangle of trees, glades and grasses; it was unkempt, unexplored, and had limitless fascinations for a child's imagination. Owls lived there, and their night calls gave it an air of special mystery. Drella and I penetrated farther and farther into this unknown territory, until one day we came upon Holland House itself – a large mansion set among green glades and garden statuary. A gardener moved across the lawns, and the sight of him sent us scuttling back home to report excitedly on our latest discovery.

Nan converted the ground floor and basement of the house into a flat for us, and there we lived a comparatively country life in the midst of busy London. Below the windows of our sitting-room climbed a huge wistaria. On Sundays, the sisters used to breakfast late, and then sit with windows wide open above the delicately-scented lilac flowers, talking all morning. They both had a philosophical turn of mind, and enjoyed discussing ideas. Their outlook was original and individual – *too* individual I sometimes thought later, when I had to fit into conventional patterns for which I had not been prepared.

They chose their friends for their talents, rather than for status, or because of propinquity, and they used their own talents to the full.

As well as converting the house, and finding tenants to occupy the other floors, Nan was at this time running an exclusive dress shop in Hanover Square. Drella and I used to visit her to see her latest models, and be regaled by large portions of Fuller's walnut cake, brought in specially for us. Later, I was commandeered to model for Nan, and many an hour I spent, standing impatiently, while she pinned her latest creation round my unwilling form. As a reward, she would give me a 'Friday night spree'. This consisted of dinner at a favourite Soho restaurant, and then seats in the pit or gallery for the latest musical comedy. I soon knew all the stars and the words of all the songs. Jack Buchanan and Binnie Hale in *Sunny* were my favourites, but I also thrilled to *The Desert Song*, and sighed with Paul Robeson when he sang 'Ole Man River'. I saw myself as the star behind those footlights, and practised the songs on the ukelele during the long Sunday morning conversations.

Politics touched us comparatively little. I remember seeing queues of people walking to work during the General Strike, and

I knew the names of the cabinet ministers in the government, and their functions, because I enjoyed Strube's cartoons in the *Daily Express*. But now Eric Muspratt, a young Australian who had hobo'd round the world, and was hoping to write a book about his adventures, came into our lives. He was an ardent Communist. He became a great friend, was admitted to the Sunday morning conversations, and arguments about politics raged above the wistaria.

My mother was basically a Conservative, Nan a Liberal, but Eric insisted that the only way to right the world's wrongs was to change its economic system. Sometimes I participated in the discussions with a few jejune ideas, which were nevertheless given a hearing. Much more, I enjoyed exploring Holland Park with Eric. Then his Communist personality would be shed like a snake's skin, and he would tell me wonderful stories of his south sea island, and the wild life he had lived there. (Later he wrote a minor classic on this topic.) He taught me to eat the young green shoots of the spring leaves, and to climb trees, but I was never able to swing, monkey-fashion, from one to another as he could. I was too young to fall in love with Eric, but nevertheless I nursed some romantic feelings about this challenging figure.

He has written, about this time:

This Irish household had a wonderful happy-go-lucky spirit, and they were all dreamers, intending, like me, to reform the world in some way ... Molly said: 'I believe above all else in dancing, in movement done with the instinctive concentration of pleasure and harmonised by music ...' She was ever young, gifted with the zest of a selfless cause. Other women over forty like herself marvelled at the sheer elasticity of her, a glamorous gaiety, essence of youthfulness. She was a deadly serious zealot of her cause, but could suddenly throw off all cares with an inner abandon to simple well-being, laughing at all the world, really laughing at it, as if laughter were the only one and complete answer to all things.

Sometimes my mother held evening musical parties in her studio. On these occasions Irene Scharrer, the concert pianist and cousin of Myra Hess, who lived across the road at Holland Park, would join us; and so would Zlatko Balokovic, a Yugoslav, who was already famous on the Continent as a concert violinist. Zlatko, as far as I know, was the only man whom my mother ever thought seriously of marrying, after my father's death. She retained her love for music, and she told me later that she felt that Zlatko's music might fill the gap in her heart. But when, with typical Central European male authority, Zlatko refused to allow her to cut her hair, she cut it nevertheless, and the engagement was off. Zlatko went to America, and later married an American heiress, Joyce Borden. Sir Cyril Atkinson, then a barrister and a Conservative MP, later a High Court Judge, and his wife Kay, were two others in this circle.

As in her youth in Dublin, my mother had drawn to herself a number of close friends.

Drella and I attended Norland Place School, a day-school nearby. We both enjoyed this school, and made many friends, with whom we played hop-scotch, and French-and-English, in our respective gardens after school hours. Television was unknown, and only a few people possessed wireless sets, so we had to create our own amusements. The games mistress at Norland Place, Miss Fagge, had the indefatigable energy necessary to keep a number of lazy little girls in motion on the hockey field. I loathed organised games. I never could run fast enough, or see the ball in time, being short-sighted. Miss Fagge used to call imperative commands out of the side of her mouth. I can hear her to this day, shouting 'Chance of a lifetime, Prunella, chance of a lifetime,' if by any miracle I got the ball. Alas! I knew it was a chance I should never be able to take.

The most exotic figures at this school were the three Brooke girls, daughters of the white Rajah of Sarawak. They lived up to their early promise by making bizarre or romantic marriages.

By 1925 the way was clear for my mother to start her training school and fulfil her ambition of training teachers to pass on her methods. Peggy and Joan St Lo were now old enough to become her first students, and they were joined by eight other girls. With typical extravagance, my mother ordered sheaves of beautiful embossed writing-paper, with the heading:

Build-the-Body-Beautiful at the Bagot Stack Health School
A training in health, grace and expression.

The title sounds old-fashioned and pretentious to-day, but at the time it expressed her aim: to create beauty through the harmonious functioning of mind, body and spirit. She intended to lay the foundations of health with her remedial exercises, while her partner, Marjorie Duncombe (trained at the Ginner-Mawer School of Dance) would build on this foundation to bring out grace and expression, through Greek and National Dancing and Mime. Some elementary Ballet was also taught to establish a dance technique, and in addition the students learned Anatomy, Physiology, Ballroom Dancing and Public Speaking.

It was an ambitious programme, and my mother was understandably nervous when the shy students assembled on the first day. She had complete faith in her own methods and the results they would achieve, but she felt deeply responsible to these girls who were now committed to a two-year training for what would be their future career.

All went well on the first morning until about midday. The students were sitting in a respectful semi-circle listening to my mother's lecture when suddenly the door of the studio burst open, and in walked Nan, naked except for several rows of beads and a few ostrich feathers strategically placed! She had been designing a cabaret costume and had been so amused by the result that she longed to share it. The students tittered politely, my mother explained the apparition as best she could, and Nan beat a hasty retreat. One look at my mother's face told her that the joke had fallen flat.

In private life, my mother might be unpunctual, impulsive and unpredictable, but in her work she was punctilious. The rest of the family had to learn that here they took second place.

When I was thirteen, I left Norland Place School, and trained at my mother's Health School for three years. The first batch of students had now finished, and passed out to take up their own private teaching, or, in the case of the St Los, to work on the stage. Peggy and Joan had suddenly blossomed into glamorous grown-ups. I greatly admired them, with their nonchalant stories of life backstage, and I felt sure they would end up as stars in their own right.

Drella went to live with her father, and I made new friends among the batch of students who had come to join the second course.

Lessons in school work continued under a young graduate friend of my mother's, Maisie Marshall, who had recently come down from Oxford. I shared these lessons with another of my mother's students, a girl of sixteen. Three times a week we walked across to Kensington to Maisie's studio for our instruction. Our education had its eccentricities. Maisie believed in studying a period in depth, so we learned the history, literature and art of a particular period thoroughly, but great gaps were left about which we knew nothing at all. We hardly touched maths (which neither she nor we liked), but she taught us to draw and paint in a decorative fashion, even though we were both most unpromising material. She fired us with a love for ancient Greece, which tied in well with our Greek dance training; and then, in contrast, immersed us in the eighteenth century. I remember ploughing through Pope's 'Rape of the Lock' and understanding very little of it.

Maisie treated us more like undergraduates than schoolgirls. It was a good system in that she awakened our interest in certain directions, and this interest survived into adult life, so that we were able to explore further later on. But our minds were not yet disciplined or educated enough to take full advantage of it. Nevertheless, she gave us scope, and did not dull us with mechanical repetitive formulae. Much depended on her personality which was forthright and energetic. At that time she was designing dresses for pageants, so her studio was filled with sketches of extravagant costumes and her hands stained with gold or silver, as she painted lengths of material. We were very impressed when at the end of our lessons she would depart for a dinner-date having painted her nails gold or silver to match.

I loved my dance training, and have always been grateful to my mother for taking me away from an orthodox school and giving it to me, at that particular time in my life, although she was criticised in several quarters for doing so.

To learn a good dance technique entails considerable self-discipline. This was a conscious achievement; but in addition emotional and intuitive qualities developed subconsciously, and powers of expression had scope at an age when many girls are poured into an unbecoming mould. My mind was not forced at the expense of my body: and so, although I suffered the usual emotional upsets of adolescence, worry about a podgy figure was not one of them. Whatever creative talents I possessed were nurtured, and I was given a lasting appreciation of music and movement, balance and harmony.

My strictly academic education suffered, of course, and this worried my father's side of the family. My father's sister May had married Professor R. W. Seton-Watson, the brilliant historian and expert on Eastern Europe, one of the men who had helped to create Czechoslovakia, Rumania and Yugoslavia after the first war. He was a friend of Thomas Masaryk, and knew a number of leading Eastern European politicians and artists who frequented his house in Buckingham Gate. It was there that my mother met the violinist Zlatko Balokovic.

The Seton-Watsons owned a house in Skye, and one summer about this time, they invited me to drive up there with them, taking a leisurely week to do so, and visiting places of interest on the way. Uncle Seton related the history of each place, and peopled it with former inhabitants; thus the Cathedral at York, the Abbey at Melrose, the exquisite late Gothic church of Rosslyn, outside Edinburgh, and finally the Highlands came alive for me. The whole family were avid readers, and during the long evenings we each sat with a book reading by lamplight, in front of a peat fire. I was filled with the romance of the Highlands, became an ardent Jacobite, and wrote poems about deserted hills and mysterious lochs. The space and austerity of Skye appealed to me deeply, and imposed a scenic standard to which I have adhered ever since.

In spite of her demanding work and commitments, my mother and I remained very close. She was still an enchanting companion – spontaneous and gay – and in some unexpressed way we each felt a responsibility for the other. We each tried to make up to the other for my father's loss.

My mother used to hold 'séances', as she called them, in her bathroom, when, if I wanted to talk to her, I could walk in through the unlocked door and converse, while she lay, relaxed and contemplative, in her bath. In this way she shared with me her schemes and hopes for the future, gave me advice, or listened to my problems.

One day, while lying there, she told me about the facts of life. I suppose, as I was now thirteen, she thought it was time I knew. Drella had found out long before, and had hinted things to me at various times, but being rather vague and incurious I had never bothered to follow up her clues. Now I was appalled. Living in a very un-masculine environment it seemed terrible to me that women could not manage to have babies by themselves. Sex was not widely publicised or discussed in those days, and it was quite possible for a city child to grow up with no knowledge of it. Just then, I had posed for a series of photographs arranged by my mother and the art editor of *The Times*, who was a friend of ours. One of these photographs showed me in the position of the famous Greek statue, the 'Discobolus.' This photograph appeared in *The Times*, and thence in many other newspapers abroad. As a result, I received a considerable fan-mail from lonely men in far-flung places, some even proposing marriage. The juxtaposition of this fan-mail with my new knowledge of masculine powers added to my turmoil, and for several days I would cross to the other side of the street if I saw a man approaching! Quite soon, I forgot all about it. I mention it here only because it is in such contrast to the mores of to-day.

By sixteen, I had finished my training at the Bagot Stack Health School, and passed out with an honours diploma. I could now have started to teach, and help my mother with her work. But instead I suffered a fit of adolescent temperament.

'I have been too close to your work for too long, I know it all too well, I am tired of posing for photographs, and helping with children's classes, I want a wider environment, what I really want is a conventional mother and a spell at a conventional boarding-school, I want to be like everyone else.' Incoherent sentences poured forth, as I tried to define the indefinable. My mother had the wisdom and unselfishness to take me seriously. Although she could ill afford it, she agreed to send me for a year to the 'conventional girls' boarding-school' of my desire, and cast around to find a suitable one. Her choice fell on the Abbey, Malvern Wells, chiefly because the headmistress was interested in music, and because of the school's lovely situation, at the foot of the Malvern Hills.

In September 1930 I was dispatched there, with a large brown trunk full of hideous school clothes.

How soon I regretted my decision! Boarding-school life with its rules and regulations seemed incredibly restrictive to me. For the last three years I had moved among girls several years older than myself, and had had freedom to think and act as I liked. Now attitudes were dictated by the prevalent schoolgirl fashion, or 'the honour of the school'. Most of the other girls had been there since they were thirteen, and had formed pair-bonds which were as binding as marriages. I was the odd girl out; and if, in arrogant confidence, I overrode one of these relationships, certain that my superior attractions would be welcomed by the friend of my choice, I found myself up against an uncompromising barrier. I was plunged into a world where I knew none of the unspoken rules, and, for the first time in my life, I experienced serious loneliness. In work, I was hopelessly behind in maths, and had to be given special tuition. My erratic schooling had nevertheless left me with a good grounding in history and literature; and the school possessed a brilliant English mistress to whose lessons I looked forward all week.

On Armistice Day, an anniversary which my mother and I always shared by laying a wreath together on the Cenotaph, I walked alone through dripping rhododendrons to the school chapel, and cried into my handkerchief as I knelt in my pew.

Sundays proved to be an amalgam of piety, boredom and indigestion. They were also the only days on which we had time to ourselves. After learning the day's Collect, we were allowed to write letters or read. In the afternoon, we went for a walk, two by two in a crocodile, wearing white coats and skirts, black woollen stockings and 'boards' (straw hats, like a boy's boater) which it was forbidden to tilt to a rakish angle. Skilful girls became adept at allowing their 'boards' to blow off as they passed the boys from Malvern College, but apart from this polite exchange, there was no contact between the two establishments. We lived in a ruthlessly feminine world.

I wanted to write to my mother more often than the regulation Sunday letter, so I sometimes scribbled a page to her by torchlight in bed after lights-out. One day a half-written letter was found on my dressing-table and I was asked if I had written it during forbidden hours. In a panic I lied. It was the first outright lie I had ever told. I tried to excuse myself to myself and to my mother by saying I had done it for her sake, but I had an uneasy suspicion she would see through this defence. Back came a letter from her urging me to confess. 'That was an awful problem for you,' she wrote, 'but I think a lie is always wrong, even when your motives are unselfish, because the *truth* is the only thing worth working for in life, and if you tell a lie you will never be trusted again.' She ended, '*Never* tell a lie to anyone no matter what it involves.'

I read the letter, realised I must act at once or not at all, and three minutes later was knocking on the headmistress's door.

Miss Judson was a terrifying figure with a booming voice and a heavy tread. (Years later, I returned to the Abbey to give a lecture-demonstration, and was surprised to find, when I looked at 'the Jud's' portrait on the school wall, a face of distinction, kindness and humour.) On this occasion she understood at once, and swiftly forgave me, only making me promise not to repeat the offence. However, she could not resist relating the story on the next occasion that the school assembled, charging my repentance to a belated remembrance of 'the honour of the school'!

During my year at the Abbey I discovered two things – the English countryside, and the glories of English literature.

We were steeped in the Elizabethan poets by our brilliant English mistress. Sonorous lines began to reverberate through my mind:

> My galley, chargèd with forgetfulness,
> Through sharp seas on winter nights doth pass
> 'Tween rock and rock; and eke my foe, alas!
> That is my lord, steereth with cruelness;

Such lines fell on fertile soil. My natural love for poetry was nourished, and I learned skills of judgment and analysis. The English mistress also supervised my reading, suggesting Ibsen, Conrad, and others who widened my literary experience.

The year spent entirely in the country was a revelation. We had always visited Ireland, Scotland, or Normandy for summer holidays, but never before had I been given the opportunity to watch the procession of the seasons at close range. Probably because I was lonely and unhappy my senses were more acute than usual, and the experience was unforgettable. The autumn walks up the Malvern Hills disclosed hedgerows full of wine-dark blackberries and cloudy old-man's-beard. Trees glowed with the colours of the dying year, and later bare branches swayed in filigree against a winter sky. Scarlet berries appeared on the holly bushes, transparent Christmas roses blossomed in the shrubbery. Winter moved into spring, and the miraculous first flowers bloomed – aconites, snowdrops, crocuses, primroses. The pale sun warmed, colours became strong and bright, and the world was cradled in bird-song. Its beauty and freshness possessed me like a vivid dream. The merging of the seasons, their inevitability, and their perfection, ran like a strong tide below my conscious life. Finally, summer burst upon us with an intoxicating rush of green. We spent long afternoons out-of-doors, and were given tea at 'the Field'.

By now I was reconciled to school. I had made some friends and had been drawn into a number of activities. Above all, I knew that I would soon be leaving.

The summer term ended gloriously. I acted in the school play, I swam and dived for the school, and I won the Prize Essay (my mother, coming down to prize-giving, spent the afternoon trying to place this P. Stack who was on the list of prize-winners but could not possibly be me).

On the last day my trump card was played. I said my goodbyes, and then my trunk was loaded into a sports-car, containing a handsome young man – my cousin, Neville King, with whom I had exchanged loving letters all year, and who was also just leaving school. In front of many pairs of envious eyes, we drove away. (I had only been able to engineer this feat because he really *was* my cousin.)

The year at boarding-school had solved my doubts. A plump schoolgirl I might now be, but all misgivings about my future had disappeared. I felt completely committed to my mother's work, and longed to join her in the exciting developments which had taken place during my absence.

I pushed my 'board' on to the back of my head and slipped my hand into Neville's. We drove through the shining countryside, and I felt ready to burst with joy. I was grown-up at last, seventeen years old, and the whole world lay before me!

CHAPTER 3

The League is Born

LIFE is not worth living without romance. Romance gives it colour: a world without colour would indeed be dull, and a life without mental colour is dull, monotonous, deadly.

We can all have this colour in our lives, for romance is not always a question of outer circumstances, such as happiness between a man and woman, between a mother and her child, but may be between the artist and his art, the poet and his poetry, the dreamer and his dreams. We can all have some inner dream, and our biggest romance will be when we make that dream come true. Some dreams are so big and far-reaching, that in this life at any rate they cannot altogether come true, but the finer the dream the greater the thrill of even partial realisation.

So wrote my mother, describing her thoughts in 1930. For many years she had wished to extend her work in some way that would make it available to all the women whom she felt needed it. In her own life, she had experienced its benefits; she had had ample proof of its good effect on her students, her private patients and the children and young people she taught. But being essentially a visionary and an idealist, she longed to use whatever talents and experience she possessed for the benefit of humanity at large. This desire was linked with her sense of dedication – a sense which made her write:

As I pass the Cenotaph, and lay flowers there, my inward prayer for myself is always the same – that this Cenotaph may be not only a monument to the glory of unselfish death, but an inspiration to the glory of unselfish living.

These thoughts and feelings pulsed below the activity of her daily life, and were the driving motive of her work.

At that time she held an evening class once a week for business girls who were employed during the day in London offices or shops. These pupils interested her more than any others, because of their enthusiasm, the results achieved, and their real necessity for her work. As she came to know the girls better, she took them into her confidence, and shared with them the thoughts and aspirations which were absorbing her mind. She talked to them about the Sokol movement in Czechoslovakia – a movement which had united the youth of the nation through the medium of physical training. The Sokols (so different from the obligatory youth movements of the dictators which were to appear later in the thirties) used no force or coercion, but inspired their members with a democratic ideal and gave them the means of training themselves for it. My mother longed to achieve something similar with the women of Britain; those 'architects of the future' who she believed could have a profound effect on the well-being of a developing generation.

But how to begin? How to turn her ideas into realities? What happened is best described in her own words:

These intangible, vague dreams had to be translated into practical action . . . I set my hard-faced friend – my alarm clock – to 6.45 a.m. When it rang with that slap on the brain which sends all day and night dreams flying, I jumped out of bed, said my prayers, had a cold bath, opened my windows, stripped off my clothes, and set going on my gramophone the gayest jazz tune I could find, and I exercised around my bedroom in physical bliss but mental blankness. Suddenly, in the middle of these bodily activities, I found I was thinking – thinking hard . . . Mental inertia was going, mental alertness was coming. I opened my windows wider, I breathed deeper, I leaped higher – mentally and physically I was bathed in gladness. Laziness – mental and physical (the root of most failure) – was going – and then – and then – the BIG IDEA came. If Energy is the source of life, and if we women want – as we all do – Life, *we must have energy*. How? – a League – a League of Women who will renew their energy in themselves and for themselves day by day. A League of Women pledged (so as to keep us lazy things at it) to *Breathe*, to *Leap*, and above all, to *THINK* . . .

There floated into my mind a phrase . . . 'building-the-body-beautiful' – the title of the book that I had just begun to write. A Build-the-Body-Beautiful League?

My heart sang all day . . .

But in the middle of the night I awoke with a start from a financial nightmare. Warfare was afoot, a very subtle form of warfare. The belligerents were Rent v. Racial Health. In the dark I lay and thought anxiously. If I dropped my private school and went into the arena of life to form a huge League, how could it be financed? The source of my finances lay chiefly in my school: my daughter had to be educated – my rents had to be paid – my – my – my – I – I – I. I was already forging my own chains, putting the brake on my own endeavour.

Then my thoughts grew hazy, my anxious head cuddled down on the pillow, my dreams came back – Beauty – The Thrill of Worth-While Achievement . . . And in the night, believe me or not, as you choose – I heard a voice saying, 'Back the League'.

My mother formed a committee (which included her close friends, Sir Cyril and Lady Atkinson and Irene Scharrer) to help her translate these dreams into realities; she confided in her business girls who were already requesting her to extend her work to their friends; and in March 1930 the first League class was held under the name which was finally chosen – the Women's League of Health and Beauty. Sixteen foundation members attended, each of whom paid £1 1s. subscription, and this, together with £8 8s. which the Committee had already contributed, constituted the League's entire capital. My mother refused to seek financial backing from any outside source.

The man who pays the piper calls the tune, [she wrote] the tune that was singing in my ears I knew was not of this earth, and that tune was a necessity to me . . . it had to draw us forward by its compelling melody.

She was convinced that if the League was really needed by the women of Britain, it could pay its own way. The annual membership was fixed at 2/6, the admission badge at 2/-, and each class cost 6d. Large numbers and cheap prices were the course my mother chose, so that no one who needed her work would be precluded from having it on grounds of expense. Expert instruction was the third most important ingredient; and here my mother was fortunate, for she had a number of fully-trained teachers already available, from the ex-students of her school. A rapidly growing membership was essential, and this was achieved by a display in Hyde Park, three months after the League began, and the opening of the League's first provincial centre in Belfast six months later.

Both these events attracted many new members. I took part in each of them and shared the excitement and enthusiasm they generated. By the time I went to my boarding-school in September 1930, the League membership had grown to over a thousand.

For the next year I watched the development of the League at one remove. Peggy St Lo, who had left the stage to join my mother's staff shortly after the League's inception, was her invaluable aide, teaching classes in London, and helping to arrange a second display in Hyde Park, and the first Albert Hall display in June 1931.

My mother's time was divided into three shifts – daytime, evening and night. Daytime, when she worked in her private school (now a school for future League teachers). Evening, when she taught League classes. Night, when she planned the League's development, and the organisation for the Albert Hall display. She worked to a schedule, sometimes sitting up most of the night until the particular stint she had planned was completed. It was an exacting programme for herself and for those around her.

I had leave from school to take part in the Hyde Park and Albert Hall displays of 1931. They were thrilling experiences for me, and gave rise to much publicity, augmented by my mother's book *Building the Body Beautiful*, which had recently been published.

With these achievements behind her, and the first year of the League's life completed, my mother allowed herself a break, and when I left school in the summer of 1931, we set off for a holiday. She had recently bought a car, a rarer acquisition in those days than now. She was immensely proud of her large sedate second-hand Austin, and was determined to learn to drive it. Choosing the most distant place she could think of – the Isle of Skye, 650 miles from London – she invited my cousin Neville King to teach her to drive there, accompanied by myself and her sister Nan.

Nan had not ceased to wish to reform the world. Her present hobby-horse was what she described as 'leisurism'.

'Leisure will be the problem of the twentieth century,' she declared. 'Soon we will have so much of it we won't know what to do with it. Machines will make human workers redundant, and then what? We will all have to find out how to occupy our leisure.'

Neville and I gave scant attention to her words, poised, as

we were, on the edge of a new freedom, the discipline and drudgery of school suddenly swept away. My mother listened and replied, but at times she seemed distrait. The summer before, three months after the League began, she had undergone an operation for the removal of the enlarged thyroid gland in her neck. This had become necessary because of an alarming increase in the swelling. The specialist she consulted recommended an operation, but was disappointed to find, on carrying it out, that the thyroid gland had burst its capsule, and it was not possible to remove all the enlargement. Without the operation my mother could not have lived. Now, the specialist hoped for a complete recovery, but if the swelling returned within two years, her condition would become serious.

My mother made light of this diagnosis, and pressed on with her work as before; but sometimes she looked tired and pale in a new way, as though her ardent spirit was burning through a shell which was becoming daily more transparent.

After two days' driving, we reached the Highlands and approached Ben Nevis. We found a camping-site, lit a fire, and sat round it, while dinner steamed in a billy-can over the flames. Twilight fell. We watched shreds of coral mist weave round the flanks of the mountain, and talked softly, unwilling to disturb the silence and space of the glen.

Next morning we were up early. The weather was fine. Ben Nevis towered above the glen. We found a path which wound upwards, crossing the slopes and bastions of the mountain. After two hours, Neville and I, eager for a more adventurous ascent, discovered a gorge which ran sheer up the face and rejoined the winding path at a higher level. We started to climb in this cleft, plunging out of the sunlight into cool depths. Sheer walls of rock rose on either side, and the knee-high heather and large boulders in the gorge made the ascent strenuous and exciting. We toiled up for about an hour, and then flung ourselves down on a grassy mound beside the burn that wound its way down the gorge. We had come out into the light again, and the midday sun shone fiercely. My heart beat rapidly with the exertion of the climb, and I tingled from head to foot as I sat, drawing deep breaths of mountain air, and gazing over the glen, already far below. The silence and mystery of high places surrounded us, broken only

46

by the murmur of the little burn, whose peaty waters lapped stones burnished by its passage.

We took off our shoes and paddled our feet in the water.

'How good to be alive!' said Neville.

'Yes,' I replied, feeling there was no need to say anything more – ever. Just 'yes' to life, 'yes' to its beauty, adventure, hardship, even sorrow. 'Yes' to friendship, 'yes' to love. Life seemed at this moment a quest and adventure for which I would never lack the spirit or strength. The present moment was all I needed. To live in the present, I reflected, perhaps that was the secret of happiness? A deliverance from day-dreaming, from nostalgia, from desires for an unattainable perfection? I remembered something my mother had written to me at school:

What you need is concentration. You live either in regrets for the past, or filmy dreams of the future, but the *present* is only here for a second, not that, and then it is past, and the future quickly becomes the present and races into the past again. *The present*, brace yourself and concentrate on the present, and draw the utmost from each second.

That was easy enough to do when, as now, I was completely happy. But what if the present brought sorrow or loss?

My mother had also written:

You are lucky; but you are sure in proportion to your luck to have big duties and responsibilities ahead. I think you are always ready to rise to them, but be sure when the time comes that you do.

'Let me accept life, whatever happens,' I said to myself.

We climbed Ben Nevis, and we reached Skye, where we stayed with the Seton-Watsons. Their house, on a wooded point near the village of Kyleakin, looked out on islands rising from translucent waters, with beyond them the rounded shapes of the Red Hills and jagged silhouettes of the volcanic Cuillins. My mother loved the landscape of Skye: few trees, rugged coastline, wide stretches of heather and peat, sunlight glancing on white crofts, sudden rain sweeping across the moor, wind moving softly over tall grasses. It reminded her of the countryside of her Irish youth. With this to refresh her, and the Seton-Watsons' hospitable home to enjoy, she became rested, gathering new strength for the autumn's activities. Neville taught us both to drive; but we found to our cost on the journey south that the deserted roads of Skye were no preparation for the traffic of industrial cities. Our trip ended when my mother, with the greatest confidence and aplomb, propelled the car straight into a lamp-post in Preston, having mistaken the accelerator for the brake.

She returned to an onerous decision. The League now had two thousand members. They were bursting out of the only halls it had been possible to find, and the acquisition of large, permanent premises was essential. But the League's resources amounted to only £180. How far would that go in financing the yearly rent and expenses of a headquarters in central London?

Suitable premises had been found – the Mortimer Halls in Great Portland Street (a few minutes' walk from Oxford Circus), a building with two large halls, office accommodation, and a rent of £2,000 a year. Most people faced with such a proposition would have set about raising a large capital sum, applying to trust or educational sources, or to charitably-minded individuals who might supply the necessary funds. But my mother felt that the League had not yet sufficiently proved itself to demand assistance from outside. Its strength lay in its own members, above all in her intuitive vision which must be allowed to fulfil itself in its own way. With the help of the Atkinsons, she tried to work out the finance involved in this new venture. If all the present members of the League supported it by attending extra classes, and introducing new members, it might be possible to secure the rent. 'If!'

That almighty IF! [my mother wrote] What a short but powerful word! It represents life as it is, one vast uncertainty, full of tremendous risk. 'If' at first became a nightmare of fear to me, but I have learned now how to twist its tail. It is quite simple. When faith comes in, IF goes out. Faith in the importance of your work, your destiny, call it what you will. It seems to me now useless to work at all, unless your work, however insignificant, has this quality of faith. 'Do the thing and the power comes.' I believe it. The great difficulty is to choose the right work and be *sure*. Indecision wrecks many lives and enterprises. Decision comes from wise thinking and wisdom depends on instinctive feeling . . . Once having thought slowly and wisely, the solution will float into the mind 'instinctively'. When it does, we should act quickly while our enthusiasm is at its height, and never look back but always forward.

I thought, and at last I knew, we must take the Mortimer Halls, whether we were really financially safe or not.

It was a brave decision. My mother *hoped* the members of the League would support her by trying to increase the revenue, but the ultimate financial liability was hers alone. She signed the lease of the premises, lodging all her private resources (including her life insurance) as a guarantee against the rent, and thus jeopardising any future personal financial security for herself or for me.

In October 1931 she wrote to all League members, telling them of her action:

As our Founder (and in order not to lose these premises, a decision had to be made within two or three days) I have decided to lend the League the first quarter's rent payment as a proof of my personal faith in the ideals of our League, and the loyalty of our members to each other . . . Had I not this faith, the responsibility for one person would be too heavy, but shared by 2,000 now, and 2,000,000 potential members, it has no terrors for me.

As salaries are down, and prices cut, and the future is in some people's estimation hazardous, it is more than ever necessary for us women to stand together, and prove that all is well, business is as usual, and we fear nothing.

She signed the letter 'yours in enthusiasm'. She needed all her enthusiasm for the days that followed. After a triumphant opening, when 600 members sat on the floor because there were no chairs, my mother found herself inundated with unforeseen expenses:

Don't suppose for a moment that now I had any time to think of Racial Health or Building the Body Beautiful. O, dear no!

I was now by some extraordinary mistake a 'business woman' in West End premises, and the only thing that mattered day after day was money.

Peggy St Lo and I manned the office during the day, and taught the classes every evening. To us, the whole venture was novel and exciting. We were stimulated by the members' enthusiasm, and by the fun of occupying these large new premises, even if they were bare of furniture. I had no real conception of the financial strain involved. When I was not working, I was enjoying myself with friends of my own age, falling in and out of love, and going to parties and dances (often after teaching until 10 p.m. first), and these activities were as important to me as my work for the League.

But for my mother the League was everything. It gradually absorbed the whole of her life.

In the summer of 1932, the third Hyde Park and second Albert Hall displays were held. The performers marched down Oxford Street, wearing an 'outdoor uniform' designed by Nan, and shepherded by resigned London policemen who at that time were not apprehensive of demonstrations. These hundreds of women in their mini black velvet skirts and capes, swinging along behind a military band, were a new sight for Londoners. The attendant publicity brought many new members, and in the autumn new centres were opened in Birmingham and Glasgow, as well as around London.

Nan also designed the uniform in which the members exercised: black satin pants, and a white satin blouse. This uniform, somewhat daring in the thirties, but flattering to every shape and size, has survived to this day. The pants have become shorter with the passing of the years, recently even reaching once more the peak of high fashion: a tribute to Nan's far-sightedness, or perhaps merely an example of the lasting quality of a practical and attractive design. The same may be said of the design of the League badge: a leaping figure, taken originally from a photograph of Peggy St Lo. It was this figure, charged to the finger tips with grace and vitality, which inspired my mother to choose the League motto: 'Movement is Life'.

In 1933 the League's immediate commitments could be met from its large increase of membership, and it seemed that now my mother's constant financial anxiety would be eased. But an even greater strain awaited her.

The swelling in her neck had returned. Early in 1933 she consulted her specialist. He told her that an operation might save her life, though he could give no guarantee of permanent recovery, but that without it she could live for only six or eight months. Faced with this stunning verdict, she wrote to her sister:

I have forty people directly depending on my efforts. I believe, in some queer way, the country is depending on them too. I believe if I desert the League now, it will go under. *I cannot desert it.* Besides, I feel so completely well . . . the doctors may be wrong . . . I think we will choose the constructive way of prayer and faith and work . . . You know how I loathe operations.

My mother had always been convinced that the body was its own best doctor. She also believed in the power of prayer, and felt certain that she would be spared for however long it took to establish the League on a sound permanent basis. She had recently written:

What shall happen to our League matters more to me than life itself.

She meant these words, and she now prepared to put them into practice.

No decision of such magnitude could be reached without hours of heart-searching and anxiety. This she communicated to no one. To me, she minimised the gravity of the diagnosis, and stressed her present good health, and her certainty that it could continue. It never occurred to me to dispute her decision. I felt anxious, of course, but her radiant vitality and faith were so strong that this anxiety soon ceased to be paramount in my mind. We went together each Sunday to Holy Communion at All Souls, Langham Place, where we prayed for her health; and she now shared a great deal of her work and plans with me, preparing me (although I was not fully aware of this) to take over if necessary.

In May 1934, League members assembled from all over the country for a rally in London. It began with a service at All Souls Church, followed by a march down Oxford Street, and a performance in Hyde Park, 1,000 strong. Then came the evening's display in the Royal Albert Hall. On the second night the huge building was packed from floor to ceiling. The performers, in their black and white uniform, marched *en masse* into the arena, each contingent carrying a silver banner inscribed with the name of their town. The Irish from Belfast wore emerald green shoulder ribbons, the Scots girls entered to the skirl of pipes. The League now had 30,000 members and fifty students were in training to become League teachers.

A murmur of anticipation ran through the hall, as my mother rose to speak. She wore a long red evening dress, her slim figure vibrant with magnetic power. She spoke of the need for constructive thought and constructive action in a world torn by doubts, and fears of another war. She said (as earlier she had written):

Life has taught me many things . . . and above all a deep sense of comradeship with humanity. It was this growing sense of comradeship, I suppose, which first gave me the idea of this League . . . Because I see a goal further ahead than Health and Beauty, in the ordinary sense, and that is Peace, and further on still stands Love – Universal Love and Service. Human Health and Beauty are but the stepping-stones to that ideal . . . Health represents Peace and harmonious balance in the innermost tissues of mind and body. Beauty seems to me to represent this idea carried out by every individual, by humanity universally . . . Peace must finally come to the world by our own determination to make it come. Each individual counts, each individual can plant a weed or a flower in 'Life's garden'. It is my belief that the health training and happy social contacts which we members find in our League are going to help us in our little corner of this vast universe to grow a few humble flowers.

How far my mother had travelled since the early days of her Dublin flirtations: since the bereavement of the war, the constant struggle to make ends meet, the efforts to establish her training school, and to widen its scope. Now she operated on a national scale. The threads of her life had been drawn into an inevitable pattern, each event preparing for this triumphant moment, the apotheosis of her work. Did she think, with a flash of prophetic insight, 'Now the League is safe'? No one who saw her that evening could forget her radiance and inspiration.

Shortly afterwards she said to her sister:

I want you to remember, whatever happens to me, *the League is going on.* And I believe I may, perhaps, be able to help it more from the other side.

In July 1934, she became critically ill. She conducted her students' final examinations through a week of increasingly severe pain, located behind one eye, until finally she was forced to give in. The specialist was called. He diagnosed a second malignant growth at the top of her spine, and gave her only a few months to live.

I was given a letter, headed 'Prunella – to be opened in case of emergency', and dated '7th July, 1934'.

If this head gets worse, and I can't think clearly – stand by the teachers and the students, see that they get a square deal. *Train* the ones I have chosen until 1935 – one more year, and then you are free to do what you choose, and go where you will. The League will be safe with about 100 teachers to carry its message of Peace and co-operation to all ends of the earth . . .

We were committed to open a number of new centres that autumn. I spoke at those meetings, and then hurried back to my mother's bed-side to tell her the results, and to read to her letters of encouragement and appreciation. She could not read. From the second day of her illness she was blind. Her pain was constant, only mitigated by injections of morphia, never really relieved. She never complained, and never gave up hope.

During that crucial autumn I looked forward with longing to Christmas, when my commitments would be over and I could be constantly at her side. At last the time drew near, but with it came a crisis in my mother's illness. She fell into a coma, from which no one thought she could recover. I knelt beside her bed and prayed with all my heart for a reprieve. I knew she was near death, but I longed intensely for a few more hours of our old intimate comradeship.

On Christmas Eve, my mother miraculously regained consciousness. Holding her hand, I felt it flutter back to life, and then the familiar voice sounded, weak and far away, but rational and imbued with the old tenderness. Her arms stretched out and folded round my shoulders.

We spent all of Christmas Day together, drawing on our store of memories, re-living episodes from my childhood.

'While I was lying here,' she said, 'I saw the man you would marry. A tall Scotsman with a deep laugh.'

Her recovery seemed miraculous, but I knew that it was a reprieve which must soon end. Towards evening she spoke of her work, of the peace which must eventually come to the world when men's hearts changed, and people finally wished for understanding rather than domination.

'The League is only a tiny drop in the vast ocean,' she said. 'But it is something. I've done it all because of what your father meant to me, because of the shattering effect of war on so many millions of lives, not only my own. You will carry on this task somehow, I know. And I can be happy, darling, truly happy. We have had a marvellous life together.'

My mother died a month later on the 25th of January 1935. The horror of her body's last hours seemed entirely divorced from her spirit, which watched the struggle with compassion, already almost free. As she died, I seemed to feel vivid wings speed through the room – up and away, up into the empyrean, high, far, free. I waited, breath suspended. She had gone.

At her memorial service, held at All Souls Church, League members from all over the country brought flowers which shone in the dim light of the January afternoon. The heavy scent of white lilac permeated the church. A wreath of Flanders poppies lay across her coffin. The atmosphere was one of deep peace. Whether or not her movement would fulfil her vision, she herself had done so. 'She overcame,' I thought.

To-morrow would dawn, and the burden of life alone must be taken up, lived through, conquered. Yet, I would not be quite alone. My mother had fashioned between us a bond which could never be broken.

CHAPTER 4

Journeys and a Meeting

♣

I WAS twenty when my mother died. The responsibility which I had already borne increased a hundredfold. But I did not bear it alone. The teachers and staff whom my mother had trained now showed their loyalty and affection by working to the limit of their capabilities. Peggy and Joan St Lo, who had called her 'Mummy No. 2', and were devoted to her, were deeply shocked by her death. But the inspiration which she had given them now bore fruit. In everyone's mind the thought was paramount – 'the League must continue'. It was well established with its own impetus of growth. But there was no denying that the prime vision and guidance had gone. My mother had given all her thought, energy and talents to the League. No one could replace her.

Fortunately, during those first five years, my mother had standardised and written down her system of exercises in her book; had left us a record of her thoughts and aspirations in her pamphlet *The Romance of the League*; and, above all, had fired a spark in the hearts of everyone with whom she had worked. In spite of trials and difficulties – and there were many – those sparks were never extinguished. The spirit which she had breathed into the League never died.

It was my first experience of loss. As in most crises, the initial effect entailed a summoning up of resources. Commitments had to be carried out, responsibilities had to be faced, interviews had to be given, letters had to be answered. My active self was glad to accept this challenge, to rise to the occasion, to see to the best of my ability that my mother's work continued. The resiliency of youth helped: powers of endurance were still fresh. But beneath the constant activity was a deep void. When I was alone I knew that a precious part of my life – the dreams of childhood, the tenderness of the maternal relationship, the certainty of being first always in another's heart – had gone, and could never return.

I had been close to death. I had seen my mother transform and overcome it through her courage and faith. I knew death could be faced without terror or despair. But now I must also come to terms with life, and I must do this alone. My mother's spirit and example had given me the strength. But her loss, and the grief and loneliness it entailed, clouded my happiness for many many months.

Her faith, and my own, sustained me. I was sure that somewhere her spirit continued, and at times I felt it very close to me, particularly in the days that immediately followed her death. She was near, and yet immeasurably far; for her mysterious presence always brought with it a sense of powerful release. I experienced this most strongly at her memorial service and at the first League centre opening which I conducted after her death. She was palpably *there*. I felt I could slip my hand into her own. Gradually in the days that followed, her presence withdrew, taking with it its comfort and calm, as though the shock of death had now been weathered, and she and I must go our separate ways.

But I still found great consolation, and a sense of her closeness, in continuing her work. And I had much help from her friends. Cyril Atkinson, one of the oldest and most devoted, wrote:

. . . of very few people can it be said that the world is definitely the richer for their having lived, but when it can be said, it is all to the good to consider how much the richer and why. Molly Stack was one of the few . . .

It seems to me that it is very important to know and understand what were the qualities which gave the League birth, which nourished it and made it what it is . . .

I would put first unselfish devotion to an ideal, loyalty to a cause. There was never thought of self, always and only of the League. All great movements have been built on this fundamental quality . . . Then I would dwell upon her faith. I frankly admit she frightened me, when she signed a lease pledging her to a rent in the neighbourhood of £2,000 a year for years to come. But it never worried her – you see, she knew! I merely hoped. But she was right. She never doubted that she had something great to give. Her faith was the sap of the tree that

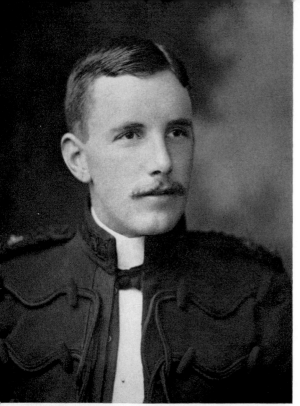

Prunella's father

Prunella with her mother

Mary Bagot Stack, founder of the League

Peggy St. Lo and Prunella lead the members into Hyde Park,
12th June, 1930

The first League Display

Prunella

has thrown out branch after branch. That is the second thing we must learn of her.

And one more thing – her courage. I always knew she was brave – ever since she saw her husband's name in the dreadful lists of 1914 – but I did not learn the half until this last year or so. I saw her smiling courage in the Albert Hall last May and it made me feel very humble.

Loyalty to an ideal; a burning faith in its warmth and beauty: a spirit of sacrifice and a courage unquenchable – these are the gifts of God that made the League and that, if held fast, will lead it to the heights of which our founder dreamed.

My mother had 'left' the League to her third sister, Aunt Norah, and myself. This legacy may have been a burden for a rather fragile woman. If it was, she never showed it. She accepted the responsibility and fulfilled it with devotion, working at the League headquarters and dealing with much of the administration and public relations.

Aunt Norah possessed my mother's determination, and her interest in people; but her life had developed on more orthodox lines. Married to a Scottish Army officer – Colonel Alec Cruickshank – she tended to equate behaviour with strictly conventional patterns. It must have been difficult for her to be thrown headlong into the turmoil of conflicting personalities and interests which the League's rapid development had produced. Difficult also, often, to deal with me; for I was always certain I knew exactly what should be done, and what my mother would have wanted. Aunt Norah achieved these tasks with tact and humour. She and her home became a welcome refuge for me during that first sad year after my mother's death. I lived alone in the flat at Holland Park, but I escaped at week-ends as often as possible to Aunt Norah's house in the country.

During 1935 the League embarked on three new ventures. In the spring the annual Rally and Display was held for the first time at Olympia, instead of the Albert Hall; and in the autumn the first centres were opened overseas, in Canada and Australia.

At Olympia, two thousand five hundred members took part: almost double the number in any previous display. We needed these numbers to fill the huge arena, used regularly to house such national events as the Royal Tournament and the Ideal Homes

Exhibition. At the first rehearsal its size seemed appalling. Items which had looked effective in smaller halls were swallowed up in vast spaces. Members, negotiating a maze of concrete corridors, got lost between the dressing-rooms and the arena. The arena itself contained dismaying evidence of previous equine occupants. Problems multiplied.

Fortunately, after several anxious weeks, the final result justified all our hopes. Performers and audience alike were thrilled; and the finale, a moving tribute to my mother, inspired everyone with the conviction that the League must, and would, survive.

In the autumn, Thea Stanley-Hughes sailed for Australia, and opened a League centre in Sydney. My mother, in recognition of her exceptional gifts, had given her permission to train her own teachers. This she proceeded to do, and her work soon spread to a number of Australian towns.

In Canada, two hundred and eighty-four members joined on the opening night. I had travelled to Toronto to start the League there, and found this response most encouraging. It proved that the League work possessed a universal appeal.

During that first year after my mother's death, my personal life was bound up almost entirely with the League. Work was demanding; and though I had many friends, and fitted in as many parties and social engagements as I could, the League always came first.

I fell in and out of love several times. I enjoyed the extra glow and excitement that being in love, or being loved, entailed. Love had always come easily to me, and I accepted it unthinkingly. Sometimes I felt remorseful if I could not return it, but this did not prevent me from encouraging it. My nature was to plunge into experience. I wanted to live life to the full, and human relationships were an important (at twenty, the most important) part of life. I dramatised my love affairs to myself, but they were not much more than romantic dreams (completely innocent by modern standards), and though I might shed tears when one ended, none had touched me profoundly. With my cousin Drella, I went to dances at the Royal Military Academy (I remember being embarrassed when I was pointed out as 'the girl who walks up

Oxford Street behind a military band'), and to the May Week Balls at Cambridge. And in the summer of 1936 I was asked to join a party for a Commemoration Ball at Oxford.

The Oxford colleges rose gently into the summer sky as I piloted my car between them, and pulled up in the square before Oriel. The late afternoon sunlight lay across old grey stone in strips of gold, while inside a silent peace pervaded the quad, with its green turf and graceful fifteenth-century walls. I walked through the entrance gate and into the courtyard. It had been a rush to get away, leaving work and responsibility behind, and I now felt slightly apprehensive about the long evening ahead with a party of people I hardly knew. I glanced up at the façade of the Great Hall, rising from its flight of steps into a majestic sweep which ended in delicate tracery silhouetted against the June sky.

A young man entered the far side of the courtyard and began to walk towards me. He was tall and moved with the easy carriage of an athlete. The sunlight glinted on his very fair hair.

'Looking for someone?' he said.

We talked, and it soon transpired that we were joining the same party. Together we climbed a narrow winding staircase and emerged into a typical Oxford undergraduate's room, full of shabby furniture, sports equipment, books and people. Soon I found myself sitting opposite the young man. His name was Alfred Albers – Ally for short – and he was to be my partner for the evening. I studied him as we talked. His face was open and pleasant, with humorous creases at the corners of his eyes. He had a ready smile, a wrinkled brow, and a manner which seemed reserved. His powerful body looked better adapted for sport and for the open air than for the conventional clothes into which it had been poured. He leaned forward as he talked to me, his elbows across his knees, and I was conscious of some quality which I could not analyse, something different from the other young men I knew.

'How long have you been here?' I asked.

'A year.'

'What are you reading?'

'Medicine.'

'And do you like Oxford?'

'I don't know yet. It's so utterly different from my own country. Takes getting used to.'

I felt a sense of disappointment and trouble behind his pleasant manner.

'Where is your country?'

'South Africa. I come from the Cape.'

I asked him about his home. He described the mountains and sea, his sports there, the beauty of the scenery. His voice, with its lilt of a faint South African accent, warmed to his topic: 'It's a wonderful climate. We live out of doors all the time. Life's free and easy. People are friendly and hospitable.'

'It sounds ideal,' I said.

'It is. "God's Own Country".' He pronounced the banal phrase with such conviction that I laughed. He looked disconcerted. I realised he had meant what he said.

For the ball, a large marquee was erected in the college grounds, where the guests danced. Outside, braziers burned on the wide lawns, attracting groups whose chatter was lost in the night sky. In the early hours some couples, we among them, drifted down to the river, found punts, and began to glide over the smooth dark water. Ally piloted our craft. I listened to the soft plunge of his pole, the onward rush of the boat, the tinkle of the drops which fell from the pole back into the river. I wondered if this excursion would end in the usual way, by hand-holding, kissing, and the deepening of a romantic attachment. Last time I had ventured on the river with a young man at a Commemoration Ball he had snored away the hour. What should happen this time?

Ally tethered the boat some way up the river, and came to sit opposite me. A companionable silence fell between us. He broke it by beginning to talk about philosophy. It was a subject which interested us both. I realised that Ally's nature was thoughtful, looking below the surface of life, and beyond superficialities. He also valued detachment. The conversation moved to the place of tradition, and its strong influence on Oxford life.

'It's very different in South Africa,' he said. 'We have so few years of tradition. We're making a country, and I suppose making ourselves at the same time, although we don't think much about that. It's a frontier mentality, always pushing on and ahead.'

'Life must seem very slow and frustrating to you here.'

'It's certainly frustrating. Not slow necessarily. But there's so *much*, a wealth of opportunities in Europe and here at Oxford. One doesn't know where to start exploring them.'

'And we take them all for granted?'

He laughed. 'Yes, you do. Unquestionably, as your birthright. And you look rather askance at people who show too much enthusiasm or curiosity.'

'It's our desire for privacy. Don't forget how many people are living here, crammed into this little island. Not many of your wide open spaces.'

'Too few. And too many set patterns of behaviour. Can be claustrophobic at times.'

I sensed the difficulty of adjustment under his light tone. I, too, had often felt restricted by conventions, but I had an ambivalent attitude towards them. I valued the security they gave, but chafed at their restraint. Evidently the convention of love-making on the river was not going to be fulfilled to-night! We talked a little longer, then Ally smiled his quizzical smile and picked up the punt pole.

The ball continued until the early hours, and ended with a mass photograph of now somewhat dishevelled participants at 6 a.m. The sun was ablaze, and the sounds and scents of early June made it unthinkable to go to bed. We drove, with some others, to an inn on the river just outside Oxford; then break-fasted, swam, and sunbathed. An intense *joie de vivre* seized us all. Nothing seemed impossible that morning. It was a long time since I had felt so happy.

Only after Ally had driven me back to London, and we had parted, did it occur to me that this happiness might have generated from the tall young man from South Africa with the amused green eyes.

Up to this point the League had developed within a charmed closed circle. My mother, like most pioneers, sought to set the pace rather than to study what already existed. Although she was aware of the work of the Sokols in Czechoslovakia, neither she nor I knew much of other European systems of physical education. The Thirties were a time of great expansion in this field, not only in the dictatorships, where physical training was often used as a means towards a militant end, but also in the Scandinavian countries, particularly Sweden. No movement quite like the League, involving such numbers of women, and run on a self-supporting basis, existed anywhere else at that time, but there was much of interest to see on the Continent, particularly in Germany. So in the autumn of 1936 it was decided that I should take two months off, and set out on an exploratory tour of several European countries, viewing the different systems of physical education, and informing myself about current developments.

I started in Munich, chiefly because a German girl who was training as a student at the Bagot Stack Health School lived there, and had invited me for Christmas. I arrived to find this city gay with Christmas decorations. Along the wide boulevards illuminated trees sparkled in many windows, while the shops displayed tempting goods. Hitler had come to power three years ago, and Germany was geared to the Nazi tempo, with a surface of spectacular expansion and success. I had no means of knowing what lay beneath this façade. Vicki, my German friend, set herself out to entertain me, and I met many of her young friends, but politics, as a subject, was taboo. It was very easy to accept conditions at their face value. Encouraged by German *Gemütlichkeit*, warmth and hospitality, I fell into this trap.

After Christmas, I was joined by Ally. His father was German and his mother South African, but her father had gone to university in Freibourg. Ally would probably have followed his example if he had not won a Rhodes scholarship to Oxford. So he felt that he had close ties with Germany, and wanted to explore it.

We allowed ourselves a few days' skiing at Garmisch, before setting out on our respective tours. It was a time of discovery for me: discovery of Germany, of the thrills of skiing, and of Ally. I found his companionship most enjoyable, but also somewhat disconcerting. He had a particular brand of light-hearted humour which prevented me from taking myself too seriously, something I was all too inclined to do. He also possessed a quality of detachment, which seemed impervious to my charms. This challenged me. Brought up as a health and beauty goddess, I was not used to lack of homage.

We stood one evening outside the ski-hut, gazing at the lights twinkling in the valley far below, and discussing our own place in the universe.

'Of course,' said I, 'people count. It *matters* what each of us does. We're not just insignificant little ants crawling about under unfeeling stars.'

Ally smiled. 'It's easy to see that you haven't had a scientific education,' he said. 'Try saying that to someone who demands proof for a statement.'

'There are some things you can't prove by science. Faith, and the life of the spirit, for instance.'

'How do you know you don't make them up? That they're not just projections of your own inner needs?'

I thought of my mother's last days, of her death, of our closeness of communion then and afterwards.

'I *know*, that's all,' I replied.

'You're lucky.'

Ally followed my gaze up to the stars, and I saw the familiar wrinkle of his brow. The black vault was pricked with innumerable points of light, twinkling and sparkling into infinity.

'When you look at that,' he said, 'how do you imagine man can have a special significance? He's just one of countless experiments of the universe. But we're all so subjective we have to make up meaning for ourselves in order to go on existing. Perhaps it doesn't matter much *what* we believe, as long as we believe something.'

We celebrated New Year's Eve together in Berlin, and then Ally left, saying goodbye with a casual charm which left me in doubt about when I would hear from him again. I settled down to life in Berlin.

I was staying with Baronin Isi von Gleichen und Russwurm, an old friend of my uncle Seton-Watson. She had a spacious apartment in Nestorstrasse, where she held a salon for musicians and writers. 'Tante' Isi, as I soon called her, was a doyen of the *ancien régime*, who had nevertheless adapted herself to modern Germany. Her husband's large estates in Tanganyika, where they had lived an autocratic colonial life, had been lost with the first war. Her family home in Dresden had perished. Her husband had died. Surviving these catastrophes with courage and humour, she had settled in Berlin, where she was now engaged in writing a book on astronomy, her life interest and work.

Isi von Gleichen started the day with pumpernickel, sausage and a small cigar for breakfast. She then took me sight-seeing in a rickety car whose radiator required constant filling from a 'little pot' which accompanied her. She was knowledgeable, cultured and didactic; and she accepted the Nazis because they had got rid of the Communists, dire enemies of her class. I feel sure she had no knowledge of the Nazi excesses. She was essentially humane and fair-minded, and would have rejected the régime, if she had known of its horrors. Like so many others in Germany at that time, she was taken in. Probably her friends, the writers and musicians who frequented her flat, felt the same. I could not speak enough German to converse with them, so I never discovered; but most likely, they also accepted the *status quo*. I taught her three Wehrmacht officer nephews to tap-dance (they were avid for American dance-tunes and rhythms), but we never discussed politics. And in spite of my practising dancing and club-swinging in the limited space of her apartment, 'Tante' Isi and I formed a life-long friendship, and became very fond of one another.

I saw various systems of physical education, among them those of Laban and Mensendieck; and then decided to study at the Medau School of Gymnastik, which I considered the best. Herr Medau had worked with Dr Bode, and with Dr Laban, both pioneers of modern German physical education, and then had broken away to found his own school.

I soon became absorbed in the new work I learnt there. It was a fascinating experience to find an entirely novel approach to my own subject.

I demonstrated the League system to Herr Medau and some of his colleagues. They were polite but not unduly impressed. Until then I had never doubted that the League system was supreme in the field of physical training. Now I experienced a different concept – plastic, flowing movement, something which was neither dance nor exercises. The balls, hoops and clubs used in the Medau system extended the possibilities of movement, and the improvised music, with its rhythms specially adapted to the movements performed, brought about a close integration between the two.

I entered Herr Medau's classes, and felt for myself the inspiration of his music, the subtle rhythm of each movement like that of a wave, rising to a climax, breaking, falling away. Professionals from several other countries were studying the Medau system. I realised that this type of movement could be a valuable follow-up to the League's basic system of exercises. I made friends with Herr Medau and his charming wife, and later, at the League's invitation, they visited one of our Teachers' Courses in London, gave some tuition there, and appeared on television with the League teachers they had trained.

From Berlin I travelled to Prague. I was anxious to see the work of the Sokols, the movement which had inspired my mother, and whose pictures she had taken with her when she persuaded George Lansbury, then Minister for Home Affairs, to allow the League to appear in Hyde Park for its first public demonstration.

I went to Prague armed with introductions from my uncle Seton-Watson, and, basking in his reflected glory, soon found myself having tea with the daughter of the president, Thomas Masaryk, in the beautiful and ancient Hradčany Palace. Prague was covered in snow, from which its baroque buildings emerged with an air of mystery and romance. History seemed written into every stone, but the city was modern as well, teeming with life. The new Republic demonstrated its vitality, in spite of, or perhaps because of, the Nazi threat from across its borders.

I stayed at the Sokolsky Dum, the headquarters of the movement, where I was given the warmest of welcomes. This extended to the porter, who surprisingly performed a cartwheel for me as he led me to my room, and the bell-boy, who astonished me by suddenly standing on his head. Assuring them in broken German that I was indeed interested in physical training, I hurried to the dining-room, to learn more about their movement in less athletic surroundings.

'The Sokols were founded in 1872 by Dr Miroslav Tyrs,' I read. 'The name Sokol means falcon, a bird of legendary courage; it became a symbol of the unquenchable determination of a people to survive in independence.' After the First World War this independence was gained from the Austro-Hungarian Empire, and when I visited them in 1936, the Sokols were consolidating their freedom. But now they were threatened once more: this time by the Nazi menace. Sitting over a meal in the *Stube*, where wooden stalls surrounded tables laden with beer mugs, and diners turned over newspapers attached to long sticks, my new-found friends told me of their problems, and of the ideals of their movement. The Sokol training, they said, placed great emphasis on spiritual values as well as physical well-being. Discipline must be learned, for the 'falcons' might have to resist an enemy once more. But self-discipline, too, was prized; the second, they felt, being the result of the first. A sense of fraternity and equality permeated the whole movement; the Sokols served each other and the nation.

Later, I visited the Sokol Physical Education Training College, and observed some of their classes. Paradoxically, the method of physical training which they used was not so advanced as the Medau system which I had seen in authoritarian Germany. There was an old-fashioned stiffness of movement, a lack of individual expression, and a monotony which the German aesthetic approach avoided. The students at the training college stood smartly to attention every time a member of the staff passed by (something I would never be able to achieve with my own free-and-easy students, I reflected, even if I had wanted to). But I made myself remember that if a military aspect was encouraged by the Sokols it was for the very good reason that freedom might have to be defended once more with lives.

My Sokol friends took me on a short skiing trip to the mountains, and then I moved on to Vienna. But alas! I saw little of that enchanting city, for I was forced to incarcerate myself indoors, completing some essential promised writing for the League. And so, back to Berlin, where one of my last experiences was to see a performance by Mary Wigman, a creator of modern dance in Germany. The hall was packed with enthusiasts, and at the end of the recital Wigman was given a standing ovation. The message of her performance stressed the value of freedom. Her dance tried to show every level of human aspiration – mental and spiritual as well as physical. From an emotional base the whole being was involved, and its tensions were expressed in movements of great drama and conviction. I was struck by the contrast between this highly dramatic and emotional performance, and the feverish reception accorded to it, and the rigid discipline and regimentation of life outside the theatre. These dual aspects of the German nature seemed to have no connecting link.

Back in London, I found it difficult to convey to my League colleagues all that I had seen and learned. Some were interested, some were insular. Innovations are never easy to introduce into an established structure, and this the League had now become.

We were arranging a display at the Albert Hall, together with the Margaret Morris Movement, and the English Folk Dance and Song Society, which the Queen was to attend. The intention was to show more specialised advanced work than was possible in a large mass display. Marie Rambert, the famous teacher and ballerina, came to watch a rehearsal. She thrilled us all with her responsive and vital personality. She admired the League's basic exercises, but disapproved of one of the dance items. As a result, this item was excluded; instead I had to take the floor alone in the centre of the large arena, demonstrating some of the Medau work I had learned. I knew I was not sufficiently qualified to do this. It was the kind of situation I hated, and which seemed only too often to occur; it set up a chain-reaction of early memories of being thrust into the limelight against my will. In the end, however, all went well. The combined programme provided an interesting and varied evening, and the Queen brought an added radiance to the occasion with her own particular grace and charm.

To my joy, Ally had been on the platform to welcome me when I returned from my Continental trip. It was not long before we were making plans to ski together at Easter. I was already committed to rehearsals for the next big League display at Wembley Stadium in June, but I could manage a week away, and Ally would be on his Easter vacation. We chose Davos in Switzerland, for our jaunt.

We travelled out third class, sitting up all night on hard wooden seats. Though we were tired after the thirty-hour journey, one glimpse of the snow slopes on arrival, diamond-bright in the sunshine, revived us; and in no time we were on them, trudging up, and sliding down again in complete absorption. I was still a beginner. Ally had had more experience but, with typical thoughtfulness, adapted his pace to mine. We were out all day – from

7 a.m. until dark, and sometimes later. Each day our skiing improved, and we tackled longer runs. Chugging up the valley in the little train, or swinging upwards in the funicular, we paused for breath, admiring the dazzling white slopes bordered by forests of firs and pines. Snow lay on the dark foliage; white paths, usually icy, wound their way between the trees. We would hurtle down these, often hopelessly out of control, skis clattering in two icy ruts, hearts pounding with excitement. The upper slopes were great wide snow-fields, where one could *schuss* to one's heart's content, following the line of ski-tracks brilliant in the sun.

We spent the last three nights at the Schwendi ski-hut, on the way down the Küblis run. Skiing down to the hut in the twilight at the end of the day, with the first star appearing in the sky and long violet shadows stretching across the snow, one seemed in another dimension, on a different planet. Sun, snow, the cold sharp air and the day's exercise combined to produce an exhilaration which tingled in every nerve. We stumped into the hut, shedding gloves, anoraks and scarves. We talked, exchanging experiences and ideas, until there seemed no ground that we had not covered. Ally had a gift for companionship which drew out the deepest level of friendship. We were comrades in the best sense of that misused word. And if, below the surface, the tides of physical attraction were gathering momentum, Ally kept them under control in order not to spoil or jeopardise the happiness of our relationship. Neither of us felt ready yet for a serious committal. It was a little over two years since my mother had died. Strange as it may seem, I had never expected to feel again such youthful joy.

CHAPTER 5

New Horizons

♣

THE League was now seven years old. Its success had been spectacular. Its pioneering spirit was still its motivating force; but now it became necessary to try to relate the League to the national pattern of physical education. I have often wondered how my mother would have tackled this problem. Consolidation is the task which the visionary usually leaves to those who follow after. The balance then has to be struck between the force of the original inspiration, and the compromises which its preservation in a continuing form entail. This is no easy endeavour. Until now, the League had been a law unto itself, developing independently of any recognised physical education system, producing its own financial resources, and gaining nation-wide recognition and publicity, which made it the target for much professional jealousy. As often in Britain, the spur for a new leap forward had come from outside official channels. This did not make the League any more welcome within them. Aunt Norah, whose diplomatic nature fitted her well for the task, now made tentative overtures for recognition to the Ministry of Education and the Central Council of Physical Recreation. This body had been formed the previous year to encourage sport, games and physical training in the sphere of adult education.

At the same time, I was asked to serve on the National Fitness Council, which was formed by the Prime Minister in the spring of 1937, with the object of improving the health of the nation.

I found myself working with experienced men and women of affairs – Members of Parliament, civil servants, figures famous in the sporting world, doctors and educationalists. Lord Aberdare was our chairman. A slight man, with a gentle manner, he possessed the tact and conscientiousness necessary to synthesise the many different elements that the Council represented; but not, perhaps, the personality to inspire. Himself a superb cricketer, he leaned towards the encouragement of games, and stressed that the Council's first task was to set in motion the provision of more playing fields, sports grounds and gymnasia. I felt that the cardinal need was for leaders to animate these otherwise inanimate objects. I spoke from experience, for the success of the League had been largely due to the quality of its teachers – hand-picked and carefully trained over a period of two years. For the first time, I came up against the ramifications of local authorities and voluntary organisations, each working in their own sphere, each touchy about their own rights, with each of whom one must seek co-operation but not duplication. The wheels of progress were obviously going to grind very slowly, while vast sections of the population would remain untouched by the fitness drive.

It was difficult to catch the imagination of the public. Anything which smacked of a mass movement, or of coercion was, rightly, suspect in Britain. Democratic processes must be used, but this meant interminable consultation, compromise and delay. The provision of facilities was not a controversial issue; the Council gratefully accepted this as its first priority. But I was sure that the fitness drive could only succeed if it was animated by trained leaders with the enthusiasm to inspire others to action.

I was asked to speak at large meetings organised by the Fitness Council in various parts of the country. Displays by groups of voluntary organisations were also arranged by the Central Council of Physical Recreation; and the local League centres, taking part in these, made contact with other movements working in the same field.

The regular Council meetings in Whitehall gave me an insight into the working of the Civil Service. Before each of them a Niagara of papers and memoranda descended upon the heads of the unlucky Council members. (Margaret Morris sat up all night before the first meeting, trying to digest them.) If we had read and absorbed all the statistics handed out to us, we should have had no energy left to speak or think. (Perhaps this was the object?) Often I felt an apprehensive catch at the heart when I realised that this kind of unimaginative bureaucracy could swamp a live, vital movement like the League.

I made friends with some of my fellow Councillors – Kenneth Lindsay, who was then Parliamentary Secretary at the Board of

Education; Philip Noel-Baker, the Socialist MP; Kay Stammers, the champion tennis-player; and Margaret Morris, whose movement and work I admired. Thelma Cazalet and Megan Lloyd-George, both Members of Parliament, arranged a luncheon-party at the House of Commons, and invited me to speak about the League's work. The spectacular increase in the League's membership – now over 100,000 – and the large public displays which it held each year, had laid it open to the charge of being a mass movement, influenced by the dictators abroad. I was glad to have the opportunity to refute this accusation. I stressed that the League's cardinal objects were to encourage the development of the individual, and to give each member greater scope for health, happiness and self-expression. 'How?' I was asked. The luncheon ended by all present practising some of the League's basic exercises!

About this time, I was commanded to an afternoon party at Buckingham Palace. I was presented to the Queen, and talked to her and Princess Elizabeth and Princess Margaret about the work of the Fitness Council and of the League. The King and Queen had promised to be present at an afternoon Festival of Youth, which the Fitness Council were organising at Wembley Stadium in July. The League was asked to provide an item. Three weeks before, we were to present our own display at Wembley, where 5,000 members of the League would perform. The programme of work and preparation for all this was formidable.

One May morning in 1937, I woke up early and went to sit in the bay window of my flat at Holland Park, which looked over the garden. The sun streamed in through the open casement, accompanied by bird-song and the freshness of new green leaves. I was hastily writing a speech, which I must deliver that afternoon when I opened a swimming-pool at a girls' school in Dorset, run by Lady Lees. I was to be flown down to the school by the Marquess of Clydesdale, whom I had met shortly before at a League demonstration in Glasgow, at which, as a member of the Scottish National Fitness Council, he had presided. Douglas Clydesdale was a first-class middle-weight boxer, who had captained the Oxford Boxing team and narrowly missed becoming British Champion, and an expert pilot, the first to fly over Mount Everest in 1933. He was now a Member of Parliament for a Scottish constituency: East Renfrew. Eldest son of the Duke of Hamilton, one of four brothers and two sisters, he was a cousin of Lady Lees.

We arrived at Lytchett Minster in time for lunch. The school occupied Sir Thomas and Lady Lees's house, which stood amid extensive grounds, bordered by undulating Dorset countryside. The new swimming-pool shimmered in the May sunshine. Madeleine Lees had built up a unique establishment; started originally to educate her own large family, it had developed into a flourishing school which practised her liberal methods of education.

A tall young man came forward to greet us.

'This is my brother David,' said Douglas.

I shook hands, conscious of a latent power and strength, evident behind a disarming shyness. This impression was re-inforced at the family lunch, over which Sir Thomas presided like a master of hounds with an unruly pack.

After lunch, I changed into a bathing-dress (Lady Lees insisted that I must dive into the pool in order to open it properly), and we all repaired to the garden. A large crowd of parents had assembled, as well as the whole school of children. I had designed my speech for children, not grown-ups. I realised I must make a hasty revision. I clasped my flowing bath-robe (bought specially for the occasion) round me, and walked with Lady Lees to the little dais erected in front of the pool. We stood there together and she turned to me.

'Take it off,' she said, pointing to the bath-robe. 'They all want to see you.'

There was nothing to do but comply. Feeling very bare, I launched into my speech, which was completed by a thankful dive into the pool.

At tea afterwards, I talked to David Douglas-Hamilton. He had come down from Oxford in the summer of 1936, and spent the time since then taking a public schoolboy tour round South Africa. He loved the country and had made many friends there. I asked him if he knew Ally. He had met him – boxing with him at Oxford the previous year. (I learned later that David had gained an Oxford blue as a heavy-weight boxer, and captained the Scottish boxing team to the Empire Games.) David accompanied us to the aeroplane, and as we said goodbye he took my hand and examined my fingernails. 'I'm glad you don't paint them,' he said. 'I hate artificiality.'

Flying back to London, the plane's shadow accompanied us, gliding below over rolling downs and wide fields of sprouting corn. It had been a challenging day, bringing me into contact with a new set of people. As I watched the evening light stretch across the country beneath, I reflected on the rich heritage of British life and on its unique variety, which brought it strength and resilience. 'There are stresses and strains, of course,' I thought, 'yet everyone combines to make a whole. And if there were any challenge to our way of life, or our deepest values, we should respond as a whole.'

The smiling landscape below me unfolded in a mellow radiance that seemed the epitome of peace. Yet suddenly I felt that it was lit by the rays of a vanishing era.

The League's display at Wembley Stadium on my mother's birthday, the 12th of June, was given by five thousand performers, drawn from centres throughout Britain; it also included two overseas contingents, one from Canada and one from Australia. There was a single mass rehearsal on the morning and afternoon of the display. Peggy St Lo and I stood beside a microphone on a rostrum, and watched the vast stadium gradually fill with women of all ages, shapes and sizes. Trained by their young teachers they had been rehearsing in their own localities for months. Now they must be fitted together into one cohesive whole.

The bright green grass of the stadium, packed with performers, was bordered by a cinder track, used for athletic events. On this (the only space available) a number of unfortunate women found themselves standing, many in bare feet. Soon, they were asked to lie down! As the day wore on, the patience and good humour of performers and producers alike were severely taxed. The climax came with the finale. This was an ambitious concept. It started with a Greek athletic dance by teachers and students in white tunics, carrying mock swords, shields and javelins (we envisaged this as being very effective on the green sward). Then continued with chariots, drawn by fiery steeds, which were to emerge from the entrance tunnel and dash round the cinder track, their drivers flourishing whips in Attic style. We had hired the chariots and drivers from a circus; during that long thirsty morning they had been refreshing themselves behind the scenes. When they sprang from the tunnel, it was to gallop, not round the cinder track, but straight across the arena. Peggy and I watched with horror as the runaway horses, their drivers pulling vainly at their reins, scattered performers in every direction. The members had not bargained for this test of their athletic capabilities.

By evening, a huge audience had assembled. The June sunlight shone across the grass, the military band of the Queen Victoria Rifles struck up, and the League members (miraculously recovered from their gruelling rehearsal) streamed on to the arena. Item succeeded item without a hitch. Daylight faded, and spotlights played over the moving black-and-white masses. The audience responded to the spectacle with bursts of applause. But there was one more hazard to come. At the very end, members were to enter from the tunnel, bearing torches of naked flame, which they would carry in two long files round the arena. There was some congestion at the head of the tunnel, and torches began to wave wildly. I had a vision, out of the corner of my eye, of Mr Herbert, Wembley's rotund manager, standing in a crucified posture with arms outstretched, trying to hold back hordes of eager women, as he shouted, 'For God's sake, ladies! For God's sake, take care!' By some miracle, all got on to the arena unscathed.

I led my file round the darkened grass. The smell of torches was acrid in my nostrils; the night air blew through my hair; high above me the arc-lamps spotted the flags of all the nations, flying round the loftiest rail of the stadium. The compelling music from Arthur Bliss's march from the film of H. G. Wells's *Things to Come* beat in my ears. I heard again my mother's voice – 'One day the peoples of the world will unite in understanding.'

I left my file to take my place in the final tableau, grouped in the centre of the arena. I climbed to the top of a column, thirty feet high, and raised my torch above the serried ranks of five thousand League members. How proud of them my mother would have been! The floodlights blazed, and a wave of applause echoed round the stadium.

Ally watched the display, and was one of the first to congratulate me afterwards. He had shared my previous apprehension, and much of the preparations. He would now sit his second-year examinations at Oxford, and then was going abroad, to join his mother in a Continental tour; later in the summer we would meet in the Dolomites.

Three weeks afterwards we were back again in Wembley Stadium, this time taking part in the Festival of Youth, organised by the National Fitness Council. Items were presented by all the large youth organisations, and by movements interested in physical training or dancing. Brightly coloured costumes and changing designs made a kaleidoscope of colour and movement, watched with interest by the King and Queen. After the performance, the organisers of each item were presented to them. Among the manager's guests, I saw a tall young man. It was David Douglas-Hamilton. We had met several times since our first encounter in Dorset, but I had not expected to see him here.

'Perhaps you will have a little more leisure, now this is over,' he said. 'Come and sail next weekend, with my brother and me.'

David's elder brother Malcolm, and his wife Pam, were living near Hamble, on the Hampshire coast. Malcolm was teaching flying at an aviation school, following a bent which had been his major interest ever since leaving school. At eighteen he had gone to Cranwell and joined the RAF, becoming the first of the family to fly. All four brothers were now experienced pilots – the eldest two commanding auxiliary Air Force Squadrons in Glasgow and Edinburgh. David had been a member of the Oxford Air Squadron, where he had learned to fly. He and Malcolm now shared a Tiger Moth.

The following weekend, David flew me down to the coast in this aeroplane. (Little did I know his limited experience!) We stayed with Malcolm and Pam, and early next morning, in Malcolm's small yacht, we nosed our way out of the Hamble estuary. Craft of every size and shape were moored there. We slipped past them and soon were in the open sea.

Small waves lapped the side of the boat. Gulls wheeled above the sails. A fresh wind sent us along at a good pace, while cloud patterns changed slowly overhead, and the coastline became hazy in the distance. David took the tiller and Malcolm brought out his concertina, and started to play and sing Austrian songs. I realised that he and David were alike and yet deeply different, each complementary to the other. Malcolm's gaiety and spontaneous approach to people countered David's more serious and thoughtful nature. There was a very close bond between them, making them more like twins than brothers, in spite of the three years' difference in their ages. They shared a love of adventure which manifested itself in flying and mountaineering, and which had already taken them to far corners of the world. David had visited Russia and climbed Mount Elbrus, in the Caucasus. Malcolm had taught flying in Hong Kong. Watching them now, as they lounged in the stern of the little boat, unconscious alike of their rough old clothes or their careless good looks, they seemed to my romantic heart like heroes from a Greek saga speeding over the waves to a future of epic deeds. They talked of their family and friends – talk punctuated with laughter and banter – and I felt as though looking in on an esoteric world far removed from my own.

After a while, we anchored the yacht, changed into bathing costumes, and dived over the side. The sky arched above us; sun sparkled on the crests of the waves. We felt at one with the elements, animated by health, youth and happiness. The future seemed as limitless as the spread of the blue firmament. Yet when we talked of it later, after our sandwich lunch, a troubled note entered the voices of the brothers.

They knew Germany and Austria well, and had friends in both countries. They spoke of the spread of the Nazi creed, and of the threat it presented to the rest of Europe. David had worked in a German labour camp, during one of his Oxford vacations, and had experienced Nazi domination at first hand.

'You don't know what it means to resist,' he said. 'If you resist, you stake everything – your job, your life, your family. Everything.' He described the plausible propaganda of the Nazis; their efficiency, their apparent success.

'They've taken in a lot of people,' he said. 'But they're utterly ruthless if you don't agree with them.'

'And the Fascists?'

'They're as bad. Look at a man like Reut Nicolussi. He's spent most of his life resisting the Fascists in Italy, and now he may be engulfed by the Nazis.'

He was speaking of a friend of his, in Austria, a professor at Innsbruck University, leader of the movement which was pressing for the return of South Tyrol, originally Austrian territory, but ceded to Italy in 1918.

'You couldn't wish for a braver man. He was a deputy in the Italian Parliament, until he was thrown out for being too outspoken about his cause. Now he can't even live in his own country. He's living as a refugee in Innsbruck.'

'There are cases like his all over Europe,' said Malcolm. 'And much worse things than just exile are happening to many of them.'

'I know. We don't realise how lucky we are to live in freedom. To be able to think and speak and act as we like. We just take it for granted. Well, we may have to defend that freedom yet.'

David's jaw set in a line of determination I was to know well.

Malcolm glanced at him, hesitated, then picked up his concertina.

'All right, old egg,' he said, 'we'll defend it. But let's enjoy it while we have it.'

The day was wearing on. Soon we must set our course homeward. My initial shyness had evaporated, and there was a happy ease of communication between the three of us. I still felt overawed by this challenging couple, but I was now brave enough not to let them have everything their own way.

We slipped back into the estuary at dusk, and glided slowly past the lines of yachts. Lanterns shone on masts, casting a glow into the hazy summer evening. Voices called across the water. The sky darkened into the velvet of night. The day had seemed unending, but now it was over. We anchored the boat, and took ourselves back to Malcolm's house, where Pam, who had been looking after their two small children, gave us dinner. The world closed in.

But later that night, as I lay awake in the little spare room, I went through the events of the last twenty-four hours in my mind and the magic of the day returned to me. A breeze blew in from the darkness outside, bearing the scents of the summer night. I heard again the lapping of the waves against the yacht, and the sough of the wind through her sails. The day had cast a spell on me. The magic remained.

Soon after, David asked me to stay for a few days at Dungavel, his family's home in Scotland. I found a house-party assembled there, presided over by David's mother, the Duchess of Hamilton. I had already met her in London, and felt drawn immediately to this tall woman with the piercing blue eyes. She was president of the Animal Defence Society, and had given much of her life to the cause of kindness to animals, leading a campaign against vivisection and playing a vital role in making humane slaughter compulsory by law. Her dedication to her work reminded me of my own mother. She had a commanding presence and a natural gift of leadership, but this was combined with a simplicity of character and generosity of heart which dissolved barriers between herself and other people. She could be unyielding and severe at times, when her strict upbringing in the home of her stern Army father, Major Robert Poore, manifested itself. But she had given her own children a great deal of freedom, and brought them up to think for themselves.

Dungavel, originally a shooting lodge, had been extended bit by bit to become the family home. It was fifteen miles from Hamilton House, where Mary, Queen of Scots, had sought refuge after escaping from imprisonment at Loch Leven. In the early nineteenth century this house had been extended to about the size of Buckingham Palace; when, filled with one of the finest art collections in the country, it became known as Hamilton Palace. After the First World War coal mining had rendered the structure unsafe and it was demolished. Only the vast Mausoleum, erected at great cost by the 10th Duke, and containing marbles brought from Greece and Italy, and treasures from an Egyptian tomb, remained.

Dungavel, which had been rebuilt in the Scottish baronial style, flew the St Andrew's Cross from one of its turrets. Beyond it stretched the Lanarkshire moors, sweeping up to Dungavel Hill; miles of bleak heather and peat, where only the cry of curlew broke the silence.

David's father had been an invalid for many years, and was confined to a wheel-chair. A naval officer, and a distant cousin of the previous duke, he had been known as 'the pocket Hercules' in his youth; he had uncommon daring and strength in spite of his small stature. When he married David's mother, soon after his accession to the dukedom, he was already a semi-invalid, having suffered from a stroke. He possessed the family's searching blue eyes, often animated by a twinkle when his keen sense of humour rose to the surface, and he gained great joy from his children, all of whom were devoted to him.

David's eldest sister, Lady Jean Mackintosh, was also at Dungavel with her husband Christopher, and their children; and so was his brother, Douglas, whom I already knew. Two young guests, Lady Elizabeth and Lady Diana Percy, daughters of the Duchess of Northumberland, completed the party. Soon we were all persuaded to walk up Dungavel Hill, led by Douglas (whom everyone called Douglo) and David, each wearing a kilt and without shoes. They claimed that bare feet were best for traversing the moor. As we mounted, they told us stories of the Covenanters, who had found refuge here during the seventeenth century, holding their dissenting services in these wild places, and thus preserving the life of the Scottish Kirk.

I went to bed bemused by all these new impressions, and awoke to the sound of bagpipes. I ran to the window of my room to see the Duke's piper striding round the house. Behind him on the horizon rose the shape of Loudon Hill, where David had promised to give me my first lesson in rock-climbing.

It took place that afternoon. I stood at the foot of a cleft which stretched upwards for about seventy feet in the steep cliffs near the summit of Loudon Hill. The rope round my waist attached me to David, who was working his way up the cleft. As far as I could see, it was bare of hand- or footholds. David heaved himself out of this chimney on to a grassy knoll. He sat there with the rope running through his hands, and looked down at me.

'Come on,' he said.

I felt the rope tighten round my waist, and looked despairingly upwards.

'How?'

'Just climb.'

I started up. There was no time to feel frightened. I was too busy holding on, wedging fingers and toes in tiny cracks, stretching, pushing and gradually heaving myself higher. From time to time I looked up to see David's watchful face framed in the radiant blue sky. I only once looked down; the unnerving drop below decided me not to repeat that experience. I was

79

stretched to what seemed the limit of my capacity when I finally pulled myself on to the knoll, and sat down beside David, too breathless to speak.

'Well done!' he said. 'It was much harder than I expected. In fact, to tell you the truth, it's the first time I've climbed that chimney myself.'

We surveyed the rolling countryside below us. Large white clouds moved at a leisurely pace across the sky, and a small wind stirred the foliage of the silver birches and rowan trees growing far down the hillside. A disturbing thought struck me.

'How do we get down?'

'Oh, that's quite easy. You just rope down. "Abseiling", it's called. I'll show you.'

David untied the rope from my waist, twined it round a large boulder, and handed the two long ends back to me. He then arranged them over one shoulder, round my thighs and through my legs, so that I was held in a cradle of rope, one end clasped in my hand, the other dangling down the cliff-face on to the ledge from which we had ascended.

'What happens now?'

'You step over the side, put your feet against the rock-face, and let yourself down, holding on to the rope. Lean well away from the rock.'

'What?' I was aghast. 'Do you mean to say I've got to step off this cliff into space?'

I looked over the edge and saw the free end of the rope plummeting away into the void. I looked at David and saw amusement but no relenting in his face. I would have to do it.

I reached the bottom with grazed hands and neck where the rope had burned them, but otherwise intact.

David followed me.

He coiled up the rope and smiled his slow smile. 'Better get used to it,' he said. 'You've probably got a lifetime of it ahead of you.'

We stayed for a few more days at Dungavel, and then the house-party broke up, and we drove north to the Highlands. David wanted to visit Kurt Hahn at his school, Gordonstoun, which had been established three years before on the Moray Firth.

Driving through the hills and glens, David sang Gaelic songs, and talked to me about the history of the Highlands, and their problems. He loved Scotland deeply, and seemed to take on an extra dimension of living when he was in his own country. He had been to St Andrew's University for two years before going to Oxford, where he had made many friends, organised Highland dancing and played in the pipe band. We exchanged impressions of Skye and he told me of climbs in the Cuillins.

We reached Gordonstoun where Kurt Hahn showed us over the school, and talked to us about the education of youth, and the need for challenge, combined with what he called 'Samaritan service'.

'Young people can be coerced into an experience, but never into an opinion,' he said. 'Youth will always respond to a real need for service. That's why we have coastguard watchers at Gordonstoun, and a mountain rescue team. And later this ideal of service can be used for the benefit of the community.'

Kurt Hahn's power of magnetism and his vision had already made themselves felt in educational circles. He was an example of one who would not compromise his values or ideals; he had recognised the evil of the Nazi régime and tried to resist it. This had forced him to leave Salem, the school in Germany founded by Prince Max of Baden, where he had been headmaster. He was now building up an inspiring educational experiment here in Scotland. He was deeply interested in the aims of the National Fitness Council, and we discussed its work.

'The question you must ask,' he said, 'is – fit for what? It isn't enough just to develop muscle and brawn. How is this fitness going to be used, and for what purpose?'

'War, perhaps,' said David.

'Perhaps. One must hope not. Peace can have its challenges, too. We must make them as exciting and testing as those of war.'

We left Gordonstoun inspired, and awakened to a wider view of the needs of youth. David was moved, and longed to throw the whole weight of his ability and enthusiasm into this cause.

'I wish we could do something of real value in the way of service to the community,' he said.

How old-fashioned such a statement sounds now, when a

Welfare State looks after the population from the cradle to the grave!

But David meant what he said. He felt that he was one of the fortunate ones, born with the proverbial silver spoon; and it was incumbent on him to use his advantages for the benefit of others.

I had seen a new side of David during this brief stay in Scotland. At times he had drawn aside the curtain of his reserve and shown me where his roots and real interests lay. He liked to say that Oxford had made him doubt the validity of all ready-made philosophy, religions and moral codes, and that he was without faith or belief. Now I saw that in fact he possessed a deep idealism which infused all his thought. He saw things clear and true, and refused to romanticise; yet the ardour of his nature gave an intense life to everything he did.

I said goodbye to him with a sudden sense of loss. I had promised to meet him and Malcolm when they went to Austria for a climbing trip later in August. Meanwhile I returned to London.

While I had been enjoying myself in Scotland, the League had gone through yet another financial crisis. Its overheads were now considerable, with salaries to pay to the large staff at headquarters, and to all the teachers. The rent at the Mortimer Halls had greatly increased. The whole building was now occupied by the League. Four halls were used for classes, and the other rooms for office accommodation.

With rapid growth, expenditure had also mounted to an alarming degree. It only took an unforeseen drop in income, such as a summer slump, to reduce the League's finances to a precarious level. Its spectacular expansion and outward success masked this reality. (Indeed, I was often accused of making a fortune out of the League. In fact, I received a modest salary, like any other teacher.) But the League still suffered from its initial lack of capital. There was no security on which to fall back if income fluctuated.

Aunt Norah had been negotiating for a loan, or gift, from a large industrial firm, who had already been generous to the League. She went to see the directors and told them of our needs. To her great relief, they offered help. This extricated the League from its present financial crisis; but it was evident that it might easily recur. What we needed was a hard-headed business manager; but somehow this concept did not go with the original aims and ideals of the League. I wondered if official recognition and consequent financial aid from the Ministry of Education would ever be forthcoming. In some ways the League's success was its own worst enemy; much of the publicity by which it grew gave a wrong impression of its work.

I put these sombre thoughts aside, and concentrated on the students' end-of-course examinations.

My mother's ambition of a hundred teachers for the League had been fulfilled. Would they 'carry its message of peace and co-operation to all ends of the earth'? I remembered her last letter: 'Then you will be free to do what you choose, go where you will.'

My life up to now had been so much bound up with the League that I could envisage no other. But recent months had brought new experiences; my horizon had enlarged. It was in a thoughtful mood that I completed my work, and got ready for the summer holidays.

CHAPTER 6

A Holiday and a Choice

I JOINED Ally in Innsbruck. Austria had recently been discovered by many English holiday-makers. They purchased *Dirndl* and *Lederhosen*, in the shops, and then wore them with an air of self-conscious bravado. They invaded cafés, and encouraged spurious exhibitions of *Schuhplattler* dancing. The Austrians cashed in on this foreign interest, how and where they could, but the tourist boom was only in its infancy. Many Tyrolese villages still conducted life on a pattern which had changed little since medieval times. Without visitors, television or radio the traditions of centuries remained unbroken.

Seis-am-Schlern, in South Tyrol, was such a village. The wife and children of David's friend, Dr Reut Nicolussi, were holidaying there. We crossed the Brenner Pass and joined them for the start of our walking tour in the Dolomites.

Ally was in gay holiday mood, fit and sunburned after his month on the Continent. I was tired from the long journey out, and my last spurt of work in London. I was also divided in heart. My life had become complicated in a way not altogether of my own choosing. I wanted time to assess the events of the last few weeks.

I was able to bring Frau Nicolussi news of her husband's activities in London on behalf of South Tyrol. He himself could no longer visit his own country. His situation was typical of the pressures then operating in Europe. His family, who welcomed us so hospitably, were parted from him only for their holiday: many other families were separated for life.

Frau Nicolussi's son-in-law looked through our maps and approved our route; then drove us to Völs, where the path began.

The way stretched ahead of us, over grassy meadows, and gently rolling countryside. We shouldered our disconcertingly heavy rucksacks, and started.

84

Ally had the capacity to live in the moment, postponing problems or choices. I envied this ability, something my mother had advised me to cultivate many years ago. We exchanged experiences of the last month, and I told him, with reservations, of my friendship with the Douglas-Hamiltons. I was equivocal, partly because I did not yet know my own mind. Like many who respond easily to affection, I had become the victim of conflicting loyalties.

We walked for four hours, until a spectacular sunset blazed ahead of us, illuminating the crags and towers of the Rosengarten in the far distance. In that Valkyrie light everything appeared dramatic and larger than life. With the slow rhythm of the mountaineer, we pushed our feet, clad in their heavy boots, up the last slopes of the path leading to the Niger hut. The silence was complete as the light gradually diminished, changing from coral to rose, to silver and to grey. London and England faded far away. Time stretched away into days which would be marked only by the distance covered, the weather, and the changing views of the mountains. I set aside the contemplation of any other kind of future, and felt content.

The hut was crowded with Austrians and Italians, and soon a guitar began to strum. Snatches of *Tiroler* songs rose and fell from different corners of the room.

'They get on well enough up here,' said Ally. 'Pity all frontier disputes can't be settled in the atmosphere of a mountain hut.'

'Yes. But the divisions really go very deep. People forget about them here, that's all, but they still remain.'

'I suppose so. But, one day Europe will have to unite. She can't continue her fratricidal wars.'

'She may continue them and perish,' I replied.

'That would be disastrous. The world would be very much the poorer without the European concept.'

Ally's conviction surprised me.

'You really think so? I thought you felt that "God's Own Country" had the answer to every problem?'

'Of course not.' Ally spoke with unusual seriousness. 'I love South Africa, but we have great problems ourselves. They won't grow any less as the years pass. The racial issue is going to become more and more dominant in the world. South Africa will have to try to find some fair solution.' He paused. 'One day I must go back and help in whatever way I can.'

Ally's sincerity impressed me. He meant what he said. I realised that he, too, could be committed.

We rose with the dawn. Layers of cloud stretched around us as far as we could see. Through them the high peaks jutted, their summits gleaming cold and mysterious in the last of the darkness. No life stirred. Slowly the dawn light crept along the horizon and over the sea of cloud. Shapes changed, as the colour warmed and chasms of shadows began to appear. The sky lightened, the morning star faded, and a tentative blue spread across the firmament. Then the Dolomite rock suddenly caught fire and blazed with radiant light.

That day we walked over three high passes, up and down steep slopes covered with scree which took us into the heart of the mountains. At each pass fresh views appeared – layer upon layer of peaks stretching away into the far distance. The great Rosengarten and Marmolada groups dominated the scene. Towers and crags of Dolomite rock reared up to the sky. It seemed impossible that anyone could scale those precipitous walls, yet we saw some climbers on the Rosengarten Spitz. We found a lake to swim in, then crossed the Grasleiten Pass, and slithered down on snow into a bleak and desolate corrie. Another pass, with magnificent views, another descent; and at last the countryside opened out into gently sloping table-land and we saw the Schlern hut ahead of us. It was almost dark when we reached it. We had walked for nearly eight hours, the way traversing passes, desolate valleys of stones, and steep turrets of rock. We were tired and hungry but entirely content. The long day's march had relaxed our minds and bodies, and we shared the peace and solitude of the mountains.

We repeated this day, with variations, for the next two weeks. We lived only for the moment, and the moment was one of unforced happiness. We heard stories of persecution and oppression; we saw some cases of poverty and hardship; but we were too carefree for these to affect us deeply. David had become closely involved with the injustices of South Tyrol. Ally and I skirted over the surface, our attitude subjective rather than objective, concerned primarily with our own enjoyment.

We spent the last three days in the Stubai Alps, surrounded by glaciers and towering snowy peaks. Our final descent brought us down to the valley of the Inn, with a panoramic view of Innsbruck, nestling below its mountain.

Mein schönes Innsbruck am grünen Inn! – the words of the song ran through my mind as I watched the twilight deepen, and the evening shadows form. We were sitting in the Mütterer Alpen hut, drinking a last glass of wine. The trip was over. Neither of us wanted it to end. Ally turned to me.

'We don't know what the future will bring,' he said. 'We can't promise ourselves anything. I've got to work hard, get a degree, get qualified. But perhaps some time, somehow . . .'

'Yes?'

'We'll be together again.'

We met David that evening in Innsbruck. The next day we parted to go our separate ways; Ally to join his mother and continue his Continental tour with her, I to climb with David and Malcolm.

Once more I was in the orbit of the challenging Douglas-Hamiltons; committed, this time, to the exposure and difficulties of mountaineering on Alpine peaks.

We stocked up with supplies in Innsbruck; met Malcolm in a village called Mayerhofen in the Zillertal; and trudged up to our starting hut through a thunderstorm, which seemed to me to be a suitably dramatic overture to the climbing tour.

The next morning we left the hut before dawn. Our boots crunched along the narrow path, each stride sending up sparks as the nails hit the stones. (Vibram rubber soles had not yet been invented. We climbed with awkward nailed boots.) We walked in single file, well muffled up against the cold, grasping our ice-axes in mittened hands. Light filtered down from a sky laden with stars; a waterfall beside the path scattered its spray into the night air. This purposeful passage through a half-lit world excited me. We seemed like figures in a ritual, trudging along, solitary and silent, while the universe around us remained totally unaware of our presence. Before long, the stars faded and a pink flush irradiated the snow. We stopped for a moment, blowing on our fingers, and gazed at our mountain ahead.

The Olperer was not unduly high or difficult – not in the class of the great Swiss Alpine peaks, in fact a good beginner's climb – but to me it looked dismayingly large and precipitous.

Three hours later I stood at the foot of a steep ice-slope, while David, ahead of me, cut steps in the hard surface. The sun blazed down, and the sparkling white of the snow reflected the light back into our faces, and up to the vivid sky. Malcolm was behind me, connected by a second rope, tied round my waist. David reached a stance, belayed his rope round his ice-axe, and called for me to come up. I ascended slowly, digging my toes into the small grooves which David had cut into the ice, balancing precariously on this steep and slippery slope. The ground below me fell away at a precipitous angle, and soon I felt poised in mid-air, between sky and snow, nothing connecting me to terra firma except these minute toe-holds dug into the uncompromising ice. An elation compounded of fear and intense exhilaration took hold of me. This slope would take at least an hour to negotiate, and during that time one slip might mean disaster for us all. David's sharp blows on the ice above rang through the silence, and little chips of diamond-bright substance showered into the sky. We crept slowly upwards, human ants on the face of this towering mountain; our activity, so intensely important to us, the only sign of life in the snowy expanse which stretched on every side. In this vivid sapphire and white world living took on a new dimension. Gradually my fear subsided and was replaced by an intensity of awareness which communicated the experience to muscles, heart and mind. At last we reached the top of the slope. We remained roped for the last few hundred feet, scrambling over snow-covered rocks to the summit; and then, suddenly we were there!

We stayed up in this magical kingdom surrounded by a frozen sea of peaks and passes, for as long as possible. The zenith of the day passed in silence. Then, in the early afternoon, we began our descent. It was necessary to leave the mountain before melting snow brought dangers of avalanche.

I was tired now, and the aftermath of the morning's elation began to take its toll. David's and Malcolm's superior strength and experience kept them confident and upright where I slipped and floundered. I became increasingly discouraged at the length and difficulty of the descent. We were traversing a steep slope, where a thin layer of snow lay over ice, when I slipped out of the tracks which Malcolm, in front of me, had made and began to slide rapidly down the mountain-side. 'Dig in your ice-axe,' David called, as I gathered speed at an alarming rate. I seized my ice-axe with both hands, and pressed the head into the skidding hard-packed snow. At the same moment I felt the rope tighten round my waist, and I came to a halt. I regained my feet and was hauled back to safety, painfully kicking steps in the hard snow.

'Be more careful how you step next time,' said David, severely. 'You ought to be able to remain upright on a slope like this.'

I felt tears of exhaustion and annoyance start behind my eyes. Why couldn't David understand? Evidently one must learn emotional as well as physical skills if one was to succeed as a mountaineer.

We reached the hut by late afternoon, and after a short rest, my damaged spirits were restored. I remembered the beauty and mystery of the summit, and said something about feeling like an intruder there.

'Nonsense!' David replied. 'You've earned your right to see it. To get there, you've lived to the height of your capacity. Intensely, stretched to the limit. That's the way to live.'

'All the time?'

'All the time, if one could. Life is meant to be *lived*, not just existed through.'

'Not everyone has the capacity.'

'Then they must crawl about in the valleys – valley-lizards. They can never know what it is to live on the heights.'

David was serious. His creed smacked of arrogance, but it was true that he put it into practice in his own life.

Malcolm intervened.

'You mustn't take life *too* seriously, old egg,' he said. 'It's such a painful, serious business anyway that the only thing to do is to laugh at it.'

David rose from his chair, and turned away from us, looking across to the Olperer, now touched with the first glow of sunset. Almost to himself, he quoted:

Who dares not put it to the touch
To win or lose it all
He either fears his fate too much
Or his deserts are small.

He turned to face us again.

'Montrose said that. The noble marquis. He didn't win. He lost. But before they killed him he had *lived*.'

We spent another week at snow-level, traversing the Zillertal from hut to hut, taking in climbs on the way. Then we returned to Innsbruck, and Malcolm flew home. David and I had two more days. We spent them in Kufstein, a little town grouped round its picturesque castle on the border of Austria and Germany. We stayed in an old sixteenth-century *Gasthaus*. Like the tourists in Innsbruck, we wore *Dirndl* and *Lederhosen*, and were several times mistaken for a local man and girl. David could speak German with a Tyrolese accent, and this added to the effect. We were immersed in Austria, purposely cut off from our real lives. On the last evening, we sat in the wooden *Stube* of the inn, and listened to an itinerant harpist, who had come in to sing and accompany Tyrolese songs. The liquid notes of the strings rippled through the smoky atmosphere; the music, evocative of mountain peaks and meadows, rose and fell. The player asked for requests, and we named our favourite tunes, including some from South Tyrol, which David had learnt from Reut Nicolussi. The other guests joined in, and song reverberated round the old oak beams. After a while the harpist rose to go, and we all tossed coins into his hat. As he passed our table he stopped, and his eyes met David's and mine.

'*Vergessen Sie nicht*,' he said. 'Do not forget.'

I have described this holiday in some detail because from it sprang a number of future events.

First, it presented a dilemma which was to occur several times in my life: that of conflicting loyalties and the difficulty of choice. Before starting it, I was committed to neither David nor Ally. Possibly I hoped subconsciously that the holiday would solve my dilemma and bring me to a clear-cut choice. Having completed it, I was left with the uneasy feeling that I had used the affections of others as a means to my own enjoyment, without in fact reaching any point of decision about the future.

I had been brought up to believe in absolute values (there was never any question of doubting their existence) and to consider them more important than conventional codes of behaviour. This did not mean that one could behave with no regard for others; rather that in any situation one must search for the truth below appearances, and take that as a basis for action. The difficulty was to choose between subjective and objective truth, not merely to choose what might be most convenient.

I had more independence than most girls of twenty-two: I lived alone, earned my own income, and had freedom to do what I chose. (Not many girls, at that time, would have been able to take a month's unchaperoned holiday abroad.) But this situation threw the onus of decision-making fairly and squarely on my shoulders. If my mother had been alive I would probably have asked her advice and confided in her; but she would have insisted on the final choice being mine alone. The price of freedom, in her eyes, was responsible action.

Second, the month on the Continent drew me much closer to Europe. I now understood the Nazi threat more clearly; I was subjectively involved with the way of life which it endangered. When the Nazis invaded Austria nine months later, the invasion came as a personal blow.

Finally, the three companions with whom I shared this holiday had permanently entered my life at the deepest level. Whatever happened subsequently, there they would remain.

I returned to an avalanche of work in London. The year's new students were being admitted into the Bagot Stack Health School. A number of new centres were scheduled to open. Plans were being drawn up for League teams to be sent to Physical Education Congresses abroad. Speaking engagements for the Fitness Council had to be fulfilled. And – most taxing of all – I had promised to undertake a tour of the existing League centres, which entailed travelling throughout the country, and speaking on an average in three different towns each week.

The League's growth was continuing at an almost unbelievable rate. There were now about two thousand classes held each week by over a hundred teachers. Sixty or so organisers were employed in the various areas throughout the country; while the staff at the

London headquarters had risen to fifty. Membership increased each year, but so did expenses. Financially, we lived from hand to mouth, with continually increasing commitments. The League had always lived like this, but now it was on a disturbingly larger scale. It was decided that I should take the members into my confidence when I spoke to them on my tour, and ask for contributions to a Reserve Fund.

Up and down the country I travelled, through long train journeys, one-night stops in draughty hotels, and the constant pressure of public appearances.

In every place, I told the members the story of the League; of our early days, its founder's vision, the need now for consolidation and financial stability. They responded with warmth and generosity. My mother's 'darling human capital' was still the vital factor. I enjoyed this close contact with them, the grass roots of the League. I had recently been too much cut off, with the pressure of committee work, Training School obligations, and speaking engagements for the Fitness Council. Like my mother, I needed to renew my enthusiasm by contact with the basic fabric of the League.

David, meanwhile, was working at the Pioneer Health Centre at Peckham. This interesting experiment, inaugurated by Dr Scott Williamson and Dr Innes Pearce, aimed to examine a cross-section of the London community from both a medical and social aspect. The centre existed for families, rather than individuals, and whole families were encouraged to join. They were given a medical examination, and then used the facilities of the centre as they pleased. Activities developed spontaneously, without superimposed direction; and through their results much of interest emerged. Medically it was established that the health of the majority of the members was below par. Even when not suffering from a diagnosable disease, few, if any, were in the state of 'positive health' considered by the doctors to be the ideal norm. By means of regular medical check-up minor ailments were dealt with promptly and consistently, and gradually people were made aware that positive health was more than a mere absence of disease and contained psychological as well as physical factors. Socially, the families influenced one another considerably. Left to themselves, the different age-groups tended to congregate to-gether. They made friends and found common interests among people of their own age. To start with, some of the Centre's facilities were defaced and misused by the undisciplined young. But when they found that their destructiveness evoked no re-sponse but indifference from the authorities, they changed, gradually became orderly, and soon began to take a pride in the centre, and to value its amenities. Families came together in social events in which some or all could participate; and before long a sense of responsibility and concern for the Centre began to emerge.

David was most interested in this experiment and in the oppor-tunities it gave him to study the problems to be tackled in the sphere of social service. He found it difficult to curb his natural qualities of leadership; to wait for the initiative for activities to come from the Centre's members, rather than from himself. He had many long talks with the sponsors, and in the process came to respect their integrity and originality. He formed a boxing club; and, as he got to know them better, he discussed with the members of the Centre their views on work, on physical exercise, on religion, and on how they thought the Centre might be improved. Dr Pearce asked me to provide a League teacher who could take regular classes there, and this became a popular activity.

The League had recently started a new venture to extend its work to the poorest areas. Advanced members were given a few weeks' intensive training, and then sent to take free classes in distressed areas and slum districts. These classes were organised in conjunction with a church or voluntary movement in the locality. They met with a good response, giving the advanced members a rewarding outlet for their enthusiasm, and their pupils some knowledge of physical training.

My work in these directions, and on the Fitness Council, gave me a wider view of what needed to be done. I realised that large sections of the population were completely untouched by the fitness drive. They participated vicariously in sporting events; but the pressure of existence left little energy at the day's or week's end for physical exercise, quite apart from the scarcity of facilities and finance. Most people also lacked incentive. In Nazi Germany fitness was compulsory; the means to achieve it were allied to the

National Socialist philosophy. In Britain, if the fitness drive was to succeed, it must be voluntary: this meant that it must appeal on its own merits to the public, and be associated, in some way, with the British way of life and the values which the nation thought important. I discussed these ideas with David. We both wanted to work in the sphere of social service, and this gave us another interest in common.

At present David was feeling his way. He had read politics, philosophy and economics at Oxford, but had no professional training, or wish to enter a profession as such. Politics interested him; the experience and insight he was now gaining would prove useful if at a later stage he stood for Parliament.

In my brief moments of respite from my tour of the League centres we met in London, and during several weekends, I stayed with him at his mother's and sister's homes in Wiltshire.

By now David had asked me to marry him, but I was still undecided. I knew that I loved him, and admired and respected him more than anyone I had met; but I did not feel ready for marriage. The responsibility of the League weighed heavily upon me; David's world seemed in many ways far removed from my own, and I could not see how I could continue my work if I entered it. Above all, I was still deeply attached to Ally and our friendship, and dreaded having to break it. David seemed like a fiery comet which could ignite me, but I was not at all sure that I would be able to match his force and flame.

In late October, I spent a weekend with David in Scotland. We stayed at the old Kingshouse coaching inn in Glencoe, under the shadow of Buchaille Etive Mor, the great mountain which guards the entrance to the glen. We spent all the first day climbing it. Autumn brought tints of tan and gold to the moors. Bracken glowed in wide patches of colour, and the small spears of the tormentil's leaves, now turning scarlet, struck points of fire from the anonymous stretches of peat. The sharp scent of bog myrtle rose from the damp ground; a curlew's or a raven's call echoed through the glen. It was easy to imagine the scene of the treacherous massacre over two hundred years ago, yet one felt that its human privation and terror must have soon been engulfed by the indifference of these great mountains. As we climbed up, a sense of peace and certainty entered my heart. The mists which shrouded

94

the future seemed to part and clear, as though a peak of destiny was emerging. I remembered my mother's words – 'I saw the man you would marry. A tall Scotsman.' All along I had felt that David was my fate, but that I might lack the strength and stamina to be equal to it. Now for the first time I saw that we needed one another, and that one might cherish and protect, as well as be challenged and stimulated.

Soon after this, I travelled down to Oxford one Sunday to see Ally. He was full of his Continental tour, and described it to me in detail as we drove into the Cotswold countryside. I thought how much more European he had become, and how his interests and powers of expression had widened since we had first met. He still had the same quizzical sense of humour and the same capacity to view a situation objectively; but much of his former reserve had vanished, and he was now able to give vent to his ideas and enthusiasms without an inhibiting shyness. We walked through the autumn fields and woods, and I thought of our friendship, and the happiness it had brought to us both. I knew that now I had a new and overriding loyalty which must take precedence. It seemed that I was standing on the threshold of womanhood, leaving my girlhood behind, and Ally with it. I was torn by this necessity, half-afraid to go on, unable to go back. In any other situation, Ally would have been my first confidant. I must now give him the means to understand.

I waited until we were driving back to Oxford; then asked him to stop the car and forced myself to be frank. Ally responded with his characteristic generosity and unselfishness; but we were both miserable, profoundly affected by the depth of our feelings. I boarded the train back to London with the sense that a carefree era was closing, perhaps for my whole generation.

In this state of inner conflict, I became tearful, jumpy and emotionally tense. At last Aunt Norah insisted that I should see a doctor. He interrogated me, and being a perspicacious man, his first question was, 'Are you in love?'

He prescribed a month's rest, and also suggested a month's separation from David, so that we could each think over our future alone. We were now on the eve of the Christmas holiday. I went to spend it with old friends in Ayrshire. David was staying about thirty miles away, over the moors at his home, Dungavel, but we conscientiously stuck to our separation. There was no communication between us, except a Christmas card decorated with Celtic interlacing designs, which he sent me, and which I treasured out of all proportion to its value.

As the weeks passed, I began to recover my equilibrium and my sense of proportion. The autumn had imposed too much strain. Now, removed from it, I realised that though love and marriage would open a new world and carry me into unknown fields of experience, nothing of the past need be lost, because it was already a part of me and would continue to be so. To give one's life to another, to share and support and uphold, was an enlargement; nothing could thereby be diminished. David's happiness and welfare had become more important to me than my own. I thought no longer of what I could get, or what I must give up, but of what I could give.

The issue became clear and simple. As the New Year dawned, I knew that David and I would marry.

CHAPTER 7

The Last Year of Peace

THE New Year was 1938 – the last year of peace. David and I started it with high hopes for the future; but looking back it is hard to understand how we could have entertained them.

War was imminent. Those at the centre of power in every nation possessed few illusions: but the majority of people still equated their horror of conflict with the delusive belief that a world war could not occur again. Europe had suffered too much during 1914–18. Such agony could not be repeated.

The democracies were on the defensive, waiting apprehensively for the dictators' next coup. Suspense saps initiative. The desire for peace was so strong that it justified almost any expedient to preserve it. Those who suffered the Nazi and Fascist evil were virtually powerless to oppose it. Those outside its orbit were possessed by a paralysis of mind and will, unable to recognise it for what it was, or to accept the inevitable outcome.

I was as blind as most, although letters which I began to receive from people I had met in Austria and Czechoslovakia a year before gave me some inkling of the true situation. In guarded language they spoke of the possibility of leaving their country, and of the likely take-over by the Nazis. Could I help them if they decided to come to Britain?

David was much more politically aware than I. He, too, hoped passionately for peace; but I believe now that he was already steeling his heart for war. He had studied the problem of German minorities in the countries bordering Germany – minorities which Hitler was now claiming for his Reich – and knew that different conditions obtained in different territories, and there could be no panacea which would bring justice to all. To be incorporated into the Nazi Reich would be a bitter, not a welcome, fate for many of German blood now living beyond Germany's frontier.

In the early days of the year the full apparatus of Nazi propaganda was focused on Austria.

'Ein Volk. Ein Reich. Ein Führer,' became the dominant theme. To those who did not know the deep divisions within Austria, and cared to forget the liberal and socialist struggle, and the contribution made to the life of the country by many eminent and cultured Jews, this doctrine of the union of German-speaking peoples sounded plausible enough. As always, Hitler succeeded in dividing his opponents, thus paralysing decisive action. Tension mounted week by week, until in March, German troops crossed the border, and streamed into Austria.

David wrote to Malcolm, who was abroad at the time:

Hitler has just marched into Austria, having decided to forestall Schuschnigg's plebiscite which he knew would go against him. Himmler and the secret police have been installed at once to ensure that the people vote the right way in Hitler's plebiscite. The usual régime of terror, arrests and imprisonment has started. What will happen to friends of ours there, heaven knows. Hitler has now made clear the price of Mussolini's acquiescence, i.e., a guarantee of the Brenner frontier and renunciation of South Tyrol. That is how the 'protector' of the Germans fulfils his word to them. If he tries anything with Czechoslovakia, I am convinced people here will not stand for it – they will treat it as another Belgium. Attempts at Anglo-German conciliation have been irreparably damaged – at least for a long time to come . . . It will be tragic to see happy-go-lucky Austria under a Prussian dictatorship. It's all very depressing, and I only hope to God we will start compulsory service and not stand any more non-sense.

A few days later David and I visited Austria for a fortnight's skiing holiday in the Tyrol. Innsbruck was sadly altered when we reached it. Massive red banners, each decorated with a black swastika, hung outside the station. Bands of Hitler Youth marched up and down the streets, singing Nazi songs and shouting slogans. The windows of many shops in the Maria Theresia Strasse had been broken, and the word *Jude* was scrawled across the cracked glass, in crude white paint. The hysterical acclamation, the arms jerking into a mechanical Hitler salute, and the din of bands promenading through the town, masked the fact that this union of Austria with Germany could only have taken place under duress. The radio blared forth Hitler's latest speech in strident staccato German. The compulsive phrases which seemed un-ending, became the *Leitmotiv* of our stay.

A plebiscite, designed to show the nation's approval of the Anschluss was about to be held. Everyone must vote. Bands of Hitler Youth marched through the streets, shouting the plebiscite slogan – *Jeder Deutsche stimmt mit 'Ja'. Nur ein Schwein stimmt mit 'Nein'*.[1]

David's friend, Dr Reut Nicolussi, was living in Innsbruck with his family. We talked frankly with him. South Tyrol's restitution had been rendered even more hopeless by recent events. Hitler's cynical desertion of the German-speaking South Tyrolese in recognition for Mussolini's support of the Anschluss showed his true feelings about German minorities in other countries. When they could not be useful as political pawns they were abandoned. David, nevertheless, promised to do what he could to arouse sympathy for the South Tyrolese cause in England. He was made a member of the Andreas Hofer Bund, the clandestine society working for South Tyrolese freedom; and he undertook to circulate propaganda pamphlets on our return.

The day of the plebiscite arrived. A fever of propaganda seized the town, which seemed entirely taken over by Nazi slogans, banners and loudspeakers. In the evening, Reut Nicolussi came to see us. He looked tired and drawn.

'How was it?' we asked.

'To-morrow,' he said, 'the Press will announce that Austria has supported the Anschluss with an overwhelming majority, 99%. There was no choice. Inside the voting booths were two cubicles, one marked "yes", and the other marked "no". Officials noted down which one you entered. I suppose almost everyone voted "yes".'

'And you?'

'I voted "no".'

We left Innsbruck feeling angry and dismayed. The Ötztal, which we now traversed on a high-level ski-tour, was as yet untouched by the Nazi fever; but we knew that it was only a matter of time before even these remote mountain huts and hamlets were affected. What we had seen in Innsbruck provided a disturbing

1. Every German votes with 'yes'. Only a swine votes with 'no'.

background to our thoughts, as our skis hissed through glacier powder snow, or creaked against their skins on the long climb upwards to the huts.

We spent two weeks in the Ötztal mountains, and then returned to Innsbruck where we saw Reut Nicolussi again. His valour and optimism were undiminished. He handed David the bundles of propaganda pamphlets, and smiled at us both.

'We must hope,' he said. 'Hope is the only thing left to us. We have come through worse than this before.'

'Remember your friends will stand by you,' said David.

Reut smiled. 'You know the old saying? In Germany the situation is serious but not impossible. In Austria the situation is impossible, but not serious. We must not forget how to laugh. Come back soon.'

At the station banners proclaiming, 'Ein Volk. Ein Reich. Ein Führer,' still decorated the platforms. The Austria we knew had vanished.

We announced our engagement in May. David had already told his mother and Malcolm, and I had told my Aunts Norah and Nan. Reactions varied. Nan with her radical views felt I was letting down the family by marrying into the aristocracy; conversely one of David's aunts asked his mother – 'Is she quite nice?' However, at Dungavel, when we reached it, a warm welcome awaited us.

Douglo had married Elizabeth Percy[1] the year before. They greeted us with congratulations and produced champagne. The next day, David's sister, Margaret Drummond-Hay,[2] and his brother, Geordie,[3] came over from Edinburgh to give us their good wishes. I knew Margaret already; her spontaneous charm had captivated me at our first meeting in Wiltshire the year before. Geordie I met for the first time. He was then practising at the Bar in Edinburgh, where he was also on the City Council. He had recently been appointed Commissioner for the Special Areas in Scotland, a post which the Government had created to bring

1. Lady Elizabeth Percy, daughter of the Duke and Duchess of Northumberland.
2. Lady Margaret Drummond-Hay.
3. Lord Nigel Douglas-Hamilton, later the Earl of Selkirk.

renewed life into the Scottish economy. Geordie was destined for politics. He had a good working knowledge of Scotland's problems, and a keen appreciation of national and foreign affairs. The penetration of his thought could be disturbing, and his manner – challenging and sometimes brusque – often induced shyness in those to whom he was talking. I felt somewhat in awe of him, but sensed an integrity of mind and spirit, and a depth of feeling which were much like David's. He cross-questioned us about our recent visit to Austria, taking a pessimistic view of the future, realising that Britain was on the edge of war with Germany.

As the weekend progressed I began to understand him better, and by the end of it foundations were laid for a lasting friendship. When he said goodbye, and added, 'I am very glad that you are going to marry David,' I knew that his approval was something to value.

David and I walked on the moors again together, faced a barrage of press photographers, and received a series of comic telegrams from various members of his family. These came over the telephone, and were handed to us by an impassive butler whose features showed no glimmer of surprise.

The one I remember best, read: 'You are letting us down – Women's League of Health and Beauty.'

I had already realised that anyone who married a Douglas-Hamilton would have to cultivate a special sense of humour.

The League still absorbed most of my time. My fears that marriage to David would limit my activities proved groundless. He, and all his family, recognised the value of the League's work, and gave me every encouragement to pursue it. Later, when the time came to make plans for our wedding, David's mother insisted that it should be held in Glasgow Cathedral, because 'then you can include everyone. Prunella is for the people. She must share her wedding with all.' I now received congratulations and good wishes from many quarters, including my League friends.

The League had been invited to participate that summer in two Physical Education Congresses abroad; one in Germany and one in Finland. Meantime, David and I planned a short visit to Czechoslovakia to see the great Sokol display there.

We flew to Prague and found it *en fête*, a festival atmosphere permeating the whole city. Over five thousand performers drawn from Slav members of the Sokol Movement in Czechoslovakia, Hungary and Rumania, were taking part in the displays. Flags flew from historic buildings; and between performances boys and girls dressed in their national costumes strolled with linked arms, laughing and singing, through the streets. In the stadium itself – a vast expanse, one of the largest in Europe – a huge and enthusiastic audience had assembled. The arena was packed with serried ranks of performers. Their movements, perfectly timed and executed, looked more like a force of nature – wind rippling through a cornfield or waves moving across an ocean – than a man-made spectacle. From straight lines they changed to circles, diamonds or squares, the different patterns flowing from one another with surprising ease. Under the bright sun, accompanied by gay folk-music, the performers drew the audience into a world of harmony and beauty. It required a strong effort of the imagination to remember that all this was taking place under the threat of Nazi domination, and that Czechoslovakia was the next country on Hitler's list. In fact, the Sokols were giving their last public display for many years. Soon the organisation would be disbanded, several of its leaders sentenced to death, and its members silenced for the duration of the Nazi occupation. This last display was not an exercise in national propaganda for a political end; rather it showed the unity and passionate desire for independence of a country which had only recently achieved freedom, and which counted on Britain and France to help to preserve it.

A few weeks later I was able to contrast this spontaneous demonstration of popular feeling with the rigidly controlled propaganda of the German Reich. The Congress to which the League had been invited in Germany was sponsored by 'Kraft durch Freude' ('Strength through Joy'), the organisation which arranged cultural activities and holidays for the German people. It consisted of a four-day stay in Hamburg, followed by a cruise for three weeks to Lisbon and Madeira, in company with teams from many other countries, on the *Wilhelm Gustloff*, the luxury liner built to take the workers of Germany on holiday cruises to the Mediterranean and the Baltic.

Peggy and Joan St Lo and I accompanied the League team to Hamburg and stayed with them on board the ship during the

Congress. The huge white liner, moored alongside the quay, in Germany's busiest port, made a spectacular setting for this concourse of thirty-two different nationalities. All the teams were accommodated on board, and they all ate together in the dining-room, where each table was decorated with a different flag. Most participants wore colourful national dress, and the variety of their languages made a cheerful noise. Whether or not they understood one another, smiles of enjoyment and goodwill were common currency among them all. At night the liner blazed with lights, three bands came aboard, and dancing – of every style and variety – took place all over the ship.

During the day, mass demonstrations of German physical culture and folk-dancing were held, and smaller displays by individual national teams were given in halls and theatres throughout the city. The League team performed twice, their neat black-and-white uniforms and slim figures contrasting with the elaborate peasant dresses of the Balkans, and the generous build of the blonde German girls.

On the last day of the Congress there was a parade through the streets of Hamburg, in which all the national teams participated. Crowds lined the pavements, and there was no doubt about the warmth with which the British flag was greeted.

The following morning, the *Wilhelm Gustloff* sailed out of Hamburg on her cruise to Lisbon and Madeira, with bands playing, crowds cheering and an escort of German planes weaving above the ship to speed her on her way. The St Los and I flew to Denmark, and then boarded a boat which carried us across the Baltic to our next Physical Education Congress in Helsinki.

The boat was small, quiet and comfortable; a welcome change from the noise and crowds from which we had just come. We repaired to the wooden-lined dining-saloon and refreshed ourselves with schnapps and the *smørgåsbord*. Before going to bed, I went up on deck. I was tired, full of conflicting impressions, and wanted to relax, in body and mind. The northern evening extended in luminous light all around me. Space and silence permeated sky and sea. The boat moved slowly across the still waters, casting behind her a wake of dancing waves. Seagulls dipped and glided, as I leant over the stern in a reflective mood. How difficult it was, I thought, to evaluate the hospitality we had just received, to differentiate between means and ends.

In many quarters, mass displays of physical fitness were suspect as being evidence of regimentation. But in Czechoslovakia I had seen the spontaneous harmony of thousands of Slavs, drawn together by their love of independence, free from any coercion. The Germans in their displays had performed with superb assurance and conviction. Apparently, the participants believed in what they were doing, but did they also believe in their rôle as the supermen and women of Europe?

The representatives from the thirty-two countries who had assembled on the *Wilhelm Gustloff* had a love of physical fitness in common, but not necessarily a love for the Nazi ideology. The Nazis had invited them there, and some of the means which the Nazis were using – increased opportunities for recreation, holidays and culture – were right in themselves. But was this of any value if the ends were evil?

I thought of the German leaders to whom I had been introduced on the *Wilhelm Gustloff*: the Reichsportsführer, Herr von Tschammer und Osten, a Nordic type with looks to match his rôle; Dr Ley, the burly leader of Kraft durch Freude; Herr Himmler, seemingly inoffensive, bespectacled, with a handshake like a wet fish, and the appearance of a minor clerk. These men seemed normal and friendly, yet to have reached the Nazi hierarchy they must possess a ruthlessness which would appal me, could I see it in action. How did this tie up with the friendliness and hospitality with which Kraft durch Freude had organised the Congress? Perhaps the key to the riddle lay outside the Party, among the ordinary citizens of Hamburg, who had cheered the British flag, and who longed for peace as much as any of the Congress participants. There were millions like them throughout Germany, voiceless and helpless if it came to war.

In Hamburg I had also met an old Oxford friend of David's – Prince Ernst August of Hanover – who introduced himself to me after watching one of the League performances. We discussed the Congress, which he viewed with some irony. He was proof against Nazi propaganda. 'Let your girls enjoy the cruise,' he said. 'They're too sensible, and too insular, to be taken in. Nothing is as good for the British as Britain.'

This was true. A strength, when it came to resisting a foreign political creed; a weakness when one tried to pioneer new ideas or methods among a maze of established practice and tradition. In Britain there was also a certain complacency to be fought. 'Things have always been like this. Why should they change?' I wished that the wind of urgency, so apparent through the Continent, could blow across the Channel.

My thoughts turned to my mother and her visionary ideals. The League had now made contacts on the Continent; extended to the Dominions. But how could this infinitesimal contribution stem the tide of the Nazi will to power? Had my mother realised the full extent and domination of evil in the world? Or realising it, had she turned away from it and thrown all her resources into her own creative work? There were many ways of combating evil. My mother had chosen an indirect method rather than a direct confrontation. But my generation might not be allowed such a choice.

I thought of David, who I knew would share these reflections. Already he was committed to resistance.

The evening darkened, and stars pricked the sky. The boat chugged deliberately on her way. Waves splashed softly in her wake, gleaming in the last of the light. 'Hurry,' they seemed to say. 'Hurry, hurry.' Time was diminishing for us all.

We spent four days in Helsinki, at a Congress called the 'Suomen Voimistelun Suurkisat', which brought together individual teams from different parts of Finland, and from the neighbouring Scandinavian countries. It was in the nature of a specialists' gathering – fascinating for those, like ourselves, who were interested in dancing and physical training. Teams gave performances throughout the city, and there was opportunity for an interchange of experiences and ideas. Our representation consisted of a small team of League teachers who performed on several occasions. They were well received, and we gained much from the fruitful discussions which followed the performance.

For the first time I saw the plastic movement of the Lithuanian countries – a style which was to be widely adopted. We made friends with Ellen Anderson and her team of Danish girls from Copenhagen, and I was delighted to find also a team from the Medau School in Berlin, where I had studied eighteen months before. Hospitality was friendly and unexaggerated, and the sincerity of this gathering of professionals was an interesting contrast to the blare and propaganda of Hamburg. Here again I found myself in a small country menaced by a powerful neighbour; this time Russia. One could sense the endurance and valour of the national character. It manifested itself in a certain dourness – different from the exuberance of the volatile Eastern Europeans with whom we had recently been fraternising – and we found little gaiety or spontaneity among the people. But, serious though they might be, their concern for the welfare and happiness of their guests was meticulous. We learned much. This Congress, run from private resources, proved that Government patronage and propaganda were not essential for success.

On my return to England, I found David deep in plans for a Fitness Summer School in the Highlands. The school was sponsored by the Northern Regional Fitness Committee, whose area comprised Inverness-shire, Moray and Nairn, Ross and Cromarty, and Sutherland. Kurt Hahn had recommended David as warden; and his assistant was Sandy Henderson, then teaching at Dollar Academy, later headmaster of Lord Wandsworth's School. Together they were recruiting a talented staff.

A location for the school had been found at Guisachan, a large house in Glen Affric, north of Loch Ness, formerly the family home of Lady Aberdeen. The house had been empty for many years, gradually falling into decay in the midst of one of the most remote and beautiful glens in the Highlands. Now, overnight, it was cleaned of its cobwebs, fires were lit to dispel damp, and doors and windows were flung open to the breezes of the glen. Camp beds were put up in all the bedrooms, musty outhouses turned into shower rooms, and the old house awoke in readiness to receive its new visitors. They were drawn from all parts of the Highlands and Islands, young men and women who were teachers for the most part, and who all shared an interest in youth and fitness training. The school planned to hold two courses of a fortnight each; and some students would stay for the whole month. Activities would include physical exercises; athletics training and boxing (for the men); Highland dancing and expeditions.

The project was an experiment; nothing quite like it had been attempted before. The primary object was to train leaders for youth work, but the underlying aim went much deeper. It was to demonstrate and inculcate fitness in the widest sense; not merely to develop health of body and powers of leadership, but also to awaken the spirit, and challenge the character of the students. The incomparable Highland countryside was to be used for this purpose, and two weekend expeditions were planned for each course where students would experience the beauty of the mountains and learn the endurance necessary to complete a long trek.

David and I discussed the programme and the plans at length. He had no previous experience of running a course of this kind, but it was Kurt Hahn's conviction that he possessed the necessary powers of inspiration; the fact that he was not a professional would enable him to take a wide view, and he had an expert staff on whom he could rely. Nevertheless, he set off for Scotland with some misgivings at entering such a new field of activity.

Before long I had received a couple of delighted letters:

This week-end we had the expeditions. Twenty-eight men did a twenty-five mile walk over to Kintail, about half of them over Ben Attow. They camped near Loch Duich, then marched back yesterday via the Falls of Glomach. They enjoyed themselves tremendously. Others went for walks in Glen Affric, and others climbed Mamm Soul and the peaks to the north of Guisachan. Many of the girls had never walked before, and some old men, over forty, did about twenty-five miles in a day.

The course ended in a *ceilidh* – a dance which included singing and Highland reels. David wrote:

I played the pipes for a sword dance, and we've got a grand Highlander, a Fraser, who sang some Gaelic songs. He has one of the softest and sweetest natural voices I've ever heard. The spirit of this course is marvellous. It's wonderful to see how 'full-out' everyone is. There are quite a number of people here who come from the Outer Isles. It is at times like these that I begin to wonder how I can ever leave Scotland again . . . I feel I must eventually fill the place required of me in Scotland. How wonderful it would be if the whole of the Highlands could be a national park for everybody and not reserved for the enjoyment of a few! That I hope will come ere long.

I joined David at Guisachan as soon as I could leave London. He met me, tanned and buoyant with good spirits, wearing an old kilt and an open-necked shirt.

We wandered through the firs, silver birches and rowan-trees, which surrounded the house, while he told me about the course. The heather was in full bloom, bees hummed, and the intoxicating sweetness of a hot summer day in the Highlands filled the air. David glowed with pride in the success of his venture and I shared his happiness. Later, I watched him welcome back the students from their treks over the hills, and listened while they gave eager accounts of their experiences. The last of them returned late at night, marching in from Kintail to the rousing strains of the bag-pipes. They had tramped seventy miles in two days across some of the wildest country in the Highlands.

David's staff included Kathleen O'Rourke, teacher of the League classes in Dublin, who brought a wealth of experience as well as her native Irish exuberance to her work; Jock Hunter, from Robert Gordon's College, Aberdeen, an expert performer at all sports; and Dr Robert Bolton from the Pioneer Health Centre, who kept a watchful lookout for any signs of over-strain. Dr Bolton had to be convinced of the value of this type of organised activity.

'It smacks too much of coercion,' he said to David. 'I don't believe anything of value can be imposed from without. People must find their own incentive.'

'But they must be given the right environment to awaken the incentive,' David replied. 'We produce a set of experiences here which challenge each person. It's up to them how they respond. They can take it or leave it.'

'While they're here they have to co-operate. They can't contract out.'

'They don't want to. They get caught up in the spirit of it all, and find themselves doing things they never thought they'd be capable of.'

'True. But does the enthusiasm and inspiration last when they return home to their own environment?'

'That remains to be seen. We hope so. At any rate, what they experience here is of value for its own sake, even if it leads to nothing more.'

The rare occurrence in the Highlands of continual sunshine accompanied the course. By the last evening students and staff had merged into a community which had shared an unforgettable experience. At the final *ceilidh* they presented David with a silver salver – Guisachan's wedding present to us both. David thanked them; then, as soon as he could, left the room, taking me with him. He led me outside, into the soft Highland night, not yet dark. We stood there silently. Light glowed from the old house; figures within wove patterns back and forth across the windows; the pipe music, and snatches of talk and laughter wafted out on the evening air. It seemed that ghosts of former days flitted among the trees, drawn by the radiance and rebirth of their home.

I was surprised to find David moved, almost to tears, by the presentation which had just been made to him, and by the affection which it showed.

I realised the strength and depth of his love for Scotland, and the extent of his sensitivity hidden beneath his layer of reserve. I, too, was moved by his response to appreciation and success; things which I was inclined to take for granted.

The *ceilidh* ended in the small hours of the morning. Kurt Hahn had been watching it in a reflective mood, evaluating its spirit and what had been achieved. His visionary eyes glowed. 'You've succeeded beyond all expectations,' he said to David. 'This project must go on.' He was convinced that something of far-reaching value and importance had been demonstrated.

It took time for it to develop. The war intervened. Many of the Guisachan students were called up for war service, and so were unable to pass on what they had learned. But the seeds had been sown. The spirit of Guisachan survived. And after the war it was born again in a movement which was to become famous throughout Britain and the world – 'Outward Bound' – whose original inspiration emanated from this Highland glen.

The summer had been one of intense activity, leaving little time for leisure or reflection. In early September we returned to London, to prepare for our wedding in October. Almost at once, we, and the whole country, were plunged into the ordeal of Munich. Since then, so many crises have afflicted the world, so much horror has been suffered, and peace has so often been shattered, that it is difficult to remember the anxiety and suspense of those days.

Psychologically, Britain was unprepared for war. Though some people realised the full implications of appeasement, many were prepared to accept peace at almost any price. The full horror of the Nazi régime, with its accompanying concentration camps and secret police, was not yet understood by the majority of Britons. Total rejection of Hitler's word had not yet taken place. Some still felt that rights for the Sudeten Germans in Czechoslovakia would be his last demand.

But even more pressing than these considerations was the fact that the country was insufficiently armed for war. David prowled round Primrose Hill one evening to inspect the anti-aircraft precautions, and found one gun mounted hopefully on the hill. If war came, he would be called up at once, into the RAF Volunteer Reserve.

At the height of the crisis, David wrote to me:

Whatever happens, I can only say that it is my firm belief that we are coming to the dawn of a period when greater happiness will be found for *all* human beings, and it is going to be our work to fight for this ideal. The exaggerated idea of nationalism will fail, as it is bound to, and the time will come when 'a man's a man for a' that'. The world is at present going through the pains of transition to that stage, but it's none the less painful at the time and may be yet more so . . . I know everything will come right in the end.

We considered putting our wedding forward, and went down to the House of Commons where Douglo was listening to the latest debate, to ask his advice. He greeted us with tears in his eyes.

'Chamberlain has just announced that he's flying to Munich,' he said. 'He may avoid war. But at what price?'

In the relief that surged through Britain on the Prime Minister's return from Munich, and his announcement of 'peace in our time', the cost of the reprieve was largely forgotten. My attitude was ambivalent. I felt unashamedly relieved that war had been avoided, but at the same time I was sick with sorrow and apprehension for my friends in Czechoslovakia.

The Seton-Watsons were deeply involved; Uncle Seton's life work had been betrayed. Aunt May, who was giving my wedding with Aunt Norah, came to see me.

'Hitler's promises are worth nothing,' she said. 'Before long he will invade. I'm sorry, Prunella, your uncle can't come to the wedding. He hasn't the heart for anything now.'

David, too, had little hope for the future; both he and his brothers were convinced that war had only been postponed.

Plans for our marriage proceeded. David invited Ernst August to come from Germany to share the duties of best man with his brother Geordie. I ordered a trousseau, and the date – the 15th of October – drew near. Looking back at our wedding now, it seems almost unreal; a last flash of the pre-war era, already threatened by unimaginable change. Just so must my mother have felt when she remembered her own marriage before the first war.

Two large pre-wedding receptions were given for us in London, one by David's mother at Claridge's, the other by the League. At the first, I met all the Douglas-Hamilton family and friends. At the second, David shook hands with over a thousand women. These receptions set the scene for the rest of the festivities, which were on a massive scale. By now, we were public figures and had to suffer accordingly, with maximum publicity. A special wedding train carried guests overnight from London up to Glasgow, among them Ally and 'Tante' Isi von Gleichen from Berlin, as well as a great number of League teachers, organisers and headquarters staff. From David's side came servants, tenants and farmers from the Dungavel estate, civic authorities from Hamilton, and students and staff from Guisachan. Glasgow Cathedral accommodated everyone with ease.

I was followed by my cousin Drella, a close girlfriend, Mary Lee Boyd, and eight small attendants, six of whom were nephews and nieces of David's. The aisle seemed immense, as I walked up it on the arm of my Uncle Alec, Aunt Norah's husband. Shafts of autumn sunlight shone through the stained-glass windows into the austere stone interior, lighting up the tartan worn by David's brothers, and his ushers, and gleaming on his own Royal Stuart kilt. I took my place beside David, conscious only of two things;

his presence on my right-hand side, and another presence on my left – that of my mother, so close that I felt my hand could slip into hers. Our marriage lines were spoken by the Reverend Arthur Buxton, vicar of All Souls, Langham Place, in London, who had conducted her memorial service.

Aunt Nan had designed a special uniform for the sixteen picked members who represented the League at the wedding. She saw to it that after the ceremony these girls followed immediately behind the bridal retinue, preceding the chief guests. So down the aisle an unorthodox procession streamed, to the pipe-tune of 'Lord David Douglas-Hamilton's Wedding March' which Pipe-Major Ross, who played us out of the cathedral, had composed specially for the occasion.

At the reception which crammed a thousand guests into St Andrew's Hall in Glasgow, David's sense of hospitality did not desert him. Responding to the bridal toast:

'I want to thank you all for turning up to-day, when I was in such great need of assistance,' he said. 'I am so glad we were able to have our wedding in Scotland. You see, I have begun to dominate my wife already! And I hope when we are settled in our wee "but-an-ben" you will all come and see us.'

'What if they do?' I said later to David, as we drove away together through crowds of well-wishers who lined the streets. But he was beyond answering or caring. All he knew was that we were alone together, headed for the Highlands, married, complete. Everything else – the glare of publicity, the anxieties of near-war, the tensions of work – could wait.

CHAPTER 8

The Storm Breaks

FROM an early age Skye had been a haven for me. My childhood visits to the Seton-Watsons at Kyle House had left a lasting impression.

The lapping of waves on a pebbled shore, the cry of gulls, the smell of peat-smoke, the spring of turf underfoot – these things brought a recognition to which my ancestry responded; a sense of homecoming at once indefinable and acute. I returned to the Skye hills from varying crises throughout the years, and found them always the same. Majestic and remote, they were impervious alike to outer events or inner moods; vehicles, for me, of a mysterious source of life.

David shared this feeling, so we chose Skye for the start of our honeymoon, adding to my previous experience there a period of unique companionship. We spent a week at Kyle House, lent to us by the Seton-Watsons. The house stood on a wooded peninsula whose cliffs dropped sheer into the loch; from the high ground above it a panorama of water and islands swept away to the Cuillin mountains, a dark range on the horizon. I knew it all well, having come here for holidays since I was twelve years old. The garden, the stretch of woodland, and the sea-shore, were all impregnated for me with childish fantasies and memories of growing-up. Each place contained its own particular magic, and had been made the receptacle of the dreams of adolescence. Now, in some miraculous way, many of these dreams were coming true.

The first week of our marriage slipped past with walks on the autumn hills and quiet evenings reading by lamp-light before a peat fire. Then we travelled on, crossing the stormy Minch, to the Outer Isles. Enamoured of all things Celtic, we carried our musical instruments – bagpipes and a small Irish harp – with us. Our long-suffering landlords in Lewis, Harris and the Uists listened, while in our hotel rooms we practised the chanter and the *clarsach*, sometimes simultaneously! David spoke Gaelic, I began to learn it, and we exchanged tunes and stories with the islanders at impromptu *ceilidhs* where whisky flowed far into the night.

Our honeymoon was a happy one. We already knew the best and worst of one another. Our period of adjustment had taken place before marriage; now that we were finally committed to each other, personal stresses and strains fell away. We forgot international tensions and the threat of war, and simply enjoyed being together in beautiful and simple surroundings.

We were brought sharply down to earth, however, when we returned to London and tried to visit the Crimea for the latter part of our honeymoon. David was refused a Russian visa. Climbing in the Caucasus a few years before, he had been openly critical of the Communist régime. Now the granting of a visa was evaded and postponed for so long that at last, having got as far as Budapest, we cancelled the trip, and went instead, via Naples and Rome, to stay in Austria with Ernst August's parents – the Duke and Duchess of Brunswick. A greater contrast to the USSR we could not have chosen.

We arrived at their large shooting-lodge at Gmunden, near Salzburg, to find a rambling, white-painted house, full of sporting trophies. Ernst's mother was a daughter of the Kaiser. I half-expected a rigid Prussian atmosphere, but found instead a welcome informality.

The Duchess was a woman of strong personality, used to getting her own way, but also witty and human, with forceful opinions which matched her lively intelligence. She swiftly put us both at our ease, talked to me about the League, in which she took a great interest, being herself an enthusiast for fitness, and discussed politics with David. Her daughter Frederika had married the Crown Prince of Greece a year earlier. Her four sons would be called up immediately to fight in the German army, if there was war. In spite of recent set-backs, she still clung to the hope of Anglo-German understanding. She spoke of Frederika's happiness when visiting the 'wild Hamilton boys' at Dungavel, and of Ernst's enjoyment of his Oxford days. 'These barriers which divide us are artificial political ones,' she said. 'We, who know both countries, must try to break them down.' But she was enough a daughter of her father to sympathise with Germany's desire for a place in the sun: a right which she maintained had been neglected by other European powers, until events had forced them to consider it.

Ernst August had inherited his father's impeccable manners. His three years at Oxford had also left their mark. He had a way of decrying his possessions which was very English. 'I hope you won't be too uncomfortable,' he said, handing me into a palatial open sports-car. 'Do keep warm in this old thing,' wrapping me up in his mother's expensive fur coat.

We drove past sparkling lakes and snow-capped mountains, the November frost tingling our cheeks. David and Ernst discussed the Anschluss. I noticed that their attitudes were hardening. They were each taking up points of view which they did not mean to relinquish. In some dimension beyond their control they were already preparing to fight on opposite sides.

At the end of our stay, Ernst saw us off in Salzburg. His mother had given us an armful of heather to remind us of the Alps. As the train began to move, Ernst thrust a parcel containing a black red-lined Austrian jacket and skirt into my arms. His pleasant open face beamed from the platform. 'A present to bring you back,' he called. '*Auf Wiedersehen.*'

Four months later Germany's rape of Czechoslovakia took place. We had planned a skiing trip to Austria, but in the event, decided to go to Switzerland instead. Ernst August met us for one night in a town just over the Swiss border. The imminence of war now coloured everything. It was impossible to communicate without political undertones and an unconscious bias towards one's own country. Malcolm was with us, and he, David and Ernst talked most of the night. I listened with a hopeless feeling that the time for conversation was past. I heard not their words, but the anxiety, the fear and the violence which lay beneath them.

Young men and women throughout Europe were talking in the same way during that March of 1939, hoping somehow by their words to change their fate. Even now, we could not believe that war would come. We clung to the hope that somehow sanity and goodwill would prevail.

The hours stretched out, and the three talked on and on, loath to end the evening, loath to part.

They laughed as well as talked that night. Malcolm described how, when the invasion of Britain took place, he and David would retire to the Highlands to act as guides to the enemy, sabotaging mountain ascents by cutting the climbing rope at the right moment. Ernst remembered dinners at Oxford, evenings in London, climbs in Scotland. At last dawn came, and we stumbled to bed.

Ernst left next morning. His train crossed the German frontier as we resumed our separate journey to the Alps. Already our evening with him had become a memory. David never saw Ernst again.

In June, the League arranged another large display at Wembley Stadium. Five thousand members took part, including some from Canada and Australia. Teams from Denmark, Finland and Germany were also invited, and had accepted. But the European situation had become too precarious to risk their participation.

However, a League team did attend one more international event – the Swedish Lingiad, held in Stockholm in July 1939. The National Fitness Council sponsored the British representation, which consisted of a number of teams drawn from the Ling Physical Education Colleges, and various voluntary organisations.

Confined together for three days, on a small boat bound for Stockholm, these teams had plenty of time to nurse their rivalries. Rounds of propitiatory drinks were consumed, followed by barbed appraisals of one another's systems of physical training. As became the insular British, each team kept largely to itself. But many sidelong glances were cast at the smart travelling uniforms of the twenty young League teachers; particularly when, on landing in Sweden, more than their fair share of publicity came their way.

Stockholm, Venice of the North, with its dazzling waters and graceful eighteenth-century buildings, made a beautiful setting for the Congress which commemorated the centenary of Piers Ling, founder of Swedish gymnastics. The Swedes, who presumably had been practising his exercises for the last hundred years, provided an eloquent testament to his methods, with their upright carriage and healthy outdoor appearance. They were rivalled by the Germans, who appeared with a huge contingent on our old friend the *Wilhelm Gustloff*. Strictly supervised, they were taken directly to the stadium and back again for rehearsal and performance, and not allowed to mix with any other teams or with the local population. Their mass display started with a mile sprint round the cinder-track by five hundred men, sun-burned to an identical deep brown colour, and continued with daring feats of gymnastics on apparatus, and a dancing item by five hundred girls who wove intricate patterns to the music of a Strauss waltz.

The British performances were much more democratic, and much less spectacular. Each team had its own uniform, method and presentation, so that the British contingent, when it lined up for the opening march past the Swedish king, presented a motley appearance.

The Swedes entertained us royally. After the day's performances our new-found Swedish friends took us 'orienteering' (running on a compass course through thick woods), swimming in lakes surrounded by pines, and dining in island log cabins. The Swedish summer nights – light all through – made it impossible to go to bed. Every moment of the week's stay was lived at a zenith of enjoyment.

The climax came on the last night. The palace had already given a reception for visiting delegates. Now the city of Stockholm entertained teams from every country in their magnificent City Hall. Gold mosaic walls reflected and magnified the lights of candelabra standing on long rows of tables set for the banquet. There were toasts and speeches. Then tables were cleared away, music began, and formality was replaced by an infectious gaiety. Hundreds of young Europeans, all dressed in their national costumes, flooded into the great hall to dance. In this babel of talk and laughter there were no barriers of race or nation. All mixed together in spontaneous ease, united by the mood of the occasion.

Round the hall ran a gallery, from which a wide staircase swept down to the room below. Representatives of every country assembled in the gallery, each bearing their national flag. When all were ready, the phalanx descended the magnificent staircase and crossed the great hall, flags gleaming and swaying to the accompaniment of the gleaming, swaying crowd. A wonderful unanimity swept over the whole assembly. Once again, I felt the power of a common interest to unite people, to create under-standing and tolerance, to drive out suspicion and fear. If only it could have lasted!

I went straight from Stockholm to the Highlands, where I joined David at the Fitness Summer School he was running at Gordon Castle. Once again, students assembled from all over the High-lands and Islands. Several had been to Guisachan the year before. They helped to carry the spirit which had been created there into this second effort. A repeat performance could never be so ex-citing; on the other hand David and his staff had learnt much from the previous course at Guisachan, and this they now put into practice. The mighty Cairngorms were the testing-ground for the expeditions. Glenmore Lodge, afterwards to become a training centre of the Central Council of Physical Recreation, was used as a camping base. Once again an old disused house sprang to life.

August was drawing to its close. We spent the last days of it at Dungavel. On the way from Gordon Castle, we had a week's climbing in Skye, joined by two of our new Swedish friends, Count Mac Hamilton, and Görel Gyllenkrok. Görel was one of Stockholm's most beautiful girls, and her character matched her looks. With her flaxen hair and blue eyes, she reminded me of Viking sagas and legends of a Snow Queen. She quickly became a close friend. Mac was as gay and debonair in Scotland as in Stockholm, and he maintained his insouciance in spite of some arduous days on the Cuillins.

At Dungavel, we found most of David's family. On the evening of our arrival, his mother presided over the long dining-table. All four brothers were there, all in Highland dress. Candles glowed on tartan kilts, velvet doublets and lace jabots. Betty, Douglo's wife, and Görel reflected the gentle light with their fair beauty, and gave it back again, touched with added grace. The dinner proceeded at a leisurely pace, each dish brought in by the butler and served by footmen, amid gleaming silver and sparkling glass. Talk and laughter circulated round the table. The occasion seemed the epitome of civilised enjoyment.

Suddenly I realised with acute certainty that it would never occur again. This life was over. The four brothers would part and would never be reunited. I looked round the room, aware of every detail, conscious as never before of the supreme value of this present moment. It brought, at one and the same time, a poignant happiness and a great fear.

We came down to breakfast next morning, to find large black headlines in the daily papers. Germany had announced her pact with Russia.

Telegrams came for Geordie and Douglo, calling them to service with the RAF. Mac and Görel made hurried plans to return to Sweden.

Our world was disintegrating. David and I travelled swiftly to London, to await his call-up.

During that September the weather was brilliant. Day succeeded day with sapphire blue skies. The barrage balloons, which had blossomed mysteriously overhead, glittered in the sunshine: far above them tracks of aeroplanes, like arrows shot from the clouds, blazoned their patterns across the sky. David and I walked aimlessly through the London streets and parks, waiting for action, unable to act.

All over Britain, the machine of mobilisation creaked into life, and individual existences, with their small patterns of problems and joys, were fed into it. People became numbers, parts of units, cogs of machines. Uniforms appeared in the streets, posters warned against careless talk, ration-books and gas-masks were issued. Preparations for war invaded every department of life. Overnight choice and privacy fled.

I loathed it all. War appeared to me to be the negation of everything I held dear. Until now, I had found it simple to accept life as it came. At times it had called for courage and tenacity, but I had never questioned my fundamental beliefs, or doubted that the task of a woman was to create and preserve life. Now the whole nation and everyone in it was being organised to destroy. I rebelled against this with every fibre of my being. If life was to become nothing but a battle for survival, individuals would be increasingly dehumanised, stamped with the mechanical responses necessary to win the conflict, but bereft of the sources of creativity and joy. I was beset by fear of loss, of danger and of separation; but even more strongly in those first days I grieved for the magnitude of the tragedy which had overtaken the whole world. The darkness of London, transformed overnight from a brilliant busy city, seemed symbolic.

David felt differently. He also hated war, but saw it more rationally than I, as a necessary evil which must be faced in order to preserve life as we knew it for ourselves and our children. He hated war, but he hated the Nazi régime more, and he accepted war as the only means which would destroy it. Until now, we had thought identically on all fundamental subjects. With the coming of war, a thin wedge, no more substantial than a layer of tissue paper, began to divide us. The blood of Border warriors flowed in David's veins. The ancient masculine challenge to prove himself in battle stirred him and roused his fighting spirit. From the beginning he wished to be where the conflict was fiercest. I could not pretend to a bellicosity I did not feel. I was silent, taking refuge in day-dreams where all would be as before, but knowing in my heart that nothing could ever be the same again.

Our thoughts often turned to our friends in Europe. David wrote to Malcolm:

... to us, it is inconceivable to believe that a whole people can necessarily be bad because of the language they speak. Some fools seem to think so about the Germans. We are told to hate the Germans. A fighting man doesn't need to hate – he should fight for an idea.

He continued in another letter:

I don't believe Hitler has an atom's chance of winning, though it may take long to beat him. On the other hand, it may not take so long though we daren't even hope for that: it all depends what the German people can do. It's so utterly mad when you think of Ernst and all our other friends fighting on the other side. How utterly wicked to plunge the world into war like that! ... Anyway, it's the end of Hitler and I trust all that he stands for. For God's sake let's hope for a just peace at the end of it all, and that we may live to see it.

On the eve of the declaration of war I wrote to my old friend, 'Tante' Isi von Gleichen, in Berlin. No reply came. The barrier had closed.

The League was one of the peacetime activities which the war decapitated. Classes emptied overnight, as teachers and members were called into war work. Our large headquarters in central London became an impossible burden, and soon had to be evacuated. As I witnessed this break-up of the work for which my mother had given her life, a new source of bitterness fed my hatred of war. I was unable to see that the seeds which she had planted would blossom in other fields, for League teachers and members took their League training with them into the Forces and their war work, where it helped many of them to carry on.

Peggy and Joan St Lo maintained the classes in London. It was due to their efforts, and the efforts of members in fifty other centres which remained open, that the League survived. But it was a question of survival – and only just survival. Gone were the days of expansion and pioneering. The League's coat had now to be cut with severely rationed cloth. Here, too, creativity was at a standstill; this department of my life, which up to then had been consistently exciting and rewarding, closed down.

David and I had been looking for a house in London, and we continued with our search, although the heart had now gone out of the enterprise. We found an eighteenth-century house in Campden Hill Square; a typical London house with two rooms on each of its three stories, and a basement dining-room and kitchen. It had a small paved garden in front, looking over the square, and a lawn behind, in the centre of which grew a large pear tree. We mounted to the top floor and looked over the roofs and chimneys spread below.

'We'll have a fine view of the air-raids,' David said.

We bought the house very cheaply, as most people were trying to sell London property, rather than buy, and moved in just after Christmas. We had no opportunity to make the house come alive; at present it could only be a base for our possessions. If it – and we – survived the war, it might yet blossom into a home.

After his call-up, David was sent first to Hastings, where pilots from RAFVR units were being sorted out and drafted for further training. There he met Richard Hillary, whose book *The Last Enemy* later became an epic account of the Battle of Britain; and Noel Agazarian, an old friend from Oxford days. I, with other wives and girlfriends, visited Hastings at weekends. We walked

beside the cold sea, and stayed in the holiday hotels, commandeered now by the Services, and adapting themselves
grudgingly to their new rôle. It was a strange limbo sensation,
living between two worlds, the old gone, the new not yet begun.
One looked round the room and realised that in a few months'
time the majority of these young men might be dead. Most of
them became pilots in the Battle of Britain and many did not
survive it.

In March, David's father died. The family assembled at
Dungavel, and the four brothers carried his coffin to the church
and then to his grave in the grounds of Dungavel. His piper
played a pibroch, as the wind whipped dark clouds across the sky.
The Duke's death carried us back to the days of peace; to gatherings round the fire at teatime, when he had sat apart in his invalid
chair, his bright blue eyes alert, and a smile ready to illuminate
his face. In death, the trials of his long illness fell away, and his
fortitude and quiet strength lived on in the memories of his
children.

It was a hurried gathering. The four sons – all on active service
in the RAF – had only a short compassionate leave. For a brief
moment, we experienced an oasis of personal life. Then the war
broke in again. Douglo became the Duke of Hamilton, the new
head of the family, and Angus, his little fair-haired son, the new
heir.

I was pregnant. In early May 1940, I travelled down to Ferne,
David's mother's house in Wiltshire, to make arrangements for
the birth of my baby there. Dungavel had been evacuated, and
turned into a hospital; the family were living in various cottages
on the estate, and David's mother had moved to Ferne. David was
to have followed for a short leave. He was completing his flying
training at Grantham, where Malcolm also was posted. But suddenly everything changed. On the 10th of May the Blitzkrieg broke
over Western Europe. German tanks rolled through the Belgian
and French defences and the war started in earnest.

The tension of the weeks that followed is now history, but we
lived through it. And all who experienced those extreme days,
were marked by them for life. Utmost anxiety, fear and triumph
succeeded one another with dizzying rapidity, as though one was

living in a violently shaken kaleidoscope. All usual barriers broke down. Strangers spoke to one another in streets and trains; everyone pulled out last reserves of energy for the war effort; and all shared an experience so deep and universal that it needed no words to understand.

Ferne was crammed full to bursting point. David's mother had given sanctuary to as many children as she could fit in; and also to a number of evacuated dogs and cats, whose howls and miaows punctuated my first night's sleep. In the morning I crept downstairs in nightdress and bare feet, to listen anxiously to the eight o'clock news. David's aunt, Lady Wilson, was listening also. She was a favourite of mine; a woman of intellect and culture who had taken a degree in history, and been something of a blue-stocking in her day. She turned to me with tears in her eyes.

'The Germans have broken through at Sedan,' she said. 'Nothing will stop them now. It's happened twice before – in the last war and in the Franco-Prussian war. They'll overrun France and Belgium. What will become of our army?'

The question was on everybody's lips. We listened to every news bulletin. At lunchtime, children, nannies and gover-nesses crowded round the large dining-room table. A French Mademoiselle sat with tears pouring down her cheeks, as the terrible events in her country were related in measured BBC tones. Churchill's speeches reverberated over the air, steeling us, in-spiring us, but reinforcing our apprehensions. The days of Dunkirk dragged past, brilliantly fine, never-ending. Our feet walked on English lawns, but our minds and hearts were on the sands of France.

David's sister Jean and her family had come down to Ferne from Scotland. She and several other members of the household went to Salisbury station to help man the mobile canteen there. The trains which rumbled into the station brought survivors from Dunkirk. It was the first time for centuries that women in Britain had seen troops arriving direct from the battle-front. Jean described the scene to me:

The soldiers sat in the Pullman carriages, heads and arms slumped on the tables, too far gone to move. They were grey with fatigue, clothes wet and torn, some wounded, all exhausted. I can't describe the sense of shock, the ordeal . . .

There were some French soldiers among the units. They had been rescued, like the rest, by the British Navy. They told Jean that France would go on fighting.

But the fate of France hung in the balance. The news bulletins increased in gravity. We heard Churchill's offer of common citizenship for France with Britain; André Maurois' poignant plea for help from the RAF: 'We ask for a miracle, but miracles can happen.'

The day after this broadcast, news bulletins were barred for me.

In a high, airy room at Ferne, my baby was being born. I was engaged on a task so exacting that if the house had burned down I felt I would hardly have noticed.

The long day passed slowly. Night came, and at last at 10.55 p.m., Diarmaid, my son, was born. The day was the 17th of June 1940 – the day France fell.

Britain fought on alone. David, in a brief leave to Ferne from his heavily guarded aerodrome, found the countryside transformed. Tank traps had been erected in the narrow Wiltshire lanes, bridges were fortified, and all signposts had gone. On the highest point of the Downs – Win Green – about six hundred feet above Ferne, a lookout was posted, night and day. All the men on the estate had joined the Home Guard. Old guns were being resuscitated, oiled and greased. Aeroplane identification silhouettes were studied. Stores of food were laid in.

I was absorbed in the selfish joy of motherhood, and insulated to some extent from the preoccupations of those about me. But I did share Jean's agonising decision as to whether or not to take her children to Canada.

We weighed up the pros and cons while she stitched the searchings of her heart into the blue baby basket she was making for my child. Her family ranged in age from five to thirteen years old. She was terrified by stories she had heard of what had already happened to children in occupied Europe. After Dunkirk, no one doubted that invasion was imminent, and that the Nazis might soon be in Britain.

In the end, her departure was a whirlwind affair – a matter of taking up passages in a ship bound for Montreal with only a few hours' notice. Events and decisions had accelerated with such frightening rapidity in the past month that we were swept up in a momentum out of our control. Jean left, and had gone almost before I realised that it might be years before we met again. At the port her booking was changed. She and her children were transferred to another ship and they reached Canada some weeks later. The ship on which they were originally to have sailed was torpedoed, and few of the passengers were saved. As it turned out, mothers and children who crossed the Atlantic were subjected to greater hazards than those who stayed at home.

The policy of evacuation was a sensible one, under the circumstances, and those who followed it required much courage to go. I did not have to make this difficult choice. Whatever was coming to Britain, I wanted to stay and experience it with everyone else. I felt very strongly that our little family – David, our son and myself – must remain together. Even if we could not be physically in touch, we could hold on to one another in mind and spirit, and that was easier to do in the same territory, facing the same challenges.

David had finished his flying training, and was aching to be on active service. He wrote to Malcolm, who had been posted to a Flying Training School in Salisbury, Southern Rhodesia:

I'm still pulling all possible strings to get to Fighters. It'll be grand to see you again, but meantime we have a lot to go through. We *will* go through it, and we'll come out and knock out these Nazis good and proper . . . The morale of this country couldn't be better, and in the RAF it's absolutely unbeatable. I'm sure that will pull us through: we're the first real nut Hitler's had to crack; though, mind you, I think few people have any inkling as to what the Blitzkrieg really means.

But David's desire to be in the thick of the battle was not yet to be realised. Instead of joining a Fighter Squadron, he was posted as an instructor to the Fleet Air Arm Flying Training School at Netheravon in Wiltshire. He remained there for a year, a period of frustration for him and reprieve for me, during which we lived in a house belonging to Malcolm on the edge of Savernake Forest.

CHAPTER 9

'These are Exciting Times to be Living in'

THE Battle of Britain was raging. I lay out in the garden of my new home, looking at the aeroplane vapour trails high in the sky. Richard Hillary, Noel Agazarian and many others of our friends were piloting Spitfires and Hurricanes up there, while down here bees buzzed lazily from flower to flower, and summer sounds and scents filled the air. Our peaceful lives were disturbed only occasionally by news of a crashed plane in the vicinity. But our survival was being decided up there beyond our vision. This dichotomy produced a sense of unreality and impotence which was as hard to bear as the suspense of threatened invasion.

At the end of August, I went up to London to stay for a week at our house in Campden Hill Square. League teachers – as many as could get leave from the Services or their war work – had assembled for a refresher course, and I wanted very much to see them all and to take part. I brought Diarmaid with me, as I was still feed' g him; and he, our young Scots nanny, and I picnicked in the house, taking refuge in the basement during one night's air-raid alarm. I was delighted to see my League friends and colleagues again and to be working with them as of old. Diarmaid acclimatised happily to his new abode, and all seemed well.

Towards the end of the week Geordie called on us. He was at Fighter Command, near London, and had access to the figures of German aeroplanes shot down in the Battle of Britain.

'I simply can't believe the numbers,' he told us. 'Making allowance for exaggeration and unavoidable discrepancies, they are still incredible. It seems our pilots are achieving the impossible, and we may yet see a major victory.'

Geordie looked tired and anxious, as most people did those days, but he had a buoyancy of spirit which was reflected in everyone to whom I spoke in threatened London. They all knew that severe bombing raids could not be long delayed. They remembered what had already happened to towns in Belgium and Holland. Yet a unity of purpose beat through the whole city.

'All the same,' said Geordie, 'I think you should get out of London as soon as possible. Get Diarmaid away as quickly as you can.'

The League course was over. I left the next day. On the following evening – the 7th of September – the first indiscriminate bombing of London began. The docks were the main target, but the whole of the East End suffered. Wave after wave of enemy aircraft came over all night. London's reddened sky could be seen for miles around, and in the morning fires still raged in many parts of the city. The news bulletins were guarded. Districts hit by raiders were never mentioned by name, and the damage was minimised. But we guessed what was happening to London; and, sitting safely in Wiltshire, it was like hearing of the agony of an old friend which one was helpless to alleviate. David chafed at his relative inaction during a time of such crisis.

Two people I deeply cared for were in London – my Aunt Nan, and Ally. Both were in the thick of the raids. Ally had gone to Guy's Hospital in south-east London, where he was doing his final year's medicine. He spent his time either fire-watching and extinguishing fire-bombs on the roof of the hospital, or dealing with casualties in the wards. Whole areas round Guy's were blitzed, and men and women were brought in shattered from the blackened streets. In this maelstrom of destruction the Cockney courage and humour did not fail. Londoners could take it, but Londoners also desperately wanted a means of hitting back.

Nan had started a clothing factory as her contribution to the war effort. In an old warehouse in the East End she was turning out battle-dresses by the hundreds, aided by a staff of Cockney workers. Gone were the days of 'leisureism'. In twelve-hour shifts she and her workers were straining every nerve to increase their quota of uniforms. Each night she slept in the Underground, in common with millions of Londoners. She had her own special bunk to which she returned every evening; and her special crony, who made tea for her, and gave her the top of the milk in it with respect for her grey hairs. Nan made friends wherever she went, and no doubt the occupants of nearby bunks got a dose of theories on 'leisureism' between the bombs.

On one of my rare trips to London I visited her clothing factory. The glass in the window-frames was cracked; several windows had gone altogether and were replaced with cardboard. Ominous splits appeared in ceilings and walls; but the factory continued unabated, everyone in it, under Nan's leadership, working to their full capacity.

A great incendiary raid had just taken place. More than two thousand fires were ignited, and the bursting of a number of water-mains destroyed the means to extinguish them. Nan described to me how half Oxford Street had been ablaze.

The next morning she was taking her breakfast cup of coffee at a café nearby. 'The firemen came in,' she told me. 'They'd been fighting the fire all night – hours and hours without a break. Their faces were black and their eyes red with lack of sleep. They couldn't talk. Just drank a quick cup of coffee and went back again.' She paused.

'And the next morning when I returned from another night of raids the same men were still at it.'

I pleaded with her to come down to the country for a rest.

'No, darling,' she said, 'my place is here. We've got to keep up our quota of battle-dresses, and I've got to be here to see that we do it.'

I returned to Wiltshire with a heavy heart. How could the people of London stand up to such punishment, night after night? The peace and happiness of our country home seemed like a reproach. I felt we had no right to such safety. My heart ached for London, the city of my childhood, bound to me by innumerable ties.

'Oh, God,' I thought, 'if this is only the beginning, what will be the end?'

Powerless to help in any other way, David and I decided to house an evacuee. We consulted Nan, who found a mother among her workers anxious to get her youngest child out of London. He was three-and-a-half years old, smallest of a family of six, and his name was Ernie Churchill.

He arrived one morning, and stood uncertainly on our country doorstep. His head was swathed in a dirty bandage, and his eyes, in a small white triangle of a face, were ready to fill with tears. He was unable to speak; his only means of communication was a shake or a nod of his head. After a few hours, however, his Cockney resilience had begun to re-assert itself. Gazing at the rocking-horse in the nursery, 'Coo, look! 'E's eatin' 'is braces!' he remarked.

We gave him his first bath – an experience fraught with terror for him – and his head was washed, disclosing impetigo caught from an infection in the Underground where he had been sleeping for weeks. This necessitated some hospital treatment; after which a shorn, but by no means subdued, Ernie returned to us, and the process of assimilating him into the household began. We wanted him to feel part of the family – he called me Auntie Prunella, and David, Uncle David – but his transition from a completely unregulated life to one of nursery routine had its anxious moments.

At first he was very homesick, crying for 'Mummy' at night and feeling lost during the day. Then his natural toughness and independence took over. He became the interested spectator – *in* our lives but not of them. He would watch me feeding Diarmaid, and remark, 'You love him more than you do me, don't you?' – not minding, merely observing. Then, as he became surer of himself and his environment, his natural capacity for love and affection grew. He wanted attention. He needed to be praised and loved. Climbing on to my knee after his bath, 'I cuddle you,' he would say. Or, 'Hug me tight,' as I tucked him up for the night.

His attitude to Diarmaid underwent the same change. At first he was merely curious, or delighted, when Diarmaid misbehaved.

'Look what he's doing! He's eating his face-cream.'

Then he took an interest in him as a companion, and soon regarded him with the mixture of pride and jealousy usually accorded to the baby by the older brother.

When Ernie arrived, he could not distinguish a sheep from a cow.

'What are them?' he asked, pointing to clouds; and, 'Bomb done that,' he remarked, as we passed a fallen tree. Before long he was proudly picking the lettuce for lunch, and weeding and planting his own patch of garden, and could recognise a dozen different vegetables. He made friends with the local country children, put on weight, and ran naked in the garden, so that the sun took away the last traces of his skin trouble, and bleached his hair gold. In a few months he had become a complete member of the family, giving us his trust, and receiving our affection in return. He stayed with us for three years.

We still often thought of our German friends, particularly Ernst August and his family. It was impossible to get news of them; but one day a letter arrived for David from Frederika, Ernst August's sister, who had married the Crown Prince of Greece. After the invasion of Greece, early in 1941, she and her husband and children fled to Crete, and from there they were evacuated to Cape Town. She was in the terrible position of having four brothers fighting in the German army, and her adopted country occupied by Germans. Her husband came to London, and brought David the letter.

I want to know how you and your family are getting on, and how you are feeling.

Are you still the same as you have been? Have you still got the same ideas and ideals, or has the war made you feel bitter and hard? What physical and moral hell are we not all going through just now! It is hard to believe that there have ever been normal times or that there ever shall be normal times again. In a moment like this I would like to compare notes with you, and tell you how I feel about things. After having done more than our best, we have lost everything we have ever possessed and our poor country is going through a terrible time of famine. Yet I don't feel bitter against anybody or anything. I can see the great tragedy of this war from a detached point of view and understand to a certain degree its origin. I blame the human race as a whole for this war.

I told you in one of my letters to you that we have been given by the Divine Spirit two sides to develop in this life: the material side and the spiritual side of our existence. Unfortunately, most of us found it much easier to develop the first and to forget the second. Materialism has been given to us only to help and support in a practical way the development of our spiritual side . . . As we as individuals make up the human race who is alone responsible for this mess, we as individuals have also got to suffer our own share. Even if it looks unjust and incomprehensible from the outside. If one looks at it like that, one can't feel bitter against anybody, because one understands. Naturally we all get angry and impatient because after all we are human. But that does not mean anything as long as we don't get bitter. I don't want you all nor my brothers nor myself to get bitter about things, no matter what the future has in store for us. When the war is over we must all find our personal friends again, no matter on which side they fought. After this war there will be so much hate and so much bitterness in the world that the only thing left to us will be our personal friends and families. With them we must find the courage to start all over again, and to link the nations together by mutual friendship . . .

I hope my husband will be able to see one or two of the wild Hamilton boys. I hear there are quite a number more now than there have been when I was last in London. Congratulations. We can do with some more Hamiltons in this world.

An extraordinary event happened about this time: the flight of Rudolf Hess from Nazi Germany to the moors of Lanarkshire in May 1941. Hess, who described his flight as a 'mission of humanity', aimed to land at Dungavel, and claimed acquaintanceship with Douglo, who in fact had never met him. David was indirectly involved, as he had introduced Douglo to Dr Albrecht Haushofer in Germany before the war; and it was Haushofer who had encouraged and supported Hess on his ill-starred venture. The story has been told fully by James Douglas-Hamilton in his book *Motive for a Mission*. At this time, it provided a bizarre interlude in the Service life of the brothers. The invasion of Russia by the Nazis soon after Hess's arrival, produced a major clue to his motives.

In the summer, David achieved his ambition, and was posted to a Fighter OTU, and shortly afterwards, to a Fighter Squadron, based near London.

He wrote to Malcolm:

What do you think? I've at last succeeded in getting out of Training Command, and am now at an OTU, training on Spitfires! . . . They are the most marvellous aeroplanes I've ever flown. They are *streets* ahead of anything else. So far, I've done quite a bit of dog-fighting and am gradually getting the hang of it. Also some air-firing and a lot of aerobatics, for which Spits are just wonderful. The other day I did a height climb with oxygen, and was told to go to 25,000, but went to 30,000. Needless to say, I had to dive down and managed to clock about 430 mph which at 20,000 must have been about 500 mph . . . It's wonderful to get out of instructing where I felt my whole personality was slowly being atrophied. Now I feel a new man altogether!

David spent the autumn of 1941 doing 'sweeps' across the Channel, harassing enemy communications and shipping. Then he joined 603 Squadron, the City of Edinburgh Squadron which his brother Geordie had commanded in peacetime. The squadron's motto was 'Gin ye daur'; a motto well earned during the Battle of Britain, when it had seen much action and lost many pilots. The squadron was now absorbing replacements and fitting together new elements before being posted abroad.

After the Battle of Greece and the capitulation of Crete, the Mediterranean became the centre of operations. This was the focal point to which the RAF squadrons were being drawn. I realised that soon David and I would be parted in earnest.

The 603 Squadron was stationed at Hornchurch near London. I visited David there, and had my first close view of a Spitfire. Poised on the runway the little machine looked unbelievably frail; much too insignificant to be the victor of the Battle of Britain.

'Want to come up in it?' David said.

We squeezed into the cockpit, meant only for one person, and circled the aerodrome. In the air, the Spitfire was wonderfully manœuvrable, fast and powerful. We banked, climbed, dived. I tried to imagine the split-second reactions, the skill and the concentration demanded of anyone who flew this aeroplane in action.

I knew that the world of the fighter pilot was unique and indescribable. David never talked about it to me, and I never questioned him. Pilots, after their sorties, like the spacemen of to-day, were able to give only limited factual accounts of their experiences. Their laconic modesty was legendary. But in action, poised between earth and stars, they came into their own. Only the aviators they fought could share the intensity of their experience; fighter pilots often had more in common with their enemies, than with many of their earth-bound compatriots.

That brief flight round the aerodrome on a winter's day, gave me some infinitesimal comprehension of what they felt. I understood David's infatuation; the exhilaration, the tension, and the lure of dazzling danger.

Shortly afterwards, David's commanding officer (who had turned a blind eye to our forbidden flight) was lost in a sortie over the North Sea, and David took command of the Squadron. It had moved up to Dyce, in Aberdeenshire. I followed, with Diarmaid.

The first signs of spring were making a tentative appearance on the wind-blown Scottish countryside. Catkins danced on the hazels as I pushed Diarmaid's pram through the woods. The clear northern light slanted through bare branches, burnishing piles of russet leaves. I reflected as I walked. David was in Fighters at last, where he had longed to be; not only that, he had command of a crack squadron. We were all together for a few weeks. 'Don't look further than that,' I said to myself. 'Be happy.'

I returned to England, and the year slipped into spring. Daffodils flowered in our garden, and a large bush of forsythia gleamed with yellow buds. With this burgeoning of nature it was hard to believe in the reality of war.

But one day David telephoned me. 'We've got our posting,' he said. 'Don't know where, but abroad, probably the Middle East. I'll get a few days' embarkation leave.'

The moment which I had dreaded since the beginning of the war had come. Often as a child, hearing my mother's stories of the First World War, I had imagined the parting of lovers who might never meet again. The experience had seemed to me then too terrible to be borne. How would the last days together be spent?

Fact, as so often in life, exploded my romantic fancies.

Our precious final days sped by in a maze of packing, family goodbyes, last-minute purchases and last-minute instructions. Suddenly Diarmaid contracted measles. My head ached incessantly. David was irritable. We even suffered the indignity of two partings: he was given an extra unexpected day. Secrecy surrounded the Squadron's movements. Their port of embarkation was known, but no more. Like my father, so many years before, David sailed under sealed orders.

He promised to send me a line at the first opportunity, and, as a sign that he was about to leave England, to inquire after Diarmaid's health.

Several days passed with no word. Then a letter arrived. I took it into the garden to open it, and stood beside the forsythia bush. It was only a page, hastily written. I read it as hastily, my eyes skimming to the postscript: 'I hope Diarmaid's measles are better.'

So he had gone! I raised my eyes to the forsythia bush. It was in full flower, brilliant yellow in the sunshine, each delicate petal unfolded. I stared at it, and its sight and smell imprinted themselves on my memory with the clarity of calamity.

A few days later Geordie telephoned me.

'I think,' he said, 'that from now on you'll find yourself taking a great interest in the Knights of St John.'

I reflected for a moment, then understood. David was bound for Malta.

This small island, about fifty miles south of Sicily, was of vital importance to the strategy of the war in the Middle East. It guarded the narrow sea corridor through the Central Mediterranean, and was essential as a link with the Allied armies in North Africa, and as a base from which the RAF could challenge hostile air power and destroy enemy shipping. It had been subject to constant air attack for the last year, and was also exposed to the threat of invasion from the neighbouring Italian ports. It was no longer possible to base the main Fleet there; convoys carrying supplies to the island ran grave risks of disaster. Malta, a thousand miles from the nearest friendly territory on either side, was virtually beleaguered; but it was vital that at all costs it should hold out and that the squadrons based there should succeed in regaining air-power over the Central Mediterranean waters.

Malta was being bombed almost incessantly. As David's Squadron steamed towards it on the American aircraft carrier, the USS *Wasp*, only three serviceable Spitfires remained on the island. The month before, half a dozen Spitfires and Hurricanes had frequently taken on up to 150 German bomber and fighter aircraft in battles to defend their territory.

David's squadron was a mixed bag. It included two Scotsmen – himself and Flight Commander Bill Douglas, who had been an auxiliary pilot with the Squadron in peacetime – Englishmen, Canadians, Americans, New Zealanders, a South African, a Belgian and an Irishman. The Irishman was my cousin Neville King, who had driven up to Skye with my mother and myself many years ago. Since then, he had gone to the Hendon Police College and become a London policeman. During the blitz he had seen his share of rescue work, and had shown a talent for de-fusing unexploded German bombs. Like David, he was determined to get into operations. He joined the RAF, and when David was given command of 603, seized the opportunity to be posted to fighters.

Neville still had the Irish charm which I had fallen in love with at the age of seventeen; he possessed a knack of getting on well with everyone, and was specially liked by the aeroplane crews who serviced the Spitfires.

After several days at sea, during which there was nothing more stimulating to drink than Coca-Cola or orange juice (all United States naval ships were teetotal), the squadron took off at dawn. Their Spitfires were fitted with four cannon, and with long-range petrol tanks. They set course to the East, flying straight into a great red sun, still low on the horizon, while patches of cloud lay on the water far below. Soon, through the early morning haze, the French-African coast came into view. They first sighted Malta as a small speck still nearly a hundred miles distant, and gathered speed as they dived towards it. David's group circled Takali aerodrome, their destination. They had been warned that it would probably be badly damaged; nevertheless they touched down with a flourish, doing a formation landing into wind in sections of four across the landing-run. Some of the aeroplanes came to a halt a matter of inches from bomb craters. They had learnt their first lesson – never to land like that again.

They were welcomed by a blue sky and a warm sun. The sea shone with brilliant colour; little yellow square houses, interspersed with stone walls, rose up from the rock. All seemed peaceful and attractive. David took a deep breath of the warm air and thought – 'What a lovely place for a holiday!'

April 1942 was the month of Malta's heaviest bombing. Three or four raids came over every day (with a few in the night) in each of which there were up to a hundred bombers, with a fighter escort of thirty to fifty aeroplanes. The three aerodromes and the harbour were the chief targets, but the towns of Valetta and Sliema also suffered considerable damage. In spite of the terrible battering they had already experienced, the morale of the islanders held. They greeted the new Spitfires with grins and thumbs-up signs.

The RAF Squadrons hit back continually, but many of their aeroplanes were damaged on the ground, and attacked when landing. After ten days on the island, out of the forty-six aircraft which had landed from the *Wasp*, only six were serviceable.

David wrote to me:

I have now been on this island for five days, and I must say it is a somewhat different life from any I have known before. You will have gathered from the Press that we have raids every day and pretty heavy ones at that, but this place still holds out and it will continue to hold out. For the first time I have heard the whistle and explosion of a bomb so clearly that I will never forget it! The boys here are simply marvellous – they have shot down masses of Huns for practically no loss – it is a real honour to be with such chaps . . . I have lived through many adventures already, but it has been great fun really and I must say I have enjoyed it all . . . England seems very far away just now, and so does the life I used to lead.

I read this letter at Ferne, where I had taken the family after David's posting to a Fighter Squadron. His mother had established us in two gardeners' cottages which were converted into one, giving us a spacious sitting-room which ran the length of the two houses. From the windows we looked over a large cornfield. This had been in turn a landing-strip for the Douglas-Hamilton sons and a polo-field for the Douglas-Hamilton daughters. Now it was helping to produce food for a besieged nation; a task into which we also entered. I planted vegetables, picked and bottled fruit, made jam and reared chickens. It was my first experience of truly rural life, and I loved it, and would have been very happy but for the constant ache of anxiety for David.

Every Sunday we went to lunch at Ferne, half a mile away across the grounds. David's mother dispensed hospitality to those members of the family and their friends who happened to be there; sometimes one of her sons on leave; often, her daughter Margaret, who was living with her children in the neighbouring village of Berwick St John.

Part of Ferne had been turned into a children's home. Crocodiles of youngsters circumnavigated the house, and raced each other

Prunella and David
Douglas-Hamilton at
the time of their
engagement

Prunella with Diarmaid aged 9 months

rmaid and Iain

The four brothers: *left to right* The Duke of Hamilton (Douglo),
Lord Malcolm Douglas-Hamilton, Lord David Douglas-Hamilton,
Lord Nigel Douglas-Hamilton (Geordie), now the Earl of Selkirk

David with F/Lt. Bill Douglas before going to Malta, 1942

up the spiral fire-escape which descended down one wing. This excrescence marred the classical beauty of the Georgian façade, but it was typical of the unexpected juxtapositions to be found at Ferne. On entering, one encountered two female marble statues, each posed in a niche in a Grecian attitude, each bearing in her uplifted hand a Belisha beacon. Farther on, in the large circular saloon stood two magnificent black marble busts of the Duchess and the late Lord Fisher, sculpted by Epstein. On the plinth of one of them rested a feather duster, on the other a child's toy cat. Copies of the *Encyclopaedia Britannica* occupied the arm-chairs to prevent the numerous dogs who roamed the house from doing so. Anyone who wanted to sit down had first to remove a heavy volume. And the theme-song which accompanied every meal was, 'The Keel Row', whistled by a fierce African grey parrot which occupied a large cage in the dining-room, bit ingratiating visitors, and produced the final note of its song flat.

The Duchess's small grandchildren and her varied selection of dogs ran through the house and up and down the broad staircase, playing unending games with one another. And she, with her large heart and commanding presence, welcomed them all, had a special present or tit-bit for each, and stood like a rock at the centre of this unorthodox ménage.

Ernie, our evacuee, took his place among the other children, and often sat at the head of the long table opposite his hostess. They would beam at one another from either end, exchanging smiles over the family silver.

So April merged into May, and the rosy English summer spread across the Wiltshire landscape.

In early May, reinforcements in the shape of another sixty Spitfires reached Malta; and on the 10th of May, a warship, the *Welshman* (a minesweeper disguised as a French destroyer) came into Valetta harbour. It arrived at night, carrying vital supplies of ammunition, and was patrolled by Spitfires from dawn onwards. In its defence, one of the greatest air battles of Malta was fought.

Spitfires pursued the enemy aeroplanes right through the defensive balloons above the harbour, and into the barrage of defensive 'flak'. 'The air was full of Spitfires,' David wrote. 'A marvellous sight after what we had been used to; as far as one could see out to sea there were Junker 87's, each with a Spitfire on its tail.'

At the end of the day the island's defences reckoned to have destroyed over forty enemy aircraft, and damaged another twenty, all for the loss of only three Spitfires, two of whose pilots were safe. The air battles during this month were decisive for Malta's future. Air superiority over the island had been gained, and was never again relinquished. The squadrons once more started to make offensive sorties against Sicily and Southern Italy, and to widen their area of attack. David wrote:

We are certainly in the thick of things here and every day has its excitements. But we have the feeling that it's a great job of work and will help greatly towards winning the war. The Germans have lost all chance of capturing Malta, I believe, and I am more convinced than ever that it will hold out. They may try and give it hell by bombing, but we are well used to that by now, and it will avail them nothing. Further, every day we hit back at them, and give them not inconsiderable losses to think about. We console ourselves by saying that every bomb here is one less at home or against Russia; and I gather they say at home that every bomb there is one less upon Malta! . . . These are exciting times to be living in, and this is an exciting island to be living on, but I cannot say that I'm sorry to be in the forefront.

But in spite of this victory, there were still great shortages on the island; shortages of material, ammunition, food, and all the comforts of life. Malta was living under siege conditions, and the danger and claustrophobia which this entailed became increasingly difficult to accept. It was essential to get supplies through soon.

In early June, two convoys set out to brave the heavily guarded Mediterranean – one from Alexandria, one from Gibraltar. The eastern convoy was so severely handled in the bomb alley between Crete and Libya that it was forced to turn back. Of the six ships that had started from the west, only two merchantmen reached the Grand Harbour. They brought vital supplies, but not enough to keep the island going for long. The governor, Lord Gort, warned that all possible savings in every commodity and stock must be made. Food and petrol were rationed still further. This grave disappointment was only hinted at in David's letters.

This island is so small it gives me claustrophobia. It was OK for the first two months, but now it is beginning to pall on me, especially in the great heat we are having just now. However, it is still a veritable fighter pilot's paradise. It's tough at times, but I have great confidence in the future, and I know all will come right in the end.

On the 1st of July, another massive air attack was launched on Malta. The air battles raged for several days. In one of them Neville King was lost. David wrote:

Neville had been flying with Sandy – his Flight Commander – and early on they had both shot up a 109. The pair of them then chased some 88's out to sea past Gozo. Sandy fired at one of them, but was hit by return fire in the middle of the bullet-proof windscreen. They decided to return, but were very low on the water and, in turning, Neville's wing touched the sea and he crashed.

I read this news in the frail sunshine of an English summer. Holding David's letter, I imagined the harsh Mediterranean light, the aeroplane's swift, steep turn, the sudden impact of wing on water.

Memories of Neville rushed at me: the schoolboy I had first known; the young policeman; the RAF pilot. I remembered the day we had climbed Ben Nevis. 'How good to be alive,' he had said. And now he was dead. Death was so final and irrevocable; it left everything unfinished. Neville was married, but his young wife had no child to comfort her, his mother no second son. This unique person had been blotted out, and could never be replaced.

The news reinforced my anxiety for David. I had started another baby, which would be born in August. The needs of this new life within me had lulled me into a false sense of security, aided by the peace of the Wiltshire countryside with its wide skies and spacious views. Now my calm was shattered and I was jolted into a painfully fresh awareness of the war.

In mid-August a second great effort was made to relieve Malta.

Another convoy approached from the west. It was attacked incessantly in the narrow waters off Tunis and suffered terrible losses. Of the fourteen ships which started, only five got through. But a number of enemy aircraft were also destroyed, and the next day the convoy was within range of Malta's fighters. David later described the final epic scene:

At last the moment came when I could watch the ships coming in so bravely. Those ships that meant so much to Malta. It was a most moving sight. First three merchantmen came in escorted by destroyers; and some hours later another big merchantman arrived, all alone, in reverse, with a gaping torpedo hole in her bows. Meanwhile, the tanker, the precious tanker that was so vital to us, had been hit several times; a Stuka had even crashed on her deck, and finally bombs had smashed her engines. She lay stationary, some sixty miles from Malta. It seemed too ironical that that ship with its essential cargo should come so near after going through such trials, and yet be so far. She was constantly patrolled by Spitfires which beat off all attempts to attack her, but nevertheless she lay there for about twenty hours, and it was not until next morning that she was eventually towed in by destroyers. The fuel was all drawn off, and none too soon, for the damage had been altogether too great; before long her back broke and she sank in harbour. Her story was typical of the heroism which brought the convoy in. What a fight those sailors had had! But their efforts had borne fruit; for the convoy had ensured the life of Malta for another three months, and eased the acute shortage of supplies which had amounted to a crisis. At that time we only had enough petrol to last a fortnight.

Meanwhile back in England my second baby was being born. I was lying again in the high airy room at Ferne, and the limbo which contains birth and death was claiming me. A new consciousness was emerging from it, something which David and I had created together, and which would soon be a person in its own right. In spite of the presence of David's mother, and her kindness, I felt very much alone, and I missed David intensely. A picture of him in RAF battle-dress with his old tartan scarf wound round his neck, stood beside my bed. As the long night dragged by, I clasped it to me like a talisman.

With dawn the first birds called, and the cows in the park below the window began to move, awaking to crop the grass, heavy with dew. Gently, mysteriously, after its night of sleep, the world was coming to life again. The vitality of the new day pulsed through the room, and outside the shadows began to fade. Suddenly the silence was broken by a baby's cry. At 4.22 a.m., in the first light, our second son was born.

The next few days brought congratulations from family and

friends, and all the excitement and happiness of a new baby, but the anxiety of David's absence increased, rather than diminished. No word from him. Did he even know that he had a son? Then suddenly, miraculously, a cable came. David was flying home! He had been taken off operations, and entrusted with a message for the Air Ministry.

A few days later he arrived. He had survived not only the air battles and siege conditions of Malta, but many farewell rounds of drinks on the evening he left the island, and the largest breakfast of his life when he landed at Gibraltar the next day. He brought Diarmaid an exotic present – three bananas. In rationed England, they were the first bananas Diarmaid had ever seen.

CHAPTER 10

'Love Alone Avails'

DAVID was back, but the strain of Malta was apparent to all who knew him. He had lost over a stone in weight, and was drawn with fatigue. The experience he had undergone was impossible to communicate. The peace of Ferne, and the daily routine of his family served only to accentuate his sense of isolation. The change of environment was too sudden for him to be able to adjust to it immediately. Part of his heart and spirit remained in Malta with his Squadron and the pilots there.

Just before leaving he had written to Malcolm:

The major part of the war is now being fought out overseas and in Russia, until such time as they start a second front in Europe, so we have just got to keep on at these blighters until they give up . . . Then what a task of reconstruction there will be! Those who have been in the fighting will certainly have to see that they get their way, as well as those who have been out of it all the time . . . I don't feel I have had my fill of operations anywhere near yet, and I expect I shall get back to them before long . . . As long as the war can be kept out of Britain I don't mind where I have to go: it will be worth it. I don't believe anybody at home can quite appreciate what really heavy bombing in daylight, such as we had here from December until May, is like; particularly when it is continuous, day after day, in the same small area. Thank God, we have now got enough fighters to put a stop to it, and make the Hun pay for what he has done.

The gulf between those who had been in the thick of action and those who had not, was wide. David did not attempt to bridge it. He was like a tightly wound-up machine, which must slowly unwind. He spent much time with Diarmaid, Iain, his second son, and Ernie, who was still with us. Absorbed as he was in the children's world, the tension gradually slipped away from his mind and spirit. It returned if he was questioned about Malta. He could talk only to his brothers about it; and he could also write it down. During those first few weeks he spent many hours pouring his thoughts and experiences on paper. I read his account and began to understand more clearly what he had been through.

David's attitude to operations had changed. He was no less keen to be in the forefront of the fight, but now it was his will which impelled him, rather than his emotion; a will which had to overcome the temptation of remaining in a safe ground job, and the poignancy of once more leaving his family. The romance and glamour of operations had worn off. David now knew what battle-strain meant at first hand; it had marked him with its unmistakable brand.

In all this, I had to sense his thoughts and feelings. It was impossible for us to talk about his ordeal. The war had driven a wedge of incommunicable experience between us, and sometimes I felt lonely in spirit, stretching the resources of my imagination to the utmost to try to understand.

David's health had suffered, and he had to spend a short time in hospital before taking up his new post of controller, at an airport near London. He had risen to the rank of Acting Wing Commander in Malta, but now had to revert to his substantive rank of Flight Lieutenant. He wrote to Malcolm:

In another month or so I shan't mind going overseas again. I feel the big battles of the war may well be fought out overseas, and I want to be in at the 'kill' . . . However, I feel I need a ground job for a short while to sort of steady myself up a bit. Fighters is rather an unsettling career, and makes one very 'unconcentrative'.

Our cottage at Ferne was a happy base for David, when he could get leave. Ferne contained many childhood memories for him. He had grown up there himself, and he now re-explored his old haunts with his sons. Diarmaid and he were inseparable and went everywhere together.

At Easter David came home on leave. Diarmaid greeted him with the announcement, 'Mummy's got mumps.' It was true – contracted from Diarmaid himself. David soon also succumbed and the result was a blessed month's leave, snatched out of the rapidly mounting war offensives of 1943. David's period as a controller was drawing to an end and I knew that soon he would be on operations again.

One evening he and I went for a long country walk. The hedgerows of the Wiltshire lanes bloomed with late primroses and the early buds of hawthorn. Twilight stretched before us, while summer seemed about to break like a wave curled over a waiting shore. Our path led up to the Downs. There sheep grazed the short turf and a chalk-pit loomed in the fading light. A lark sang its evening song, the notes falling like crystal pebbles into the pool of silence. We were walking hand in hand, but had no need of further contact, or of speech. The slowly lengthening evening carried us into a harmony beyond words. The strain and tension of the last few months fell away, and the war receded as though we moved in another world. I reflected on how different our experiences had been: David's the active, mine the passive rôle. His activity had drained him almost dry. Now the mysterious regenerative powers of nature, symbolised in the vigil which was woman's task, could heal him. For the first time since his return, I felt he was completely at peace. We walked on in the quiet twilight until gradually night deepened and we turned our steps homeward. Stars began to appear as the lights of our little cottage gleamed through the dusk.

'It's wonderful to be back,' David said, at last. 'Home again. I can't believe I'm here with you and the children. And Iain safely born, too. How lucky we are!'

I was still closely connected with the League. By 1942 it had overcome some of the great difficulties with which it had been faced on the outbreak of war. Most teachers, and many members, had been called up into the Services, but a nucleus of centres remained. The League was forced to operate on an infinitely smaller scale than in pre-war days, but it was still alive. That it existed at all was no mean feat, in view of the adverse conditions which prevailed: shortage of teachers, strain of air-raids, the black-out, and the lack of transport facilities.

During the war, three people were chiefly responsible for the League's continuation; Peggy and Joan St Lo, and the new Treasurer, Torquil Macleod. Macleod was a determined Scot with a penchant for knight-errantry. He was a partner in a firm of City Chartered Accountants when he took up his duties as the League's financial manager just after the outbreak of war. He found the London headquarters bereft of staff, all of whom had left to undertake war work, and the League income virtually at a standstill. In spite of a moratorium on the rent of the headquarters, and its subsequent evacuation, insufficient funds existed to meet the League's creditors. Macleod explained the situation to each of them, and gallant efforts were made to honour existing obligations. But the crisis of war conditions, to which the League was hard put to adapt, was too acute. Early in 1941, the League was forced to go into liquidation.

This was a sad blow, and an unpleasant ordeal for all concerned. Macleod and Peggy St Lo bore the brunt of it. They faced the necessary litigation, and then set about making plans for the League's recovery. Under Macleod's guidance the League was re-formed as a limited liability company (it had been registered as a Friendly Society in 1938), whose shareholders were drawn from its members, and whose profits (if any!) would be used for the benefit of the organisation as a whole. This new constitution came into being in July 1941, and served to provide the necessary framework within which the League could operate. Four directors were appointed – Macleod, Peggy St Lo, myself, and a representative of the League members, Edyth Ormsby-Taylor.

An important factor in keeping the League centres together at this time was the League magazine. Founded originally by my mother, and edited by my aunt Norah Cruickshank until 1940, it too had suffered a severe set-back. Aunt Norah died as the result of a car accident in June 1940, two days after the birth of my son Diarmaid. This was a grievous loss for myself and for the whole League, which in consequence lacked her guidance at a critical time. The magazine lapsed until January 1942, when I became editor. It was then possible to produce a slim publication four times a year which circulated among the members and kept them in touch with one another.

Fifty centres remained open. As the war continued, and more and more teachers were called up, many of these were taken over by practice class leaders – advanced members who were given special training, and a licence to enable them to continue classes in lieu of a trained teacher. News from these centres reached me, as editor of the magazine, and I realised how much enthusiasm and loyalty to the League's work and ideals still existed throughout the country.

In London, classes never ceased. In spite of the heavy bombing and fire-raids of 1940 and 1941, and the flying bombs and rockets of the later war years, the London members assembled week after week. Often their hall was changed at the last moment because of air-raid damage; often they had to take cover during a class. Nevertheless back they came, inspired by the example of their teachers, Peggy and Joan St Lo. The London Centre reached its apotheosis in September 1945, when its members gave a display in Trafalgar Square before 15,000 people, which was reported in the press as the main attraction of London's Thanksgiving Savings Week.

As many League teachers as possible assembled each year for the summer refresher course, held first in London, and thereafter at a country house in Surrey. Never, perhaps, was the League spirit so strong as at these gatherings. The teachers were all young; they were all experiencing the same anxieties; all having to summon up deep reserves of courage and endurance to withstand them. Many of them suffered personal loss and bereavement as the war years rolled by. But in class, exercising together to the well-known rhythms, anxiety slipped away. They drew strength from one another, and the war, for a brief period, took second place.

I could sense this myself in the classes I taught once a week in the Salisbury centre of the League. I took over this centre when I came to live at Ferne, and continued it for three years. There was a core of enthusiastic pre-war members who were determined to carry on; a number of young mothers who found the classes a welcome change from housework, baby-minding and rationing; and a floating population of girls from the Services who were stationed in Salisbury, or home on leave.

I was able to put my mother's principles on exercise during pregnancy to the test by conducting classes until within two months of Iain's birth, and continuing again a month afterwards. By then my figure had returned completely to normal. This experience helped me to share the results of the League's training in relaxation and posture with other young mothers; and to appreciate for myself the efficacy of the League system as a basis for successful childbirth.

The Salisbury centre soon enrolled over 200 members, and in

the summer of 1943, we were asked to give a display in the market square in Salisbury during 'Wings for Victory' week. Similar invitations were received by many war-time League centres. The huge national demonstrations might be at an end; but at the local level the League still had something to offer to the public. And many of the public were delighted to welcome back the familiar black-and-white League uniform, with its happy association of pre-war days. Those who wore it had perforce acclimatised themselves to war. But they still hoped for peace, and some still dreamed of the part they might play in helping to build a better world.

In June 1943 David applied to return to operational flying. He was accepted for Photographic Reconnaissance work, and joined the General Reconnaissance Course at Squire's Gate, near Black-pool. Though he was there for a number of weeks, it was impossible for me to join him. He found the course hard work after the comparatively easy mental life of a fighter pilot, but he threw himself into it whole-heartedly and passed out very well at the end. He then went to the Photographic Reconnaissance Operational Unit at Dyce, and there trained on Mosquito aircraft, which he flew from then on. I took the children up to Dyce, and stayed there for three weeks; but I could only see David occasionally, as his training was arduous and exacting.

Malcolm was by now back from Rhodesia, and had been posted to a Photographic Reconnaissance Squadron, also flying Mosquito aircraft. David hoped to join him, when his preliminary training was completed. He wrote to Malcolm from Scotland:

I have now managed to fly one of the little chappies [Mosquitoes] here. They are great fun, and I like them almost as much as a Spit – better in some ways. I am very lucky to be on them . . . It is grand to be flying again.

Operations had claimed him once more, and demanded all his concentration and thought.

I returned to Ferne.

The domestic life in which I was immersed gave little opportunity for mental stimulation or for leisure. The claims of the children demanded most of my time and thought. Our young Scots nanny had been called up. This left me with three children and the house to look after, so regretfully we parted from Ernie. Air-raid danger had abated in London, and it was safe for him to go back to his family. His last gesture was a smart RAF salute.

The children and I lived close to Nature, conscious of each variation in the year's cycle and deeply attuned to it. We watched the cornfield behind the cottage grow as the year grew, burgeoning at harvest time into a rippling sea of gold. We walked through the woods which led to Ferne, aware of the red sheen of buds in early spring, the canopy of summer leaves, the brilliance of autumn's dying colours, and the shape of bare branches moving against a winter sky. As the war years continued, I took comfort from these unchanging processes, the same now as for generations past.

I often thought of my mother and her experience in war. Her bereavement had come at the beginning, and she had had to endure four long years with no hope of reunion at the end. She had lived those years in London, bereft of the country joys or family protection with which I was surrounded. But I knew that she must have felt much as I did, and that she would have understood the foreboding that often possessed my heart.

Alone in the evenings, with the children tucked up in bed and the chores of the day over, I was able at last to read. I turned to the poets of the thirties, and re-read Auden, Spender, Day-Lewis and Louis MacNeice. I discovered an anthology of Air Force Poetry, which contained a poem by Vernon Watkins called 'Song'. The first four lines haunted me:

> Do not tempt me from this sky
> That yet seems to you a stone;
> A hand, if on the dead it lie,
> Shall put out the sun and moon.

I remembered the Spitfire flight with David when I had glimpsed for the first time the obsession of the aviator. I knew I was powerless to withstand that lure. I found another poem, by John Pudney:

In times when bullets prove, when deeds decide:
Nor the cool laughter of the youthful corn
Nor brief hot poppies hide
Earth trodden and torn.

In times when smiling eyes and lips tell lies,
And only dead men tell no tales, no tales
Casting their last disguise
Love alone avails.

Hold hard to the dear thought. For courage less
This tenderness is but a dress worn thin
Against the cold. Love's dress
Is blood-deep under the skin.

The poems spoke to me and I to them. They lived in my mind, joining me to others like myself who were suffering the same anxiety, longing for the same peace. The stillness of night closed round the cottage: mysterious night, grave and silent, calming the world to sleep.

Outside, a huge moon lifted itself from the cornfield, and gazed quietly down, shedding silver light on familiar objects and touching them with mystery. The wind stirred, and with it my spirit moved. It reached towards the night, towards the moon, and towards the spaces of the sky. The clamour and preoccupations of day fell away. Nothing existed but a measureless calm which drew me to its orbit and suffused the night with peace. With certainty I knew, *love alone avails*.

In contrast, days at Ferne were busy and active. David's sister, Jean, had arrived back from Canada with her four children, and they were continually in and out of the cottage. We lived an extended family life. Jean stayed at Ferne, and Margaret (David's other sister) occupied a house at Berwick St John, our nearest village. Our respective children, two of mine and four each of Jean's and Margaret's roamed through the three homes, which they regarded as interchangeable; while Jean, Margaret and I pooled our resources of clothing, food, wisdom and cheer.

Sometimes, David's mother arranged an alfresco lunch for us all. She held it on the large lawn in front of Ferne, and it resembled nothing so much as a barbecue from the then popular film *Gone with the Wind*. But a barbecue without meat. My mother-in-law lived up to her principles as president of the Animal Defence Society, and no dead animal's flesh passed her lips. To make up for this, there was every kind of vegetarian dish. The old butler, carrying mountainous trays, plied back and forth from house to garden, and finally spread out the feast on the lawn; salads, fruits, nuts, cheese, milk, cream, and a series of delicious puddings. Our children gathered round, the small ones naked like sunburned cherubs, and helped themselves with delight, sometimes carrying their spoils away to a secret glade of their own, or to the top of a tree. In after life they must often have remembered these picnics as a veritable Eden.

We shared Ferne and our lives with a number of American pilots, who were quartered in the neighbourhood. The American Air Force had taken over a local hotel, and ran it as a rest home, where fighter and bomber pilots could recuperate on a short leave after a spell of operations.

The bomber pilots were involved in daylight raids over France, using Flying Fortresses, unaccompanied by fighter protection. These arduous sorties entailed many casualties and intense nervous strain. It was the first spell on operations for most of the pilots we met; they had been thrown straight into one of the toughest assignments of the war. When they reached Wiltshire they were more than ready for a rest; ready and eager, too, for friendship and visits to English homes. Margaret offered her horses to those who would like to ride, and she, Jean and I rode with them almost every day.

A car-load of Americans would arrive, all set for 'horse-back riding', punctilious as to time and transportation. Their first shock was to discover that the horses were still in the field, and had to be caught and saddled, before we could proceed. Some had never ridden before. Those who had, as a rule were used to cow-boy saddles, in which, as they explained, 'you have a pummel to hold on to.' They tended to find the English saddle precarious and the horses' habits unnerving. 'That horse was against me from the start,' said one of them to Jean. 'I didn't like the look in its eye. I got up on it, and what should it do but make for the first tree and try to rub me off against it.'

We rode over the Downs, and through the Coombe Chase woodlands which spread across the top of the chalky hills. Cantering down leafy rides, galloping across the short-cropped turf, with the Wiltshire countryside spread out below like an eighteenth-century print, these American pilots were given a new glimpse of England, and contrasted it with the tense operational life of their aerodromes.

'It's good to be in a home again,' they would say, stretched out on the lawn after the ride.

We talked to them about their own homes and families, and wrote to their wives and mothers giving news of them. We formed close friendships, even in the short space of a week. Our contact was in the context of the war and this gave it an extra urgency and depth. We talked little about the actual fighting, or the purposes or ideology of the conflict. These were taken for granted. What the American pilots needed was the warmth of a home, and the simple welcome which they might have found among their own friends. They played with our children, told us about their kid brothers and sisters, bartered petrol for eggs, and brought us exotic cans of food from their PX canteen.

David came back for a weekend's leave, and found one of them with his arm in a sling.

'Poor chap,' he thought, 'probably shot down in the Channel.'

'You wondering what this is?' said the American. 'Just one of Lady Margaret's horses.'

David had now joined Malcolm at Benson aerodrome in Oxford-shire. He soon rose to be a Flight Commander in his squadron, No. 544, and began to undertake long distance sorties over enemy and enemy-occupied territory. The Mosquitoes used on photo-graphic reconnaissance had no protection but the aircraft's height and speed. The engine, specially tuned to achieve these qualities, tended to be unpredictable, and many pilots were lost through unexpected engine failure.

The photographic reconnaissance sorties penetrated far into Europe.

In March 1944 David wrote:

I did two trips on consecutive days last week. The first one took me over the Ruhr by mistake, where I was greeted with an unpleasant volume of flak, and then chased away by a fighter. The next one was over Norway, and went off very pleasantly although I was fired on again slightly.

David came home quite often on leave during this period; usually for a weekend once a fortnight. The adjustment between service life and home life was always difficult to make, but these brief leaves offered some respite from the strain of operations. The pressure of the war was mounting, preparations were in hand for D-Day, and everyone knew that the ultimate test of a landing and assault of the French occupied coast must be near. The Second Front, for so long a subject of controversy and surmise, would soon be a reality.

David was also concerned with the menace of the flying bombs, Germany's 'secret weapon', whose base at Peenemünde had first been located by a photographic reconnaissance aeroplane.

'London is having a bad time again,' he said, talking to Jean about the flying bomb raids. 'This new attack may be very damaging to morale.' He paused, then continued, 'The right weapon at the right moment is terribly important. In Malta, our Spits were so good that they gave us tremendous confidence. The Mosquitoes I'm on now are equally good in their own way.'

'But aren't they very temperamental?' I asked.

'Yes, they are. For photographic reconnaissance they have been tuned up to fly long distances, and to fly very high. But they do the job all right. They're wonderfully adaptable.'

'I think the pilots behind them have something to do with their success,' said Jean.

'Of course they have. In the end, they count for everything. But as the war gets more and more mechanised, the right machines at the right moment, and plenty of them, are vital.'

'I sometimes wonder if we won't all end up as machines, with no more private feelings or desires,' I said.

'A fighting man can't afford the luxury of private feelings. Once he's on operations he has to put them behind him. They're there, of course. They're the basis of all he does, and of the will to fight. But they have to go into cold storage for the duration.'

'You don't think they'll be irretrievably frozen by the time the war ends?'

David shook his head. 'I think peace would revive them pretty quickly. But it won't be easy.' The muscles in his jaw twitched as he bent his head to light his pipe. 'We don't know what the world will be like after the war or how we'll feel. We've got to win it first. That's the job of a fighting man – to win.' Then he caught sight of Diarmaid. Swiftly he picked him up, and threw him high above his head. 'We've got to win,' he repeated. 'But when we do . . .' The child's high-pitched squeals of delight mingled with his father's deep laugh.

I thought how far we had come since the days when we planned Utopias and imagined that we had the strength and hope to create them. This war was eating away the bases of human belief and human happiness. What would it ultimately do to the human spirit?

In May 1944 the Second Front was launched. The evening before D-Day, the sky over the Downs was filled with aeroplanes; a great airborne armada droning through the dusk and on into the night. Their lights moved across the firmament like a giant constellation. We watched, at once elated and apprehensive, our minds expanding to take in the meaning of this huge offensive. The beginning of the end of the war? The momentum of the landings and the subsequent successful advances swept the whole country into a mood of confidence and elation.

In late July David came home for a weekend's leave. He was tired, and I gave him breakfast in bed, and his favourite dishes. He had been doing many long-distance sorties, and more lay ahead. He told me he had found a hotel near the aerodrome, where he thought I could stay if I came to visit him, and we arranged that I should do so as soon as possible. He had flown over from Benson and landed in a field near Ferne. When the time came to go, he was anxious about the take-off, as the field was on the small side. He said he would give it a trial run. I watched while he measured out the field, gauged its length, and taxied the plane to the position for take-off. Dusk was falling and there was not much daylight left in which to fly back to Benson. The engines revved up, and the plane ran along the field to the end, turned and came back to its starting position. David leaned out of the cockpit and waved goodbye. This time the engines revved to full speed. The plane started forward, gathered speed, and at last lifted itself slowly into the air, and lumbered off through the dusk. He had gone. I watched the empty sky while silence settled again on the countryside. How many more partings? I wondered. How much more of this severing could one stand?

Twilight crept slowly over the landscape. It was cold and lonely. The familiar fear seeped into my heart, as I looked at the empty field and the empty sky. David had gone and neither he nor I knew if he would return.

A few days later the telephone rang. It brought bad news. My Aunt Nan had been killed in a raid on London. She had been riding on a bicycle up Kensington High Street when the sirens sounded. Before she could take cover a flying bomb fell. She rode straight into the explosion, which demolished a cinema and caused many casualties. She was killed instantly.

The funeral was to be held several days later at Goudhurst, in Kent, where cousins of hers and mine lived. I telephoned David to give him the news. He had just returned from a long sortie over Germany, and was off on another one the next day. We arranged that I should drive over to Benson, and we could then go on to the funeral together.

I wondered where Nan's mocking spirit would be during the ceremony. I could not yet face this end of her courage and humour – her death was just one more loss, adding to the total of senseless destruction. I pushed away the realisation of it. One had to continue with daily existence, looking after the children, running the house: life had to go on. I knew that until I reached David I must not let myself dwell upon what had happened.

The next day I set off for the drive across country to Benson aerodrome. The children waved goodbye; my last sight of them, playing in the garden with the sunlight glinting on their fair heads, remained with me for some time as I drove. Then I began to think about David: about the snatched opportunities for meeting which was all that we now had; about how the war had invaded our lives to their roots; about the way in which operations had claimed him again. Peace and the leisurely things of peace seemed so far away that they might have happened on another planet. The present held not peace but war, and that meant a tightening of emotions past the point of tears, a constant anxiety, and the impossibility of sharing the heavy shadow of continual fear. I drove through the flowering countryside, blind to the beauty of high summer, and the sunshine, with its evocation of other summers, seemed brittle and unreal.

I arrived at Benson in the afternoon and drove to the officers' mess, where David had arranged we should meet. I waited in the car for half an hour or so after our rendezvous time, and then got out hoping to find someone who could tell me where David was. A young pilot officer passed by. I stopped him and asked if he could find David and tell him I had arrived. He stared at me uncomprehendingly. His embarrassment and obvious discomfort puzzled me. I repeated my words – 'Could you find my husband, David Douglas-Hamilton, and tell him I am here?' He stared at me again. The silence between us lengthened. At last he broke it.

'Don't you know?' he said.

I shook my head.

'David was killed an hour ago.'

The young pilot officer took me into the officers' mess, which was a long oblong room full of furniture. He left me there, and I walked up and down the room waiting for confirmation of what he had said. After a while David's squadron commander came. He had just been to the airfield, and told me that the news was true. David had returned from a long sortie over the South of France, and was actually in the circuit of the aerodrome when both his engines failed. He turned down-wind for the only open country available, but could not avoid a belt of trees, one of which his wing struck. The aeroplane crashed, and both he and his navigator were killed instantly.

'There is absolutely no doubt.'

The squadron commander took me to his house, and put me in his wife's care. David had so often had to do this sort of thing for relatives of pilots in his squadron who had been killed. I knew how much he had hated it. I moved in a limbo of disbelief, the habit of responding politely to other people acting as a kind of shield between myself and the catastrophic news.

After two hours or so Malcolm arrived, having flown over from his RAF station in a Mosquito. I could not meet his eyes, but I heard him say that he would fly me back to Ferne. We stood on the airfield, joined by Margaret, who had somehow got a plane lift over to Benson and who now would fly back with us.

Malcolm turned to me.

'Nothing will ever be the same again,' he said.

We climbed into the Mosquito. The strong wings vibrated as the engines pulsed with power. This was the aeroplane David had flown. It lifted into the sky, bearing us with it into the element David loved. We flew through the darkness in a void between fear and grief; each of us separate and silent. I wanted nothing but for this plane, too, to crash. But I knew that it would not. This strange disembodied flight would end. We would land. Life would engulf us again, with its agony, terror and joy.

I could not imagine life without David. I could not imagine telling the children, going on alone. But one thing I knew with complete certainty. David had gone beyond this life, beyond this world, and in no way must I try to call him back. There was a last service which I could render for him: to let him go, unhampered and free.

> Give them their wings:
>   They cannot fly too high or far
> To fly above
>   The dirty-moted, bomb-soured, word-tired world.
> And if they die they'll die,
>   As you should know,
> More swiftly, cleanly, star-defined, than you will ever feel.

CHAPTER II

Post-War World

WITH David's death a certain kind of life ended for me. I often remembered Malcolm's prophetic words: 'Nothing will ever be the same again.'

It was not merely a question of now being alone, and of having to make decisions and a way of life by myself. It was not even the necessity of shouldering the sole responsibility for my sons and their upbringing. It was rather that a certain outlook, a sharing and an inspiration had gone, and could never be replaced. David's ardour for life and his integrity of spirit were unique. I would never find them again.

Kurt Hahn, the headmaster of Gordonstoun School, wrote:

His country can spare David less than almost any other young man I know. His strong convictions were deeply rooted in his great heart. When I spoke of the best men born in these isles I always said that they were more than great patriots, they were also good Europeans. And ever so often I mentioned David and his struggles on behalf of the South Tyrolese who loved him as a brother. To me, too, he was a 'brother-in-arms'. I shall miss him at every turn of a long-drawn-out battle on behalf of the young, on behalf of justice and humanity.

Several nights after David's death I climbed to the top of the Downs at Win Green. The space and silence of night surrounded me, as I stared into the dark sky, searching for an answer to my desolation. None came. In the infinite cold firmament I could find no pity and no peace. I felt, as in the Mosquito flying back from Benson aerodrome, that David's spirit had travelled far beyond my reach, and there could be no legitimate return.

After my mother's death, I had been upheld by the Christian creed of immortality. Her faith had sustained me, and I had known a warming presence which brought comfort, and the certainty of life after death. Now I could no longer believe this, or

believe in communication between the living and the dead. The
war had sapped my faith. It had confronted me with stark facts
which seemed inexplicable in Christian terms. I could no longer
delude myself with the idea of a loving personal God, or imprint
Nature with my subjective needs. I had experienced the cutting
down of a life in its prime; the loss of a husband and a father. This
was what I must now accept; and accept in its uncompromising
reality without pretence of spurious comfort.

The impersonal night extended on every side. Stars sparkled
with frosty indifference. The silent spaces of the universe seemed
immense.

Nevertheless, I was unable at first to realise the full implications
of David's loss. I clung to his family, as extensions of himself.
They helped me most generously. I went with Malcolm for a few
brief days to Skye, and there, climbing among the mountains
David had loved, we found some measure of peace. The lonely
high places had not changed. Remote and inviolable, they
remained indifferent to man's war, agents of healing and strength,
who could be regarded as symbols of eternal verities. The shock
of David's death began to seep away into the anonymous stretches
of peat and heather; and Malcolm, who at the other end of a
climbing rope a few yards distant up the hill, might have been
David himself, shared my loss so intensely that between us we
conjured up David's figure to walk beside us as before.

I had not the heart to continue living at Ferne, so at Douglo's
and Betty's invitation I moved to Scotland, to live in one of the
cottages at Dungavel, where my children could share a nanny
with their two small sons of nearly the same ages.

From Dungavel I taught League classes in Edinburgh, and, as
so often before, drew strength from this activity to try to rebuild
the pattern of my life. Finally, I went to stay with David's sister,
Margaret, who had recently come north to occupy her husband's
family home in Perthshire.

Seggieden was a large Georgian house, standing on the banks
of the River Tay, about two miles outside Perth. Margaret filled it
with her vivacious family and their friends, and established her
ever-increasing herd of horses in the surrounding fields and stables.
Her children rode from the moment they were old enough to sit

on a pony. At Seggieden the foundations were laid for their brilliant successes in later life. During the fifties, Jane Drummond-Hay, the eldest daughter, became one of the most prominent riders in Three Day Events; while Anneli, her sister, later achieved international renown in the show-jumping world, riding her famous horse, Merely-a-Monarch, discovered and trained by herself.

I remember Anneli at the age of about seven, galloping her pony down to the fields where we were making hay. She had no saddle, only a light bridle, and already her hands used a horse's mouth with authority and inborn sensitivity. Her long fair hair flew in the wind; her face, often shy and withdrawn, wore an expression of effortless happiness.

As at Ferne, Margaret's and my children soon merged into one large family, and Diarmaid and Iain, now aged five and nearly three, were surrounded by energetic cousins, ready to protect them, play with them or scold them as the case might be.

One day in May 1945 Jane galloped into the stables where I was unsaddling a pony. Her cheeks were bright with excitement and her eyes shone.

'The war has ended,' she cried. Her triumph was infectious, but perhaps only a fourteen-year-old could feel such unmitigated joy. The six years of privation and suspense could not so suddenly be swept away. The habits of war died hard. And for many, like myself, the absence of those most loved gave to the peace celebrations a hollow ring.

A few weeks later campaigns began for the 1945 election.

Malcolm had decided to stand as a Unionist candidate at Greenock, a traditional Labour seat near Glasgow, and was given leave from the RAF to do so. His family gathered to support him, and Margaret and I travelled down from Perth and soon became immersed in canvassing and the heady paraphernalia of electioneering. With typical feminine logic I deserted what radical principles I possessed (strengthened by reading the *New Statesman* and left-wing poets during the war), and changed into a Conservative for Malcolm's sake. In those days, before television, and in Scotland where politics were traditionally taken seriously, election meetings were packed. Heckling was acute; canvassing demanded a real knowledge of local conditions and of the problems of housing and education. I read up these subjects, expounded the party line with fervour, and enjoyed the mental challenge involved. But Malcolm and his entourage were amateurs compared to the professionals who opposed him. Later, after years of apprenticeship and study, he achieved a splendid victory at Inverness; but in 1945 he had little chance of success. Nevertheless, the intoxicating tide of battle swept us along until we were almost convinced that we would win. On Election Eve, Philip Noel-Baker (whom I had known in my Fitness Council days) came up to speak for Malcolm's opponent. We passed one another in the hotel lounge, each bound for opposite meetings. He gazed reproachfully at the enormous red-white-and-blue Unionist rosette which I wore.

'You mustn't think that your party is the only one synonymous with Britain,' he said.

Another friend of mine was involved in this election: Priscilla Grant (now Lady Tweedsmuir of Belhelvie), standing as a Unionist candidate in North Aberdeen. I first met Priscilla when David was stationed at Dyce during 1942. At that time she was managing her husband's historic home, Monymusk, in Aberdeenshire, as a war convalescent hospital. She became a close friend. Her husband, Sir Arthur Grant, was serving abroad, and later was killed in France at the same time as David lost his life. I went to stay with Priscilla soon afterwards, and she told me that she had resolved to stand as Unionist candidate in North Aberdeen in her husband's place. It was a courageous step. Priscilla was young and inexperienced, unversed in politics, just widowed, and shadowed by her husband's death. But she was also resolute, beautiful and very intelligent. She set herself a course of study to which she rigidly adhered, and by the time the election came she had a good political grounding. She also possessed a valuable knowledge of local conditions in Aberdeenshire, having worked in a factory there during the war. She asked me to come and speak in her campaign.

I had already discovered that political loyalties were stratified according to class; the poorer the district the more left-wing the views. Canvassing for Malcolm I had knocked on a number of Communist doors, and held my own in face-to-face debate once inside. But now I found myself confronting a large, boisterous left-wing audience in one of the poorest parts of Aberdeen, and it was out to draw blood.

I opened the meeting for Priscilla, and started by saying somewhat precipitately that rights should be accompanied by duties.

'What about the rights of the miners in Hamilton!' shouted a heckler from the back of the hall. 'Much you know or care about them!'

This first shot was followed by a volley of machine-gun repartee which crackled across the hall. I stood mute on the platform, trying in vain to understand the Aberdeenshire dialect, unable to reply or to gain control. Priscilla arrived to find her meeting in an uproar. She calmed it with great skill. Exhibiting a quiet authority, she took over, answered each question with knowledge and conviction, gave evidence of her serious concern, and soon had the audience listening attentively to every word.

Priscilla and Malcolm, like many Conservative and Unionist candidates at that time, lost their campaigns. The election ended in an overwhelming Socialist victory. But Priscilla had proved herself. Not long after she was given the safer seat of South Aberdeen, which she fought and won in a by-election, and subsequently represented for the next twenty years, finally being awarded a peerage in the House of Lords: a well-earned recognition for a distinguished career.

Soon after this election, I decided to return to London and to live in our house in Campden Hill Square. It had suffered some bomb damage, but once this was repaired I was able to move in, and in the autumn of 1945 the process of making a new home there began.

In spite of my rebuff in Aberdeen, I was sufficiently bitten with politics to wish to continue in that field; so I resolved to stand as a Conservative for the Kensington Borough Council. I fought in a local authorities contest, and was elected (with five others) to represent the Redcliff Ward.

The Council met in palatial surroundings in Kensington Town Hall. Flushed with my success in the poll, I started with the best intentions (immediately, unfortunately, somewhat marred by my leaving behind, on the top of a bus, the first batch of confidential papers with which I was issued).

But I, and the Council, soon realised that local politics were not for me. I found myself tongue-tied in debate, unable to express myself in the formal atmosphere of the Council chamber, and restricted by having to support my party's line, when, truth to tell, I often found myself more in sympathy with the opposition. Most major issues were settled at respective party meetings before the Council assembled, and it needed more knowledge and courage than I possessed to strike an independent note thereafter. It was obvious that my political talents were few; in fact the only useful contacts I could make were in canvassing, when I came face to face with people's problems in their own homes, and the personal touch could be of value. It is an anomalous feature of democracy that those best equipped to fight election campaigns are often those least suitable for life in Parliament. I remained on the Council for over two years, but during that time made scarcely one significant contribution to its deliberations.

Perhaps one of the reasons for my failure in this new field was that I was living in a void, without faith or happiness. I had determined to make a new life in London for myself and the children, breaking away in some measure from David's family to do so. I realised that I must learn to stand on my own feet again, and this I could only do by being alone.

London was also going through an awkward transition from war to peace. Although the black-out had disappeared, Londoners still suffered from shortages of food, from ration cards, bomb damage and lack of transport. Men and women were being demobilised to find that peace presented no easy choices or solutions, and a general air of disenchantment prevailed.

In Germany, hunger and privation were acute. As soon as it was possible to do so, I sent food and clothing parcels to 'Tante' Isi von Gleichen in Berlin. She told me later that they had been the means of keeping her alive. She had been bombed out three times during the war, had survived the Allied air-raids, and finally had experienced the Russian occupation. Through it all she had preserved her courage and humour, and continued to write the book on astronomy which was her life-work. At last, when she could enter East Berlin, she had visited the library there, where reference books which she urgently needed were stored. The same commissionaire greeted her with a smile at the entrance. She took the reference books from the shelves, opened them at the accustomed pages, and found notes in her own handwriting still there. Scholarship had survived the worst that war could do to Berlin.

Reading her account, I reflected that there was a lesson in it for me. I must get back to my own life's work, and not be diverted by personal loss, or the apparent charms of other activities.

In June 1946 the League staged a victory display at the Empire Pool, Wembley. Eight hundred members took part, and the occasion also attracted a number of teachers, returning from the Forces. But many of these girls now had other ties and responsibilities, and could not teach League work full time, if at all. It was vitally important to renew League teacher training, and to produce new experts who would maintain the high standard of the League's work, and make further expansion possible.

During the immediate post-war period, the climate in the physical education world changed dramatically. The old-fashioned Swedish Ling system was replaced in the Women's Physical Education Colleges by the Laban Art of Movement method, imported from Central Europe, and by modern dance. This entailed a freer approach to movement, and to teaching methods, extensive use of music, and more opportunity for self-expression. All these were ingredients the League had advocated for many years; but instead of being first in the field of recreative physical training, it now found itself up against much competition. Keep Fit classes appeared in many localities, financed by local authorities at prices below those which League teachers could afford to charge. The Central Council of Physical Recreation which had been formed in 1935 to extend and correlate every form of sport and physical training in the recreative sphere, took the Keep Fit movement under its wing, arranged courses for leaders staffed by specialist physical education teachers from the physical education colleges, and encouraged local authorities to start Keep Fit classes.

The League was affiliated to the Central Council of Physical Recreation but, as the League advocated a different system of exercises from that taught in the physical training colleges and the schools, no financial help for it was forthcoming from the CCPR or from the Department of Education. It was the classic case of the pioneer in a field being overtaken by government-sponsored competition. The League had two choices. It could adapt its methods to suit official policy, lose its identity, and become part of the Keep Fit movement. Or it could remain independent, and find the finance to run its teacher training and its administration from its own resources.

The League chose the latter course. Its identity was preserved, at the cost of much financial anxiety. But it was unable to expand as much or as fast as it would have wished. Nevertheless, girls were recruited for a new teacher training course, the Bagot Stack Health School reopened, and Kathleen O'Rourke, the League teacher in Dublin who was also a fully qualified physical education specialist, having graduated from Liverpool Physical Training College, came over from Ireland to act as principal of the school. I found myself teaching students once more. At my suggestion, tuition in Medau Rhythmic Movement, which I had so much admired in Berlin before the war, was introduced in the curriculum. This was carried out by Peggy Secord and Molly Braithwaite, who had started to develop Medau work in England: work which has since spread widely and has grown into the Medau Association, with a number of teachers and many devoted followers.

I became more and more involved in activity for the League. As well as teaching the students, I travelled to visit League centres, continued as editor of the magazine, taught a London evening class once a week in Fulham, wrote articles on health and beauty for the press, and did a series of television programmes which involved a fortnightly appearance in BBC *Woman's Hour*.

Like many others I was trying to adapt myself to the post-war world, and finding the task difficult. The simple virtues of patriotism, loyalty and self-sacrifice, which had governed life during the war seemed no longer important. For six years, living on the brink of catastrophe, they had been paramount. Now they were replaced by an amorphous flux in which disillusion, self-interest and apathy thrived. My life seemed to have shrunk to a condition of standing in queues in Notting Hill Gate to buy food for the children, pushing my way on to crowded buses to take them to school, and fighting an uphill battle to get the League re-established.

The house in Campden Hill Square had come alive, and was now being used for a number of activities. The children occupied the top floor, with a Swiss girl who helped to look after them. My bedroom, which looked out on to the square, was on the next floor, while the ground floor contained a long drawing-room, stretching from the front to the back of the house, with garden views from each window. In the semi-basement was the dining-room and kitchen; and as it seemed to be frequently necessary to ascend rapidly from there to the top floor, in response to some call from the children, Rosa, my Swiss girl, and I were kept well exercised.

Students from the Bagot Stack Health School came to the house once a week for public-speaking lectures, which I gave them; young members of the Douglas-Hamilton family used it as a London base, and gave parties there; and my own friends gathered to meet and talk. In the summer, we spilled into the garden to sit under the pear-tree. In the winter, we repaired to the kitchen, and ate there by candlelight, trying to keep warm in the freezing and sometimes fuelless post-war climate.

The Square was a neighbourly place to live; one of those typical London corners where a village existence can flourish. There was a pretty Christmas custom: the lighting of candles in all the houses round the Square on Christmas Eve. On our first Christmas we joined into this ceremony, and then the children and I went outside into the Square, to watch the candles twinkle in the surrounding windows. Standing among the bare winter trees, I looked at the small pinpoints of light gleaming through the night shadows, fluttering yet constant, and longed for a similar flame to illuminate the darkness I felt within. I was disoriented, searching for a means of expression, unable to find in the League the all-absorbing work of the pre-war period, unable to give myself wholly to anything else. The deep attachments and ideals by which I had lived seemed no longer valid; in the brittle post-war period they had lost meaning.

I made several new and lasting friends; my circle of interests widened, and, like any other young woman in her early thirties, I responded to affection and admiration when they came my way.

I longed to share my heart and life, to marry again, and to fill the void left by David's death. But his powerful memory still encased me like a second skin, and prevented me from committing myself finally to anyone else.

One day a taxi drew up outside my Campden Hill Square house. Watching through the window, I saw a fair head emerge and then a burly form alighted and paid the driver. It was my old friend, Ally. I rushed to the hall door to welcome him into the house.

'Ally! After all these years!'

'It's good to see you, Prunella.'

He brought a sense of space, of the out-of-doors and of simple certainties, into the dark London room.

'You look just the same.'

'Much older. A lot has happened.'

'Yes.'

Ally's reserve was protecting him. I, too, was reserved, for my life now had moved into very different channels from those we had shared. It was a long time since I had seen him. During the latter years of the war he had served in Italy as a captain in the South African Medical Corps. Now he had come to London to study for his fellowship at Guy's Hospital, and would be here for some time.

'I saw an announcement of David's death in an army news-sheet which came round to our field-hospital,' he said. 'I felt so desperately sorry for you. How have you been, Prunella?'

Here was a chance to share my loneliness; to explain the lack of meaning and the depression which clouded my life and from which I was unable to escape. But I could not take it. Ally's simplicity and transparent sincerity seemed unrealistic beside the cynicism of post-war London. I replied non-committally.

We slipped into our old rôles of the experienced mentor and the grateful recipient; when in reality Ally had so much more to give to me, than I to him.

Looking back, I realise how vital timing is in human affairs. This first post-war meeting came at the wrong moment for both of us. We each had other commitments. We lived at opposite ends of London. Transport was difficult. Ally was working and study-ing hard and had little free time. I was taken up with friends who were very different from him. After one or two desultory dinners together, we drifted apart.

I had one source of unfailing satisfaction in my life: mountains. During the summers of 1946 and 1947, I was lucky to have two seasons of climbing in the high Alps. The 14,000 ft and 15,000 ft giants of Switzerland were in a different class from the moderate Austrian climbs which I had experienced before the war, or from scrambles on the Cuillins in Skye. They required expert knowledge of snow conditions, and stamina to survive long days of exposure on the glaciers and on the icy rocks above.

At that time most parties climbed with guides, few English climbers having the expertise to dispense with them. The climbing huts were full, but much less crowded than to-day, and the classic ascents had not yet become banal.

I was fortunate in finding an English friend to climb with, who was an experienced mountaineer of many years' standing, and who had climbed in the Himalayas as well as the Alps. Together we ascended the Dent Blanche (by the difficult Vier Esels *grat*), the Zinal Rothorn, Pitz Palü, the Dom, the Obergabelhorn and finally the Matterhorn. Each of these peaks was reached from a mountain hut, three or four hours' walk up from the valley, in which we stayed overnight, starting at dawn the next morning for the ascent. As the climbing season progressed I became used to the altitude – at first a cause of exhaustion and nausea – and to the exposure. Making a way along a high ridge, with a precipitous drop of thousands of feet on either side, must be one of the most exhilarating experiences in the world. The ridge stretches ahead, rising interminably to the summit. The rope coils between you and your leader, sometimes taut, on a difficult climbing passage, sometimes slack, always your lifeline connecting you to terra firma, without which, you feel, you might fly away into intoxicating space. Every nerve, muscle and heart-beat is working to its utmost capacity. The effort needed stretches you to your physical limit. And with this effort, sustained for many hours, comes also a fusing of mind and spirit, an awareness, and an expansion of consciousness which seems to carry with it an extraordinary insight and release.

Although not the most difficult, I found the Matterhorn the most exciting mountain to climb; largely, I suppose, because of its reputation and its spectacular silhouette. The Matterhorn stands alone, at some distance from the other dramatic peaks of the Zermatt area, one foot in Italy, one in Switzerland, striding the wide glaciers with superb assurance and challenge. 'The old Matterhagger' my companion called it; a disrespectful allusion which I hoped would not bring Nemesis upon us as we struggled up the icy rocks of the precipitous north face. The Matterhorn is famous for falling stones which descend intermittently day and night, and which make it imperative to get off the mountain in early afternoon. As we climbed, I remembered the celebrated first ascent of the mountain by Edward Whymper. This was the climax of an obsession which had brought him to Zermatt year after year, in passionate attempts to be the first to conquer the Matterhorn. He succeeded on the 13th of July 1865, outwitting his Italian rival, Alexis Carrel, who was also attempting the summit from the Italian side that very day. Whymper triumphantly reached the top. But his unwieldy party of eight, summoned hurriedly for fear of being superseded, came to grief on the descent. Four men fell to their deaths from the vertiginous north face to the glacier, 4,000 feet below, while Whymper watched appalled, unable to save them. This accident and the subsequent scandal broke Whymper's spirit and turned him into a remote, bitter man, a solitary wanderer in the far places of the world. Thus did the Matterhorn avenge its first conqueror.

Since then tourists have flocked to the mountain from all corners of the world, and many have been dragged up it by long-suffering guides. Day by day a little more of its impressive pile crumbles away. But in spite of violation and decay it still retains an unsurpassed magnificence; and the little human beings crawling up its slopes, erecting ski-lifts on its glaciers, and hammering pitons into its rocky walls, seem no more than insects, powerless to impair its grandeur.

The ascent of the Matterhorn crowned my Alpine season. I returned home to give my children graphic accounts, spreading a map on the floor, and showing them the terrain I had covered. They, my only audience, were duly impressed, although they could understand little of what I described. But perhaps my stories sowed in them the seeds of future mountaineering exploits, since carried out in several different parts of the world. Years later

Diarmaid climbed Mount Kasbek in the Caucasus, and Kimabalu in North Borneo; and Iain made an ascent of the severe north face of Mount Kenya.

David's sister Jean was now living in Sussex, near the village of Rusper. She and her first husband, Christopher Mackintosh, had divorced shortly after the war, and Jean had married an old friend of the family, Leo Zinovieff, whose parents had come to England as Tsarist refugees from Russia in 1917. Leo, a brilliant engineer, was one of David's best friends, and I was very fond of him and his ebullient Russian family. I spent a number of weekends with Jean and Leo; the children thrived in the country air and I began to think seriously of moving them out of London. Just then, a house to rent became available on the outskirts of Rusper. Encouraged by Jean and Leo I decided to lease it. I let the Campden Hill Square house to a friend, and in the autumn of 1947, we all moved down to Sussex.

It was November, dank and cold. Nevertheless, I breathed the chill air with a sense of relish and relief. Here was peace; release from the city tempo and strain, a chance for the spirit to expand. Jean's house was only two miles distant, reached across country by a walk through woods and fields, and we visited her frequently.

One evening, soon after our arrival, I was riding home on a pony of Jean's which she had promised to lend to my children. Twilight fell as I cantered along the verge of the road. A large yellow moon rose from behind bare trees and climbed into the sky. It shone with confident brilliance, scattering dark shadows across the landscape. Shreds of mist lay above the fields, deadening sound, and the pony and I moved in a mysterious silence, broken only by the faint thud of hooves on the damp grass. The night closed quietly around us, bringing with it a curious comfort and peace. All at once, life seemed simple; as clear and simple as the moon's radiance.

'Don't strive,' a voice told me. 'Don't worry. Don't be anxious. Just accept.'

Accept, accept, accept. The words followed the rhythm of the horse's hooves. I felt that the moment was decisive. Somehow a change had taken place in the depths of my spirit and my burden of doubt and grief began to fall away.

How strange is the realm of the subconscious! Unknown battle-ground of so much that is at one and the same time valuable, trivial, meaningless or vitally important. Decisions which form themselves in this region often take time to emerge to the surface. But when they do, they have the assent of the whole personality and are not questioned or resented by any one part of it. They dominate circumstances, and inevitably find their own fruition. My strong instinct for life had led me to look for happiness in the wrong places, sometimes to the detriment of others. I had forced events, imposed my will upon circumstances, and refused to wait in faith for whatever fate might hold in store.

Now the silent country night told me to relax, to be calm and patient, to open my heart to its beauty, and to live in peace. I listened to its message, and trotted home through the darkness, happier than for years past.

Some months later I met Ally again by chance at the house of a mutual friend in London. This time our paths did not diverge. I asked him down to the country for a weekend and he, like myself, revelled in its space and peace. He was working very hard as a registrar at Guy's Hospital, assisting the Medical Superintendent's operations and helping to look after his patients, as well as study-ing for his final fellowship examinations. Once these were achieved he would return to Cape Town and practise there as a surgeon.

Ally drew me into the life at Guy's and I learned to admire its reality, and the dedication shown by the doctors and nurses whom I met. Here there was no lack of meaning, no questing for values, no self-doubt or tiresome self-analysis. Confronted by the issues of life and death, Ally and his friends responded with expert skill, giving practical help where help was most needed.

A routine grew up between us. Ally came to Sussex most week-ends and we met in London to go to the ballet or opera. He loved music, and introduced me to Wagner and the modern Russian composers, while I initiated him into the joys of the Royal Ballet then building up its world-wide reputation.

In Sussex, he constructed an aerial railway for my children, and thrilled them with tales of Zulu wars and demonstrations of Zulu dances and war-cries. It needed little encouragement for Ally to return to childhood's estate himself. As before, we took our companionship for granted and lived in the present, letting the future take care of itself. Ally was thirty-three, a month younger than myself, but still unmarried, and with no apparent thoughts of settling down.

We visited the Continent together, and spent a memorable holiday in Italy, starting on Lake Como and continuing in Venice and finally Florence. Our own *risorgimento* flourished in the ebullient Italian atmosphere; not even conscientious sight-seeing could damp our *joie de vivre*.

We climbed Pitz Palü, in the Engadine, and Ally had his first taste of mountaineering in the high snows. And the following spring we skied at Kühtai, a tiny village in the Austrian Alps, which at that time possessed no funicular, and had to be reached on foot or by sleigh. On the way there, passing through Innsbruck, we met Dr Reut Nicolussi, David's old South Tyrolese friend. Reut had aged, but still possessed his indomitable optimism. Neither the exigencies of war nor the apparent failures of peace could shake his belief in the cause of South Tyrol, now sadly in abeyance, and likely to remain so for the foreseeable future.

The months contracted towards Ally's time of departure. He gained his fellowship in the autumn of 1949, but was loath to leave. Ally's reactions to Britain had come full circle. He now delighted in the values of a mature civilisation. His appreciation of art and music had deepened, and he valued the experiences which the galleries and concert-halls of London could provide. He had proved his worth at Guy's, and taken his place among his colleagues with a success which brought him a warm confidence. At last he felt that he belonged in Britain. His intimate connection with one of the great teaching hospitals, and the circle of friends which we shared, had given him a stake in the community and an understanding of the British way of life. All this was hard to forgo. In addition, there was our own relationship to consider. Its future now hung in the balance.

Could I leave Britain, with everything it meant to me, take the children to South Africa, and make a new home in Cape Town?

Could Ally desert his own country, forsaking his elderly mother, fail to honour the implicit responsibility to return to

South Africa conferred on him by his Rhodes Scholarship, and stay in England?

Suddenly these questions loomed urgently before us.

We went for a last holiday to Cortina in October 1949, telling ourselves that we would consider them there. In fact, we were too absorbed in climbing the Dolomite peaks of the Cima Piccoli, the Cima Grandi, the Cinque Torre Grandi and the Punta Fiames to think of anything else. Once again, life accelerated as we clambered up firm, hard rock, roped down cliffs on to narrow ledges, and stood victoriously on spiky summits.

But our companionship was coming to an end. One sad winter day we travelled down to Southampton, and Ally boarded a liner for Cape Town. We had agreed that he must return to South Africa; but I had promised to visit Cape Town in a few months' time, to see for myself what living there would entail.

I knew that in Ally's absence I would have to consider many things: the children's future, my responsibility to the League, the reactions of David's family . . . Life could do cruel and unexpected things to two people once they parted.

I watched the liner pull slowly away from the shore. Across the ever-widening gap of water Ally's figure, one of the many that leaned over the rail, diminished until I could no longer see his waving hand. He became unrecognisable, merged with the people on either side, and finally was lost in the outlines of the departing ship's structure. The vessel steamed on, her white wake ruffling the grey sea. Smaller and smaller she grew, until she, too, was no more than a blur, a shape vanishing into the horizon, bound for a land six thousand miles distant. I turned and walked slowly along the cobblestones of the quayside, recognising in myself an unconsolable sense of loss.

CHAPTER 12

A New Committal

By 1950 the League had built up a large membership, and was gradually receiving recognition in a wider sphere. Over a thousand classes were held throughout the country each week, and most of the practice class leaders who had kept the centres going through the war years had now been replaced by trained teachers. Torquil Macleod, the League treasurer, whose wise guidance had been of such value since 1939, felt that the time had come to change the League's constitution.

For nine years the League had operated as a private Limited Company, a form adopted to meet wartime circumstances. But by 1950 it was felt that a different kind of constitution would be more suitable to the League's growing needs: that of a non-profit-making Association, which would have charity status, was chosen.

The new Association would be governed by a council of people prominent in the field of physical education and social service, while its administration would be conducted by the directors of the former company, who would become its first Executive Committee.

Plans for this change of constitution took some time to mature, and during the process I often wondered what my mother, who had started the League with such verve and vigour as a purely individual extension of her own vision and personality, would have thought of them. Pioneers who inspire new movements and carry out their first expansion often see only half of the game. They seldom experience the tedious work of consolidation which must follow; a period when it is often difficult to maintain the original inspiration and at the same time carry out the steps necessary to achieve stability and permanence.

About this time, the League received a valuable tribute to its work from Professor M. L. Jacks, Director of the Department of Education at Oxford University, and a former headmaster of

Mill Hill School. Speaking at a League display in the Midlands, he said:

I have long regarded the Women's League of Health and Beauty as one of the outstanding educational movements of our time.

In the education of the body we must begin with the stage of physical literacy, and teach people the mastery of the essential physical skills – how to breathe, how to sit, how to stand, how to walk, and how to move, and how to do all these things with the greatest economy of energy and with the maximum of satisfaction. In so far as this is a Women's League of *Health*, I believe it to be concerned with this first stage in physical education.

But we cannot stop there. We must go on to the stage of physical culture. Here we gain an appreciation of physical beauty, of the grace and poetry of motion: we learn the enjoyment which comes from harmonious and rhythmical life, and the satisfaction to be derived from the exercise of some active skill. And in so far as this is a Women's League of *Beauty*, I believe it to be concerned with this second stage in physical education. Physical education of this kind has far-reaching effects in the intellectual and moral and spiritual sphere: it is indeed one element in the co-education of body, mind and spirit. It produces better human material, and so it makes a vital contribution to the good of the community – and not only that, but also to international understanding and the peace of the world.

I am one of those who believe that peace will only come to the world through the making of better men and women. The aim of this League is 'Health leading to Peace', and this is how it strives to achieve that aim.

Other well-known figures came forward to support the League's work, and were invited to join its Council: Lord Aberdare, the former chairman of the National Fitness Council; Sir Cyril Atkinson, my mother's old friend who had taken the chair at each League display since its inception; Sir Noel Curtis-Bennett, chairman of the National Playing Fields Association; Professor Winifred Cullis, Emeritus Professor of Physiology at London University; Miss K. Curlett, director of the Girls' Training Corps; Mr R. H. Gummer, a prominent business man whose firm ran League classes for its employees; Lord Sempill, famous in the world of aviation, and later chairman of the League Council; Brigadier T. H. Wand-Tetley, former Commandant of the Army

Physical Training School; Marjorie Duncombe, my mother's partner in the early days, and trainer of all the pre-war teachers; and the Countess of Selkirk. Audrey Selkirk was an old friend of mine, who had married Geordie, David's brother, in the autumn of 1949. A world champion skier, one of the first women pilots to fly an aeroplane from Britain to South Africa, and a member of the Air Transport Auxiliary during the war, her qualities of courage and imagination have been of great value to the League up to the present day.

The League was now financially stable (the new Association started with a capital of £1,000 donated to it by the shareholders of the former company), and was in the process of building up a reserve fund from which its teacher-training could be financed.

Abroad, the League system was being taught in Canada, Australia, New Zealand and Eire. The Canadian members remained in close touch, carried on practice classes during the war, and were supplied with a teacher from Britain soon afterwards. In Australia, Thea Stanley-Hughes developed on somewhat different lines with a greater emphasis on the League's role of preventive medicine, and its ability to help those who were in poor health. In New Zealand classes had opened in 1937; and in Eire, Kathleen O'Rourke ran her own training school for Irish teachers in Dublin.

Overall, by 1950, there was an encouraging picture of post-war growth. But was some sparkle and sense of adventure lacking? Did the League now need the impetus of some exciting new venture?

I turned these thoughts over in my mind as, early in 1950, I leant over the rail of a Union Castle steamer bound for South Africa. I was on my way to my promised visit to Ally in Cape Town: a visit which might make profound changes in my own life, and might also provide a new means of expansion for the League. For days the ship had moved calmly across wide seas, and this leisurely progress had given time for rest and reflection. By day flying fish gleamed among flashes of spray. By night the tropical moon cast a sheen on dark waters, and the Southern Cross printed its crooked pattern among galaxies of brilliant stars. Slowly the ship drew near to the southernmost tip of Africa. And at last, early one morning, I awoke to the knowledge that her engines had ceased.

I leaped out of bed. Framed in the porthole of the cabin I saw the spectacular panorama of mountains with which Cape Town greets the voyager. In the half-light of dawn, shreds of cloud still clung to Table Mountain and Devil's Peak. Strung like a necklace round their feet shone the lights of the city. I ran up on to the deck. The mystery of a new land, a vast continent pulsing with a strange unknown life, stirred from across the water. I shivered, not only with the dawn wind, but also with a deep excitement, a premonition that my future was bound up with this place, that here much of my heart and spirit would remain.

Ally came on board. Delightedly we met, and I landed.

I had moved from the north to the south; from a rain-swept wintry island to the heady bloom of African summer. My senses, starved of sun and colour, opened to receive a myriad impressions. Foremost among them were the dark faces on the quayside; the gleaming brown skins, the startlingly dazzling smiles, the soft deep voices.

In early 1950 the Nationalist Government had been in power for only two years. Its policy of Apartheid had yet to be fully implemented. The 'coloureds', the half-caste population of the Cape which makes up the majority of its non-white citizens, were still allowed to vote, own their own houses, and live in districts where dark and white intermingled. The Africans, mostly transient labour, but some from established families who had lived in the Cape for one or two generations, were permitted to work and stay in the area. The cruel policy of forced repatriation to the African Bantu homelands had not yet taken place. Fear and hostility, which now divide the races and bring unbearable tension, not only to Johannesburg, but also to the sleepy Cape, existed only in embryo, and had not yet erupted into everyday life, although they were very shortly to do so.

Friendly smiles on dark faces greeted me as I stepped ashore. The African tempo – easy-going, laughter-loving, leisurely – dominated the busy quay. Sandwiched between the sea and the mountains the white buildings of the city sparkled in the clear air. Table Mountain's precipitous cliffs lifted to a sky of dazzling blue.

'What a paradise!' I said to Ally, whose pride and excitement rivalled the sun's radiance. Warmth enveloped me. Cold northern attitudes and responsibilities fell away. A profusion of colour, light, space, and sun assailed me. The southern hemisphere opened its embracing arms, and within an hour of arrival I was in love with the Cape.

Looking back, it was not only the scenery, the people and the climate which charmed me. It was also an old-fashioned, almost Edwardian, way of life. This was summed up in Ally's mother and her ménage. Born and brought up in the Cape, she had the un-questioned authority and self-assurance which being a white person in that society entailed. But she also possessed an amused understanding of her coloured dependants, and an indulgent generosity towards them which created a kind of symbiosis, essential for their mutual existence. She needed them and they needed her. Cookie, her diminutive energetic temperamental coloured cook, and William, her coloured chauffeur who looked like a seedy film-star, were essential props. She could more easily visualise the sun never rising again on Table Mountain, than life without them. They, on their side, were truly attached to their Madam, whom they always addressed in the third person; proud of her possessions and her handsome appearance, and zealous to preserve her status in the social life of Cape Town.

Her table, loaded with shining silver and glass, glowing fruit and amber Cape wine, was as lavish as her ample self. She had Ally's sense of humour, and as she retailed to her guests the latest piece of Cape gossip, or some scandal which had taken place in the coloured community, the same amused gleam shone in her green eyes as in her son's.

The ease and informality of life in the Cape delighted me. I welcomed its absence of pressure, and its enjoyable sense of relaxation. Only later did I realise how restricted, in truth, it could be.

Olly, as I learned to call Ally's mother (her name was Olga), with her bridge parties two afternoons a week, her lunch parties every Sunday, her ceremonial drives with William in attendance, and her bevy of elderly girlfriends, cronies since their mutual school-days, represented something entirely new to me: the traditional existence of a Cape Town lady of leisure. This existence depended on an unchanging order of white superiority, something which Olly and her friends accepted without question. They had been brought up in this environment and were perfectly adapted to it. In common with many other citizens of the Cape, they pushed the thought of any fundamental change out of their minds. But inescapable pressures were already mounting against their way of life.

The colour problem loomed larger every day. It was the inevitable topic of conversation which dominated every gathering; and the views expressed on it were as various as the races which had helped to populate the Cape – Dutch, Afrikaans, English, French, Hottentot, African, Indian, Malay. Socially, these races were rigidly separated into European and non-European categories. The whites could talk about the colour problem, but only among themselves. Very seldom did they hear views from the other side of the barrier.

Ally hated the restrictive racial practices and policies of the 'Nat' government, and was determined to resist them, so far as he could, in his own field of medicine. I was equally determined that if I did decide to return and live in the Cape permanently and the League came to South Africa, its work should be made available to *all* members of the community; coloured, black or white.

We spent the first week of my visit exploring the Cape countryside. Ally took me to camp under the Hottentots Holland mountains, where we slept in the open, below stars so vivid that it seemed one could reach up and pluck them from the sky. We woke during the night and watched the changing constellations: Orion, the bold hunter, here upside-down, his dagger above his belt; Cygnus, the swan, spreading her starry wings; the Serpent, coiling across the Milky Way; and Leo, my own constellation, rising in the small hours to move majestically across the heavens.

Evening brought a patina of golden light to the veldt, illuminating every leaf and flower. Stabs of colour glowed gem-like among the yellow-green foliage, while the proteas, heraldic emblem of South Africa, captured the last gleams of the sun in their generous pink cups.

We drove to Cape Point, a game reserve at the tip of the Cape peninsula, where buck and eland grazed among the flowers and grasses. We walked softly across the veldt, unwilling to disturb them, our only companions. Here man was an interloper. Even after three hundred years of white civilisation, the country still belonged to the animals and the birds.

On either side of the peninsula towering waves crashed on to ash-white sands, or foamed against rocks and cliffs. Near the city the beaches had been developed (Apartheid was enforced even on the sands, in strictly delineated white and non-white areas), but farther along the coastline we found deserted bays which no one else knew. We surfed on the crests of the huge Cape rollers, or dived into their curving green walls as they thundered with a flurry of spray on to gleaming stretches of sand. The brilliant beaches, quivering under the sun's heat, shaken with the surf's roar, seemed as deserted as on the day of creation. Running naked into the sea, we felt as free as the first man and woman in the first world.

The Cape of Good Hope – romantic words which drummed in my ears. The spectacular beauty of the countryside exceeded my highest expectations, and swept me off my feet. After our week's exploration I returned to Cape Town, and poured my impressions into the ears of my old Swedish friend, Görel: now Görel Macleod, wife of a Scottish naval officer whom she had married during the war, and with whom she had emigrated to South Africa. She was less enthusiastic.

'You can't exist only on scenery, you know,' she cautioned me. 'Have you thought of all you'll miss if you settle here? Not only your family and friends, but Europe – Europe which you know and love, where you have put down so many roots, and where you belong.'

'Perhaps I can put down roots here as well. After all, I will have Ally to help.'

'Of course. But he belongs here and you don't. You've never experienced suburban life. Do you realise how restrictive it can be? And another thing. South Africa is becoming more and more Afrikaaner-ised. Now that the "Nats" are in power, the English-speaking element will be gradually pushed out. We and our friends will have no influence on the way things develop.'

My euphoria began to evaporate.

'And what about the colour question?' she continued. 'Do you want to live in a police state, or among violent racial disorders?'

I was silent. I had thought of these problems, particularly the last one, and had discussed them with Ally, but they were still on the fringe of my Cape experience, not at the centre. At the centre was Ally's love, and the warmth and happiness which it generated. This, I felt, could overcome all obstacles.

Görel gazed at me contemplatively.

'I know you,' she said, at last. 'Whatever I say, you'll act from your heart, not your head. But see the other side first.'

I decided to explore the city. Ally took me to the locations on the Cape Flats where the Africans lived. Here, within sight of Table Mountain, and a few miles from the prosperous suburbs, was a place called Cook's Bush, where houses were little more than a dump of old petrol-cans, nailed together under a tin roof, and lined with newspaper. One water-tap sufficed for fifty families. Small children played in the dust among flies. They appeared sturdy enough, but they were the survivors of a shockingly high child mortality rate. Their mothers, moving at the slow African pace between the squalid *pondokkies*, looked sullen and dispirited. In the summer, fires raged among these flimsy structures; in the winter they were flooded when the rains came, and their occupants lived in water, sometimes inches high.

We visited 'Cafda', a charity run for the Cape coloured population by Oscar Wollheim, an Afrikaaner with a sense of vision and dedication. Cafda had established a Centre, where it was helping many destitute people, and Oscar Wollheim was hoping to achieve an ambitious re-housing scheme. Ally promised whatever support he could give. Subsequently he worked at the Centre, and arranged for university medical students to help man the St John Brigade mobile clinic which visited 4,000 Africans living below the breadline on the Cape Flats. Ally was disturbed and upset by the conditions we had seen: the obverse side of the beautiful, prosperous Cape.

Apartheid was rigidly enforced in education, but within their community some of the Cape coloured population received a good training. I visited Zonnebloem College in District Six (reputedly one of the worst areas for crime and disturbances), where teacher-training and the groundings of a nursing training were given. I saw classes at the Technical Institute in Cape Town, where coloured boys and girls learned skills which they could pass on to other members of their youth clubs; and Ally and I visited a large school in District Six, run by Dr Golding, one of the leaders of the coloured community. There, five hundred boys and girls greeted us, lined up on the playground in immaculate white shorts and shirts, ready to give us a PT display. The quality of the display, the discipline, and the whole spirit of the school were most impressive.

Dr Golding explained to me the difficulties under which his community laboured. Traditionally the coloureds were attached to the white population in Cape Town, partly by origin, but wholly by sentiment and culture. Unlike the Africans, they still retained the vote, but now they were classed by the Nationalist government as non-white and non-European. This meant that many intelligent Indians, Malays and Cape coloureds (who had little in common with the African community which possessed its own traditions and culture) were now forced to live isolated lives; their children educated only to a certain circumscribed level; their inferior status emphasised by such procedures as standing in separate non-white queues at post offices and railway stations; and their opportunities for contact with the white community sadly diminished.

Could I live in a country with such contrasts: at once so beautiful and so harsh, so friendly and so unjust, so hospitable and so ruthless? No previous European experience could guide me. Life here was something entirely different, if it was to be lived on any but the most superficial level. If I came, I could not turn a blind eye to what went on around me. I would have to be involved.

In the end, as Görel had foreseen, it was my heart which decided the issue. My heart said an emphatic 'yes' to Ally. Together, I hoped, we could face all problems. Together, we might even have something of value to give to this disturbing fractured community.

I wrote to David's mother, telling her of my decision, and asking for her blessing. She cabled back her good wishes, and we announced our engagement. We had a happy few days of celebration and congratulations. Then I flew home, to make preparations for a permanent removal to the Cape.

The next few months needed all my resolution. The wrench of

leaving England was much greater than I had anticipated. In addition, there were work commitments which had to be carried out first. For several years, I had been closely connected with Outward Bound, the movement which had grown out of David's pre-war Fitness Training Schools in the Highlands. Kurt Hahn, its original inspiration, had established the first Outward Bound School at Aberdovey, in Wales, during the war. This aimed, through adventure training on the sea and in the mountains, to extend the awareness and capabilities of its pupils, to foster their self-confidence, and to stretch their capacities for endurance and self-discovery. Boys (for the main part from industry) came for a month's residential course: a valuable experience in community living, which threw them on their own resources among a group of their contemporaries from many different backgrounds and localities.

To-day, adventure training has become part of our educational system and is widespread throughout the country; but in 1950 Outward Bound was doing pioneer work. Its growth depended on the vision and enthusiasm of a few men: Kurt Hahn and Lawrence Holt, who had founded Aberdovey; Spencer Summers, who became chairman of the Outward Bound Trust in 1946; and the associates whom he gathered round him.

I served on the Management Committee from the beginning, hoping that the day would come when the training could be extended to girls. Some of the outdoor activities would have to be modified to suit their capacities, but I was sure that girls could benefit from the challenge and community spirit of Outward Bound.

When I returned from South Africa, Spencer Summers asked me to form an Advisory Committee of women, to discuss running Outward Bound courses for girls. I gathered together representatives of various organisations, including the Central Council of Physical Recreation, the National Association of Girls' Clubs, the Girls' Training Corps, and others. Diana Reader-Harris (later headmistress of Sherborne School) was one of the members of the Committee, and when I left England she took over the chairmanship.

Although I was not to be there to see much of it happen, a number of courses for girls were subsequently held, which proved very successful, and the benefit which girls could derive from the Outward Bound experience was firmly established.

There remained my responsibility to the League. Sometimes in the past my attitude to the League had been ambivalent; occasionally it had seemed a burden too heavy to carry, an exploiter of my goodwill and vitality. Now that I was to leave it I suddenly realised how inescapably it was part of my life. With its new Council and constitution, and its efficient Executive Committee, there was every chance that it would continue to develop satisfactorily; but for my part I must leave behind my colleagues the teachers, and the many hundreds of members, from whom I had received so much affection throughout the years.

These thoughts were much in my mind as I stood before the microphone in the Empire Pool, Wembley, where in May 1950 fifteen hundred League members had assembled for a twentieth birthday display. I gazed at them all, lined up in the arena in their shining black shorts and white blouses, the Scottish contingent flaunting gay tartan shoulder-ribbons, the Irish girls with their emerald green, the Canadians – twenty-five of them who had travelled all the way from Toronto for this display – making a splash of colour in their scarlet blazers. What could I say that would fit the occasion?

I spoke of the League's beginning, its founder's vision, its survival throughout the war, and its subsequent development. I stressed its independence, free from political or State control, and the enthusiasm of its members, by whom it was entirely financed.

Then I spoke of the future. I reminded the members of the League's motto 'Movement is Life'.

'We must live up to that motto,' I said. 'We must not be content merely with past achievements. Already the League has spread to Canada, Australia and Eire. Now I hope to carry it to a new continent, and to establish its work in South Africa.'

Confident words, but on what reality were they based? ('*You are going to South Africa as an ignorant stranger,*' an inner voice told me. '*Will you be able to make even a dent in the prejudices which exist there?*')

'The world of 1950,' I concluded, 'may be radically different from that of 1930, but it is the same in one respect. Its most urgent need is still a spirit of goodwill and tolerance, a Christian outlook, and a common humanity which can overcome barriers of race, class and nationality . . .'

It was the last occasion on which I saw my League friends. I said goodbye to them, promising to return the following year for the League's twenty-first birthday celebrations, and taking with me many good wishes for my South African venture.

My sons, now aged ten and eight, were wildly excited at the prospect of our removal to Cape Town, and at the thought of living permanently with Ally, whom they regarded as their greatest friend. Diarmaid went to stay for the last few days with his grandmother at Ferne. I took the opportunity to visit the churchyard in the neighbouring village of Berwick St John, where David was buried. It was a place I seldom went to, because David was still so close to me, that I required no tangible reminder of him. But now, with a new life ahead, and serious new commitments to face, I needed this act of remembrance.

The churchyard was remote and still, silent except for some desultory bird-song, and the whisper of wind through the summer leaves. The words of a poem moved through my mind, as I looked at David's grave, marked with its simple RAF cross.

> This quiet finish from a quiet beginning
> Is seldom with us: seldom we conceive
> That life's insistent flight from the eternal
> Death with a simple gesture will retrieve,
> Placing the body home in friendly earth
> Where it may rest and flower to different birth.

The paradox of death possessed me: the mysterious fact that physical removal of a body could make little difference to the realms of the mind and spirit. David was as real to me as ever; but the numbness of his loss had receded, the forces of life had reasserted themselves, and dictated for me new channels and new loyalties. I knew it was not goodbye. I would take David with me wherever I went.

So, at last, the children and I boarded the SS *Edinburgh Castle* and started our voyage to Cape Town. Two bull-terriers and a black

National Festival of Youth at Wembley, 1946. The League contingent marches past the Duchess of Kent

Coronation Year Display at the Albert Hall, 1953

South African League members in Cape Town

Barbara Keys

Prunella with her Zonnebloem coloured girls' class, 1951

Prunella taking a class at the League's 40th Anniversary, 1970

cat, whom Iain had refused to leave behind, accompanied us, as well as a mountain of luggage, and sheaves of farewell telegrams.

As the ship steamed slowly out of Southampton, leaving David's sister Jean and her family waving goodbye from the quay, my nerve suddenly failed me.

'*You are making the greatest mistake of your life,*' an inner voice proclaimed.

Was I? Or was I sailing to a land which would provide un-dreamed of happiness and fulfilment? I did not know.

But when Ally met us in Cape Town, scintillating with excite-ment, and the children fell upon him with whoops of joy, all doubts fled.

He drove us to an old Dutch Colonial house in the country, belonging to a painter friend of his, Neville Lewis, and there we stayed for a few weeks joined by Görel Macleod and her children, acclimatising ourselves to South Africa, and making plans for our wedding.

It was the season of the Cape winter, with alternating storms and sparkling clear weather. The 22nd of July, the day we were married, was brilliantly fine. I drove through Cape Town to the Cathedral in a glow of mellow sunshine, which seemed a reflection of Ally's and my happiness and committal.

The small St George's chapel shone with the soft light of candles as we stood before the altar, and the Dean of Cape Town, the Reverend Michael Gibbs, pronounced the marriage words. It was a quiet and lovely ceremony, uniting us before God and our friends; a sacrament, performed by a holy man.

Görel Macleod and her husband gave us their house for the wedding reception, and Hubert Kidd, headmaster of the Diocesan School, where Ally had been educated, proposed our health. The warmth of good wishes with which we were surrounded, com-pensated for the absence of my family and friends. Ally was radiant. That morning, he had written to me: 'I can't tell you how much happiness the thought of this afternoon is giving me. After all these years my wildest dream is about to come true.'

I thought of these words as we drove away into the spectacular Cape sunset. I knew that the future which now opened up before us would be shared in deepening comradeship. At last, we could look forward to life together. Our happiness was complete.

CHAPTER 13

The Beautiful Cape

THE gentle murmur of doves, rising and falling in lazy cadence, and the whisper of wind through poplars: these above all other sounds evoke my home in the Cape.

It was situated in Constantia, a country district about fifteen miles from Cape Town, famous for its vineyards and its old Dutch Colonial houses. Poplars, gum-trees and oaks gave shade to the dirt roads which wound through the Constantia valley. Wine was pressed and barrelled in several of its farms. And though many two-acre plots had been sold off, and white, thatched-roof houses sprouted among the vines, the whole district still retained the neighbourly traditions and easy-going relations of a farming community, whose common experience grows from the land.

The doves were seldom silent; their soft trill mixed with the warmth of sunshine lying like a carpet across the lawn. As day ended the shadows of the poplars lengthened, and egrets in an echelon flew up the valley, winging their way from the sea-shore to their sleeping place inland. The first star trembled above the mountain, and then night – the mysterious, magical African night, ancient and enchanting – slowly enclosed the landscape, and opened its canopy of stars.

The house we had chosen was a modern one, built only two years before; spacious and light, with large plate-glass windows which framed magnificent views. The garden swept down to the valley, beyond which rose the fir-clad slopes of Devil's Peak; while behind the house a path wound up to the Vlaakenburg, a wild boulder-strewn mountain, which the boys and I soon explored. In half an hour's climb from the house one could be standing on high slopes amid the abundant Cape flora, the only movement the passage of clouds overhead, or the wheeling of a bird through the foliage.

We had found and bought this house before I left for England, and Ally had already partially furnished it. Soon crates of my own furniture arrived, and we set about making it into a home. We cultivated the garden with zest. Flowers grew very quickly and easily, and bloomed all the year round in the Cape. There were already beds of glowing cannas, geraniums cascading over walls, mesembryanthemum which opened their brilliant star-shaped petals amid succulent leaves in the spring, and tobacco plants whose delicate white blossom scented the summer evenings. Hibiscus, bougainvillaea and oleander flowered in Mediterranean profusion; a lemon tree and a pomegranate produced exotic fruit; a plot of ginger-plant with its sweet heavy smell sprawled under a loquat tree; and the flame trumpets of a bignonia creeper climbed round the house, making a ceiling for the traditional *stoep*.

The profusion of colour and fertility delighted me. Every morning I awoke to brilliant sunshine. Every evening stars littered the sky. But beneath this glittering surface I sensed an alien violence. The hard bright light destroyed subtleties of tone; in the same way nuances of sensitivity and gentleness, bred in an older civilisation, were often lacking.

Every Saturday morning Ally's mother paid us a ceremonial visit. Handed carefully out of her shining car by William, and dressed as though for a garden party in hat, pearls, and immaculate white gloves, her generous presence radiated pleasure and goodwill. She would cast a discerning eye over the house and garden – 'Your hydrangeas need watering, Prunella; and don't forget to put down some ant poison for that little stream of ants coming in through the window' – and then would inquire after our coloured servants. 'How is that rascal, Timothy?'

Timothy was our garden-boy, procured for us by William from a mission school up country; a gay, energetic youth, passionately devoted to our motor-mower which he would rev up to its fastest pace and then chase round the garden, a pair of loose white shorts descending in inverse proportion to his speed of progress.

'He's fine, except that he gets drunk every Friday night.'

'I suppose he visits that old man with the illicit still up the hill?'

I nodded.

'Try to keep him off it. He's a good boy with good country ways. We don't want Cape Town to spoil him. Make him save some of his pay each week.'

I agreed. 'But so many of the non-Europeans get drunk at the weekends,' I said. 'It's shocking to see bodies lying beside the road, and cars driving past unconcerned. No one thinks of stopping to investigate.'

'I know,' Olly replied. 'It's the "tot" system that's to blame. The workers at the vineyards are paid partly by a tot of wine when they come in the morning, and another at the end of the day. On an empty stomach that soon goes to their heads and gives them a taste for drink. Poor rascals, they haven't much to remain sober for, anyway. The system ought to be changed, but I'm afraid we all just take it for granted.'

Like so much else, I thought.

I tried not to embarrass Olly, and other members of Ally's family who lived and farmed in Constantia, with my liberal views. But it made me homesick and unhappy to feel myself part of a community with such alien values.

On the 1st of September 1950, a few weeks after our wedding, the great Jan Smuts died. I had met him briefly the previous March, on my first visit to the Cape, and had been much impressed by his extraordinary vitality and youthful appearance. When he talked, his gimlet sailor-blue eyes pierced to the core of his listener, and yet retained the capacity to range over far horizons. Although 'Slim Jannie' had often been a prophet without honour in his own country, needing the wider canvas of world affairs to show his true stature, many South Africans felt that with his death an era ended.

The Nationalist government, already isolationist, became steadily more suspicious of the outside world, its alienation growing in proportion to its policy of segregation.

In April it had announced a Group Areas Bill which assigned separate areas to the different races of South Africa. In spite of demonstrations, inter-racial riots and protests from the Native Representative Council, this Bill later became law, forcing a number of the non-white population to leave their homes. In an area like Constantia, where coloured and white had lived side by side for generations, depending upon one another for labour and sustenance, this policy caused great hardship. The coloured people needed emancipation: better schools, better medical care, better houses. Political segregation was no answer to their problems.

Several of the new friends we made were well aware of these facts. One of them, Sir de Villiers Graaff, who came from an old Afrikaaner family, was a leading member of the United Party, the official opposition to the Nationalists. De Villiers had been at Oxford with David and knew Ally well. He and his beautiful wife Ena invited us to their old Dutch home at Tygerburg, near the Cape, and to their holiday house on the coast at Hermanus. De Villiers, at heart a farmer, had entered politics from a sense of duty, and felt deeply about discriminatory measures. He was elected Leader of the United Party in 1956, and thereafter undertook the thankless task of guiding it through many long grinding years of opposition, during which the Nationalists became ever more firmly established in power. De Villiers needed all his charm, imperturbability and sense of humour to withstand this depressing political situation.

Catherine Taylor, another friend, was also a keen worker for the United Party. Brought up on a mission station up country by English parents, married to a doctor husband also of English stock, Catherine had known the primitive Africa as a child: the Africa of burning sun, parched veldt, wild animals. She and the African children had grown up side by side, playing together in the bush, living the same life of free exploration, until school clamped them into different categories. She felt deeply about the way her country was going. 'We have to do something to stop it,' she said, 'if only for the sake of our children. What sort of a South Africa are they going to grow up in?' Later she entered Parliament, where she had a distinguished career as a member for the Wynberg constituency of the Cape.

Catherine introduced us to Morris Broughton, editor of the *Cape Argus*, the evening paper of Cape Town. Morris, newly appointed to his position, was giving his paper a liberal tone. He, also, was English, but had come to South Africa as a young man and lived all his life there. He understood South Africa's problems and knew that there was no easy solution. He admired much about the Afrikaaner: his independence, his strength of will, his love of country.

'Don't forget,' he would say, 'the Afrikaaner is utterly committed to South Africa. If the volcano blows up, the English can always go back to England. There is nowhere for the Afrikaaner to go but the sea.'

He knew that fear was the basic element which separated the races: the poison below the external prosperity, the cause of violence and mistrust. His home in Constantia, near ours, was a lively centre of discussion, and we often visited him and his family.

These contacts gave me mental stimulation, and some insight into the country's problems. Ally's love and companionship sustained me, but I was still homesick and ill at ease in my new environment.

What could I do to integrate with this community? I remembered Zonnebloem College which I had seen on my previous visit, and Mrs Roman, the warden of St Clare's hostel. Mrs Roman had asked me to take a class for her students, who were training to become nurses and teachers, several of them from other parts of South Africa. Here was an opportunity for contact with the non-Europeans.

I drove down to District Six, demonstrated some exercises to a group of these girls, talked to them about the League in Britain, and soon a weekly class began.

The girls were shy at first, but excellent material, graceful and supple with natural rhythm. A sense of purpose and a mutual affection soon built up between us. By Christmas, after three months of weekly classes, they were ready to give a small display. They invited their friends to an 'At Home' at the College, and performed a half-hour demonstration, clad in the League black-and-white uniform.

The Dean of Cape Town presided, and spoke of the League's work in sympathetic and encouraging terms. The coloured audience gave them a friendly reception and the girls were delighted. So was I, particularly because the League had started among the section of the community which needed it most. Now I had no hesitation in making preparations to open the League officially in Cape Town.

I formed an Advisory Committee of interested friends, gave talks and short demonstrations to employees in shops and offices, and arranged an inaugural meeting at the City Hall on the 7th of February 1951. I had no idea how many people would come; but in fact a long queue formed before the doors opened, and soon women and girls were streaming into the hall, filling it to capacity. I could hear, from behind the scenes, a buzz of anticipatory conversation. I peeped round the curtain and saw Ally sitting in the front row of the audience, with my old friend, Görel Macleod beside him. He radiated confidence and excitement. I, too, was deeply excited. At last my hopes of extending the League to another continent were to be put to the test.

The speakers took their places on the platform and the meeting began. The Mayor of Cape Town was in the chair. Professor Brock, of Cape Town University, and Lady Packer, wife of the British Admiral at Simonstown, and a cousin of Ally's, spoke in support of the League; I followed, and then the demonstration of exercises began. Almost at once it drew applause from the gay and enthusiastic audience. I had two League members to help me; one an older woman from Birmingham, Winifred Hotchkiss, on holiday in the Cape; the other a very attractive girl, a previous London member, Kay Berg, now living in Cape Town. The three of us, in the twenties, thirties and forties, showed that the League could appeal to a wide age-range. As we performed the familiar sequences, interest and sympathy grew. At the end of the demonstration, thirty of the audience trooped up on to the platform for a trial class, and ninety subsequently joined. After the first week's classes, I had over three hundred members, and this number soon rose to five hundred.

The South African women were a joy to teach. Unselfconscious and relaxed, laughter predominated in the crowded classes, as I initiated them into the intricacies of the League system of exercises. I was fortunate to find a first-class pianist in Estelle de la Ville, a concert pianist of virtuoso standard. Her improvised music, in turn lyrical, amusing or dramatic, inspired the members to their best efforts.

Three weeks after the City Hall meeting, the non-European section opened officially, with a demonstration by my Zonnebloem students to a large non-European audience. Lady Mary Baring, wife of the British High Commissioner, presided, and sixty-five members subsequently joined.

So now the League was launched in Cape Town, in both the white and coloured sections of the community. For the moment these had to be kept separate, but I hoped in the future to be able to integrate them in a combined display. However, both the white and the coloured members belonged to the same organisation, and were learning the same work from the same teacher.

Meanwhile, Ally was building up his practice, and was finding the medical world of Cape Town very different from that of London. At Guy's he had lived in a community where excellence was taken for granted. The standards of medicine and nursing were first-class, and after years of training and practice, these were Ally's criteria. He valued the free exchange of ideas at Guy's as well as the professionalism and the camaraderie that gave this great London hospital its unique flavour.

But now he had left these things behind and was on his own, in an environment which disappointed him by being often prejudiced and restrictive. It was hard going to build up a specialist practice. It required much patience, for Ally had to make his way slowly and carefully, fighting against no small measure of competition and mistrust.

Dr John Currie, one of the senior specialists in Ally's field, with whom he often worked, understood the difficulties.

'You'll have to realise that this is a fractured society,' he said. 'It's full of stresses and strains, and these are reflected in medicine, as well as everything else. Doctors aren't immune from fear and prejudice.'

The colour bar also operated in medicine; at international conferences, visiting doctors, if they were non-white, were excluded.

'It's crazy not to welcome specialist experts and hear what they have to say because of the colour of their skins,' said Ally.

He was pacing up and down the lawn in front of our home, rehearsing to me the speech he intended to make denouncing this policy at a forthcoming meeting of the South African Medical Association.

'Of course, if I continue to object it may affect my practice,' he went on. 'Rich Nationalists won't be so keen to consult a chap who opposes the colour bar. I can't help that. I'll have to say what I feel.'

At the meeting, Ally registered his objection. As a young consultant, just arrived from England, he had a mixed reception. Some of his colleagues supported him. Others considered his intervention a piece of unrealistic presumption. But in fact the medical world was helpless in altering the policy of the Government. It had been irrevocably decided. Visiting experts, whether sportsmen, actors, or doctors, must be white.

The one place where Apartheid did not operate was the church; although even there non-Europeans tended to sit in the back rows, and take communion after the whites. The church was very active in Cape Town, with large congregations at the Anglican and Roman Catholic cathedrals, and in the big suburban churches, and crowded services in the locations outside the city where the Africans lived. The Anglican Church was in the hands of two exceptional men: Geoffrey Clayton, the Archbishop of Cape Town, and Michael Gibbs, the Dean of the cathedral. Both these men had a rare spiritual insight and power, and their influence extended throughout the whole community. They were very different in character. The Bishop was forceful, irritable, a politician who maintained diplomatic links with the Government but who, when it came to a crisis, adhered with a rock-like strength to his principles, even to the point of being prepared to go to prison for them. The Dean was a saintly character, gentle, sensitive, compassionate, a scholar with a bent for theology, and yet the most readily accessible of men, unsparing in his work as a healer of souls.

The hospitality of the deanery was open to everyone, particularly to those who needed it most, and there were usually several down-and-outs camping in the kitchen or its adjacent buildings, and being ministered to by the Dean's indefatigable wife. Michael Gibbs and his family became great friends, and we made a point of attending the series of Lenten lectures which he was giving in the cathedral.

On Good Friday, Ally suggested that we should go to the three-hour service of vigil which commemorated the Crucifixion. Neither of us had been to this before, nor were we committed Christians. Ally's scientific training had made him sceptical of religious belief; while I had lost my earlier unquestioning faith during the war, and it was only slowly returning. We came to the service with open minds, as onlookers rather than participants, and we chose a small church in one of the suburbs where the Bishop of Cape Town was giving the addresses.

The church was full. Row upon row of people knelt in silence, in an atmosphere of reverence and prayer. Into this silence, Geoffrey Clayton's words fell, quiet, meditative, and ringed with thought.

'You have come here to share a vigil,' he said. 'And now you are kneeling at the foot of the Cross. You are witnessing the same scene as on the first Good Friday. Together we will think what that means.'

True meditation brings an insight which is at the same time profound and simple. The Bishop's words were infused with this kind of clarity. He shared with us the fruits of his contemplation, bringing us close to an understanding of the final mystery of sacrifice and acceptance which lies at the heart of the Christian faith. In the face of the Cross, as he described it, the egoism of selfhood dissolved. Three hours passed.

'*It is finished.*'

This final saying from the Cross brought to me an emotion of such profound pity that I was moved to tears. The contrast between the sacrifice we felt we had witnessed, and man's indifference to it, tore my heart. I had been one of those indifferent people.

Stumbling out into the Easter sunshine, I could see that Ally had felt the same. We were both too moved to speak. We walked slowly to the car, and drove home in silence.

Looking back over the years, one can recognise turning-points. This Good Friday service was a turning-point for me. A door had been opened, which before was closed, and one day I might venture through it.

The following morning – Easter Saturday – Ally and I were walking along a track at the foot of Table Mountain. The sun, not long risen, cast beams of light across Table Bay, while above us towered massive crags and cliffs, silhouetted against a brilliant blue sky. Pine needles crunched underfoot and the pungent mountain smell of pines filled the air. It was a glorious autumn morning, with a freshness which heralded the change of season, but with enough warmth already in the sun to promise a hot day. The ubiquitous Cape wind, always present in summer, had dropped, and a trance-like calm enveloped the landscape. We were at the start of a day's climbing expedition with two climbing friends, Tom Bright, one of the best mountaineers in the Cape, and Sir Evelyn Baring, the British High Commissioner.[1] A few Saturdays before we had shared with them a splendid ascent – Yellowstone Corner, described in the guide-book as 'a severe and sensational route'. We had all enjoyed the day so much that we were determined to repeat it.

During our first nine months in the Cape, Ally and I had climbed quite often on Table Mountain, doing easy scrambles with my sons, and harder ascents, up to a very difficult standard, with other members of the Mountain Club. Ally, who had had little previous experience of mountaineering, was learning fast, and showing great aptitude and enthusiasm for this new sport. He had started in the right place. Climbing conditions in the Cape were ideal. The rock was hard and firm, and almost always dry. The walk up to the foot of the climb was seldom long. It usually took only an hour or less, just enough time to get one's leg muscles in trim. And the weather was fair. One could nearly always wear light clothing – shorts, a shirt, and 'tackies' (rubber-soled tennis shoes) – without fear of sudden storms or weather deterioration.

Already we had explored much of Table Mountain, and were gaining an affection for its rough, veldt-covered slopes and its precipitous cliffs.

On this particular day, we were to try a route on the eastern side of the mountain, where the great bastions of rock known as the Apostles sweep down to the Atlantic Ocean. We took the Kasteelspoort path from the Saddle between Table Mountain and Devil's Peak, and gradually gained height as the track wound upwards. On either side of the stony path the Cape flora bloomed; a variegated green, gold and grey, stabbed by the scarlet of a crassula, a yellow patch of *leucadendron*, or the blue of the beautiful *Salvia africana*. Proteas and heaths added their pink and purple hues, and the richness and variety made a lush contrast to the great lichen-covered boulders which from time to time reared up, stranded like marooned ships in this sea of fertile green. The sky was cloudless, and the sun as it mounted shone with increasing

1. Now Lord Howick of Lyndale.

fervour. Few birds sang. Occasionally a starling's blue-black wing flashed past, or one caught the trill of a mountain thrush, or the haunting cry of the *piet-my-vrou*. But as we climbed higher, even these sounds fell away, the silence deepened, and we seemed the only inhabitants of a hot still world.

We stopped to draw breath and mop our brows. On our right rose Postern Buttress, a large rock-face, three or four hundred feet high. It was partly bare, partly clothed with sparse scrub, and across it ran several wooded ledges, green scars on the precipitous grey stone.

'That's our route,' said Tom, shading his eyes with his hand, and looking over a slope of loose boulders which divided us from the rock-face.

'We follow one of those ledges across the cliff, and then round to the other side. That's where our climb begins. We can't see it from here.'

'But here we leave the path?'

'Yes,' Tom replied. 'All well and happy?'

'Never more so.'

The walk up had warmed our muscles and stretched our lungs. I glanced at Ally and thought how bronzed and fit he looked, how happy to be here on Table Mountain, in his own country, the country he still loved best in the world.

We struck off to the right of the path, across the slope of stones, and soon entered a patch of thick woodland scrub. Here the bushes and small trees grew so low that we had to stoop double to make our way between them. The ground was covered with moss, deadening our footsteps, and small twigs brushed against our arms and faces. We blundered through, our rucksacks catching on low branches, our feet tripping against hidden roots, and slowly made our way upwards, bending between slim tree-trunks which hid our view. The gloomy light, filtering down through the leaves, grew stronger, and gradually we emerged to find the cliff-face before us. We scrambled up a few large rocks, and reached a green ledge. It was three to four feet wide, covered with grass, ferns and vegetation, jutting out from the mountain and running horizontally across its face. Above the ledge rose cliffs, masked by overhanging boulders and small bushes, but extending upwards for several hundred feet. Below it grew more shrubs and bushes, concealing the sheer drop which fell ninety feet or so to the stones beneath. Walking along the ledge one was completely unaware of its exposed position. It seemed a pleasant easy place which required no special attention. The idea of roping up never occurred to us.

We proceeded in single file, Ally first, followed by Tom, then myself, and lastly Sir Evelyn. Before long we reached a small face of bare rock, which filled the ledge, and extended to another ledge below. We slid carefully down this, and continued along the new path, still confident of our pace and direction. Suddenly I saw Ally hesitate. We had come to a place where the ledge was broken by a small gully. It necessitated a step across, about a stride's length, but there seemed to be good handholds on the rocks above. Ally turned to face the cliff, felt for a handhold above his head, and stretched out his right leg to bridge the gap. He swung his weight over, and as it transferred from left foot to right foot, his rucksack jerked out from his shoulders. At the same moment his hands slipped on the rock, his head fell back and suddenly he was peeling off the mountain, as though he had been plucked from it by some unseen force, falling backwards and downwards, until in less than a moment he was lost to our view.

We remained frozen, gripping the cliff behind our backs and gazing below. We all three uttered the same exclamation. 'My God!' Then Tom tore across me and with Sir Evelyn raced back up the path, leaving me alone, staring down at the green vegetation with its trembling leaves. I felt life draining out of me as I, too, turned and followed the others along the ledge. I came to the place where the face of rock lifted to the other ledge above. Tom had dropped his rucksack here, for greater speed.

'I'd better pick it up,' I thought. I slung the heavy rucksack across my shoulders and climbed slowly up the face. I found myself trembling in every limb. 'I must be careful,' I thought, 'it's a very exposed place.'

In the thick woodland, I could hear someone blundering through not far from me, but I couldn't see him. I came out on to the stony slope, and turned to the left to make my way back to the foot of the cliff where I knew Ally must have fallen. Tom was there before me, and when I reached him, he was already kneeling on the rock with Ally's head cradled in his arms. I could tell at once by the way Ally was lying that he was mortally hurt. His head, legs and arms were at odd angles, and his face was a yellowish grey colour. He was unconscious, but his heart was still beating. Tom and I moved his head into the shade, made a pillow for it, and covered him with our anoraks.

He had fallen ninety feet. No tree or ledge had stopped him. We guessed later that his head had been hit almost at once, and that he was most likely unconscious as he fell. I imagined to myself his last glimpse of the world; a brilliant sun reeling away in a cloudless sky, pinpointing the extremity of the final, fearful moment.

There was nothing we could do for him. We could only try to get medical aid as soon as possible. The Mountain Club Hut, not far above us, was the nearest source of help. It had a telephone, stretchers and first-aid kit. Tom and Sir Evelyn swiftly left to climb up to it, and I waited beside Ally.

It was midday. The sun blazed down, draining all colour from the landscape, hardening every outline, and emphasising the alien quality of this alien land. Under the fierce sun life quivered, longing for a cool quiet refuge, for the sound of water, for shade and peace. The bare rocks were hot to the touch, the merciless light dazzled the eyes.

'How could it end like this?' I thought. Waves of incoherent feeling and memory passed over me as the minutes dragged by. The day seemed to be one of interminable waiting. Waiting for Tom and Sir Evelyn to return: then waiting for the doctor who had promised to come up from Cape Town, but who never arrived; and at last waiting for the final verdict when the stretcher-bearers who carried Ally down, had reached the foot of the mountain.

Waiting, waiting – when had I experienced this before? I remembered. At the time of David's death. I had waited then in the officers' mess at Benson in exactly the same way; waited for confirmation of what I already knew.

Seven hours after Ally had fallen, I drove to Görel Macleod's house, a rope and some carabiners still round my waist. She opened her front door.

'Have you had a lovely day on the mountain?' she said. Then

she saw my face. I fell into her arms, and from that moment she took over. Together we went back to my house, and later that evening the Dean of Cape Town called. The nightmare of the day still possessed me. I was filled with an inconsolable regret. I spoke to Michael Gibbs in broken sentences of how I wished I had done more for Ally, of how I had put my own interests before his, failed to hide my homesickness, been discontented with life in the Cape. All now matters of no concern, when the only concern was his death.

'But love need never die,' said Michael Gibbs, 'you can always keep it alive. Unless you squander it.' He told me that I need never be separated from Ally's love. I could find it again in the love of God. We knelt together and he prayed; simple traditional words for the comfort and healing of souls in distress. Then he rose to his feet. I remained kneeling, and he put his hand on my head, to give me a blessing. With that touch and those words peace entered my heart. It was as palpable as light which illuminates darkness. The agony of Ally's loss remained, but I realised that it was no longer necessary to strive against it or to rebel. All that I had to do now was to accept.

The words of the Good Friday service came back to me. I remembered the emotion I had felt, the sensation of a door opening. Ally's love had brought me to the verge of this door, but I had hesitated before it. Something still held me back. Now I was released. With Ally's death, quietly but inevitably, I walked through.

CHAPTER 14

Ideals put into Practice

YOUR husband's death was a great shock to many of us who did not know him personally [the Bishop of Cape Town wrote to me]. There seemed to be so much promise of continued and increasing usefulness, and this country does not seem to be able to afford the loss of such men. I do try to believe – not that God orders everything that happens, but that He does bring good out of evil, and causes even bad things to work together for good. It is very hard to believe this, but it must be true if Christianity is true, and therefore it must be true of yourself and your sons.

The day after Ally's death was Easter Sunday. I lay on my bed, gazing across the garden at our view of Table Mountain. I felt myself lifted into a sphere of being which I had never known before. It seemed as though all earthly material things had ceased to matter, even to exist, as though nothing existed but an extraordinary lightness of spirit, an intense recognition of the unity at the heart of all things. In this sphere there was no division between life and death, and I felt Ally so close to me that I was filled with confidence and peace. Paradoxically, with the greatest loss that I could have sustained, came also the greatest gift. It was as though God had taken everything from me, left my heart an empty void, and then filled it with Himself.

Doubtless this state of mind can be explained in psychological terms as a protective mechanism, a phase of self-delusion necessary for the deeply wounded psyche to recover its equilibrium and to avoid breakdown, a reflex from the intolerable shock of sudden death. I can only say that for me it was completely valid. It made me a committed Christian, something which I have remained ever since. And though with time the vision faded, the faith which it inspired never altered, and has continued as the basis of my life.

This sense of supernatural comfort lifted me out of the terrible ordeal of Ally's death, and over the first few days of loss; but I knew that it could not remain long. Soon the heavy load of grief returned, increased by the effect of the tragedy on those nearest to me.

My sons were deeply shocked and saddened. Ally's mother was heart-broken. The loss of her only son was something too heavy for her to bear. She never fully recovered. In the years that followed she increasingly regarded me as her daughter, and my sons as her grandchildren, but nothing could take Ally's place.

The mountain shrouded itself in mist; for days it remained hidden, withdrawing into its own secrecy. The clear autumn weather ended and winter rains fell, while the boys and I tried to adjust ourselves to life without Ally.

He had been the pivot of the family, his own special brand of humour ironing out bad temper, his unselfishness oiling the wheels of family life. Companion in so many of their adventures, it was he who had given the boys their delight in the Cape. Now, not only the house but all our favourite places in the Cape countryside, were bereft of joy. After a few weeks the boys went back to their preparatory school, and I was left alone with my burden of inescapable sorrow.

I was still living in the inner world of the spirit, which seemed to me far more real than the world of everyday life. I read William Temple's *Readings from St John's Gospel*, and St Augustine's *Confessions*. For the first time I understood the response of the disciple, Peter, when he realised that Jesus was the Christ. 'Depart from me, O Lord, for I am a sinful man.' I longed to be cleansed, to make a new start, to throw off the burden of past wrong-doing.

Many people in deep distress have felt the same. It is for them that confession and communion, the sacraments of the church, exist. Once belief is absolute, once one has taken the step through the open door, these sacraments become living realities. But the step cannot be taken by the will alone. The will can bring one to the threshold, but love is the only agent which can take one through; the love of God reaching out to the soul in the depths of its suffering.

These first weeks after Ally's death, alone in my house in

Constantia, were a kind of vigil. Senses sharpened by grief, I felt the beauty of nature as never before. Leaning from my window at sunrise, I saw cobwebs spin a silver glimmer over the lawn, and dewdrops flash with emerald and diamond fire. Every leaf and flower appeared to have been newly created. I visited the beach, and perceived it for the first time. The curve of a breaking wave, the breadth of the shining shore, seemed marvels of power and light.

> To see the world in a grain of sand
> And heaven in a wild flower;
> Hold infinity in the palm of your hand,
> And eternity in an hour.

I felt, like Blake, that the doors of perception had been cleansed.

The obverse side was a depression of mind and heart so intense that when it came sorrow weighed down every limb, as heavy as a physical object. Sometimes this lasted for weeks. Then I had good reason to be thankful for the kindness of the Cape community and my Constantia neighbours, shown to me in many acts of thoughtfulness and generosity.

The Barings became close friends. Molly shared her library with me, and gave me not only books to read, but a generous measure of her faith and insight. Evelyn took me for walks on the mountain, and taught me the names of the Cape flowers. Unfortunately, before long the Barings were posted to Nairobi, and Evelyn was appointed Governor-General of Kenya. They remained there for seven years, weathering the Mau Mau storm with characteristic courage and intelligence. In their brief leisure moments, Molly made a beautiful garden at Government House, while Evelyn continued to climb whenever possible. I stayed with them in Nairobi several times on my way to and from England; on each occasion being regaled by Evelyn with a detailed account of his latest climb, every move dredged up with astonishing accuracy from his extraordinary memory.

In July Catherine Taylor took me for a short holiday to Natal. We drove north on the Garden Route, through George to Pietermaritzburg, and thence across the wild Ciskei, one of the African reserves. Sun-scorched bush stretched on either side of the road, broken by African villages – small collections of mud and wattle huts – whose inhabitants stared at us as we passed, the men swathed in long red blankets, the women flashing smiles and bright bangles, the children waving with skinny arms.

Erosions of the red earth gaped like wounds. The spiky silhouettes of thorn-trees and cactus gestured against vast spaces.

This was a new Africa to me, the Africa of Catherine's childhood, primitive and ruthless, a country inimical to man. I began to realise the size of it, the extent of the huge continent stretching northwards, of which we in the Cape were only the tip.

We drove through the Ciskei and reached the Drakensberg, the great range of mountains which separates Natal from Basutoland. Primeval masses of rock towered up without shape or form, very different from the picture-book Alps to which I was accustomed. For a week we rode across these mountains on small, sure-footed Basuto ponies, following narrow and often precipitous trails. Yellow wattle, like mimosa, was in bloom. I picked a spray and tucked it into my pony's bridle, needing to make a human gesture to counteract the overwhelming space around me.

I had thought that living in the Cape peninsula, a small island world, might become claustrophobic. But this glimpse of the African interior, exciting though it was, sent me back to the Cape's green paradise with relief.

I did not know then what I know now: that Africa can haunt one until the memory of her vast plains, ringed by blue mountains, becomes so obsessive that it may no longer be put aside or denied.

I returned from Natal to my League classes in the Cape. They were growing rapidly. After five months the membership was 670, with 150 members in the non-European section. The necessity for a second teacher was imperative, particularly as I had promised to attend the League's 21st Birthday Reunion in England in November. I pleaded with London to send someone to help me, and in August, Barbara Keys, who had recently returned from running the League in Canada, arrived.

Barbara came for two years and stayed indefinitely. A professional, deeply interested in all aspects of her work, Barbara has a special talent for expressive movement, and this was the side of the League which, helped by Estelle de la Ville's choice of music, we developed together. In the classes, we worked for a close integration of music and movement, using improvisation or classical themes for accompaniment, so that the members grew in musical as well as kinetic appreciation.

This approach, akin to Modern Dance, introduced a new element in the work; a creative factor of which I felt sure my mother would have approved, for she had always regarded her system of exercises as the basic technique on which to build further means of expression.

Like many dancers, Barbara came truly alive when she moved, and her example inspired her pupils. Her Irish sense of fun stopped them from taking themselves too seriously, while her tactful personality smoothed out difficulties. Our partnership was a very happy one, and I was lucky indeed to share with her the League's fortunes in the Cape.

Barbara acclimatised herself very quickly, and two weeks after her arrival I was able to fly to England, leaving my classes in her capable hands.

It was September. The English countryside was in its late summer dress, warmed by a golden autumn sun. So safe, so secure, so gentle it seemed. So far from the unrest and violence of Africa, with its strident colours and hard, bright light. I was home! I slipped into life in England, like a hand into a glove. And yet something was missing. A certain spontaneity and vitality, a friendliness with which the Cape community, so much smaller, so much younger, was endowed. Was I now to be divided in heart between two countries? Fortunately, I had little time to ponder this point, because I was swept at once into the activity of the League Teachers Summer School, and not long afterwards, of the 21st Birthday Reunion.

'It is not everyone that can muster six thousand guests to their 21st Birthday celebrations,' I said, as once again I stood on the platform at the Albert Hall, greeting members from all over Britain who filled the arena before me. So much had happened since our last gathering there! The ambitions I had then nursed

had been fulfilled. I could report that Cape Town had just enrolled its thousandth member.

'The League's continued success depends on two things,' I
went on. 'Our unity and our faith. We started with faith, we have
grown through faith, we must look to the future in faith. We
started with unity – a band of pioneers who believed in the
League and its work. We must preserve this unity, and that can
only be done with a group of individuals like the League, if each
person gives her loyalty to something greater than herself. Unity
and faith, these are the two thoughts I leave with you to-night,
and I link them with the spirit of youth, which is the spirit of a
21st Birthday, and I hope may be the League's spirit for many
years to come.'

I found that Britain was recovering from her post-war depression.
Rationing was over at last, and there was a cautious optimism in
the air. The Festival of Britain had brought many visitors to
London: concerts at the new Festival Hall were an exciting event.
Many more people were doing many more things. There was a
boom in further education, with applicants for classes in a host
of different subjects, physical education included. Keep Fit
classes, run by local education authorities, proliferated, and
brought the League up against some stiff competition. The League
work and system of exercises were still not recognised in terms
of any grant-aid from the Government, and the training of its
teachers still had to be financed from its own resources.

Nevertheless, the policy of using only fully qualified teachers
was continued. One can see now that it was the right policy. It
maintained the long-term interest of members, and preserved the
high standard of the work; but it was often difficult to pursue in
the face of increased competition and demand. The new Council,
and the Executive Committee were functioning well, and a
number of new centres had been opened. Pioneering in South
Africa rather than supporting the *status quo* in England seemed to
be the most valuable activity which I could undertake for the
League at the present time.

But there were other considerations to bear in mind. I had to
think of my sons and their future.

'Of course you must bring the boys back and educate them

here,' said some of my friends. 'You can't continue alone in a strange country, without Ally's help. The whole reason for your going to South Africa no longer exists.'

Many ties of affection and sentiment also pulled me back to Britain. I stayed with David's sister Jean in Sussex, and swiftly became one of the Douglas-Hamilton clan again, fitting into the family as though I had never left it, adopting its outlook with a familiar ease. My sons would do the same. Was it right to deprive them of this traditional upbringing, and of the advantages of an English education?

Then I thought of the house in Constantia, the home which Ally and I had made together, and of the freedom of life in the Cape which the boys had already experienced and enjoyed. They were happily settled in their school. To remove them would subject them to yet another major upheaval, when they were only just recovering from the shock of Ally's death.

So the arguments hammered back and forth in my mind, while autumn cast its glow on the gentle countryside, and the year waned.

Should I stay or go?

To stay in South Africa was a risk. But life is not life without risks. To refuse a risk is like refusing to make a choice. Both are inevitable. Evasion is merely a means of false reprieve.

I knew this. And I knew also that the moment of decision had come. Yet my divided heart hesitated. I felt as though my will had been stretched like a piece of elastic, too far for too long, and there was no resiliency left. Something stronger than my will must make the choice. Then I remembered the peace and beauty of those weeks immediately following Ally's death; early morning communion at the small Constantia church, the uplift of spirit, and the sense of being borne in stronger hands than my own.

> All will be as it was before:
> The patient stars, the abiding hill,
> Relinquish the uncharted shore,
> Return, and let the conflict still.

The river of life had flowed on, and could not be entered again at the same place. But the certainty of faith remained.

And so I took the risk. I staked our future on staying in South

Africa. I said goodbye to David's family and the peaceful English countryside, and returned to the Cape.

That December, nine months after its inauguration, the League in Cape Town gave its first display: an outdoor demonstration, which included an item by non-European members. Wearing the same uniform and badges as their white fellow-members, the coloured girls performed a sequence of exercises which was well received by the large heterogeneous audience. So far so good. The League had established in public that it was meant for all sections of the community, and for the moment this principle was accepted. Questioning and recrimination could wait.

Meanwhile I was becoming more deeply involved with the coloured community. I served on the committee of the Institute of Race Relations and was asked to organise a charity evening at the City Hall to raise funds. Dulcie Howes, the talented and energetic head of the University Ballet, promised to produce the programme. I knew it would be of a high standard, for Dulcie's work was renowned. She had already sent several of her dancers overseas to join the Royal Ballet Company in London, where they had become stars: Nadia Nerina, David Poole and Johaan Masavel, among them. In the world of entertainment, as everywhere else, Apartheid was strictly enforced. But Dulcie Howes refused to be brow-beaten by the authorities, and some of her most talented dancers were coloured. The City Hall was one of the few places in Cape Town where a mixed audience could assemble. We filled it to capacity and made £600 for the Institute of Race Relations.

Coloured and African representatives – among them my old acquaintance the schoolmaster, Mr Golding – served on its committee, so that its views were truly representative.

But even so the Institute had an uphill struggle, constantly fighting unfair legislation, and protesting against discriminatory measures such as the Pass Laws, which forced all Africans to carry a pass at all times; if they were picked up by the police without one, prison was the penalty.

Each week I went down to District Six to take one of the League's non-European classes there (by now there were three). Driving through the crowded, colourful streets, with their Indian bazaars, and stalls of brilliant fruit, their constant chatter and press of dark lively faces, I had the impression of intense life and vitality. I soon realised that some dedicated work was taking place in District Six: that of elderly Miss Seth-Smith at the Marion Institute, a community centre which catered for every member of the family, from the youngest to the oldest, and under whose auspices the League classes were run; and of the Cowley Fathers – Anglican priests of the Society of St John the Evangelist – whose lives were given in service to the community around them. In District Six there was no Welfare State, or even the beginnings of one. The welfare of the many still depended on the charity of the few; but I saw that Miss Seth-Smith and the Cowley Fathers gave charity in the true meaning of the word – *caritas, agape*, love – and that the inspiration for their work sprang from the chapels attached to both institutions.

It was one thing to deal with the colour problem as a teacher from a platform instructing a class of keen participants: quite another to cope with it on one's own doorstep. My garden-boy, Timothy, the charming lively eager youth from up country, continued to get drunk every weekend, and had now taken to following me round the house when in his cups. If I forbade him entrance, he serenaded me from outside, and disturbed all the neighbours.

'He must go,' said my South African friends, even my indulgent mother-in-law. 'You can't manage a boy like that by yourself.'

I persisted, nevertheless. Timothy was such good material, and an excellent worker when sober.

The climax came one evening, when I returned home to find that Timothy had upset the neighbourhood yet again, singing and shouting outside the house. A neighbour telephoned offering help. At that moment I could hear no sound, so I replied that all was well and went to bed. But at about 2 a.m. I was woken by roars from Timothy on the lawn below my bedroom window.

'Maa-daam,' he carolled. 'I want to see maa-daam! Nobody loves me, but God and my maa-daam.' Furious, I leapt out of bed, seized a dressing-gown and ran down to the kitchen. 'Timothy!' I called, as loudly and severely as I could. Timothy came in from outside and advanced towards me unsteadily, still lamenting his lot.

'Go to bed at once, Timothy!' I scolded.

He showed no sign of obeying.

'Nobody loves me . . .' he began again, drawing closer.

'At once, Timothy!' I reiterated. 'What do you think you're doing, disturbing everyone in the middle of the night?'

Still no response. The singing rose to a roar of frustration and suddenly I lost my temper. My hand leapt from my side and struck Timothy sharply on the cheek.

'Now, go to bed!' I shouted. 'Turn round and go to bed!'

Timothy's eyes widened in distress and disbelief. His hand flew to his smarting cheek, and then, with a bemused expression, he turned and staggered towards the door. His sleeping quarters were over the garage on the other side of the kitchen yard. I followed him, urging him along, as he climbed up the rickety staircase. He lurched against the door of his room, opened it, and finally disappeared. I returned to my bed, as chastened and upset as Timothy himself. My surprise at giving him this blow was as great as his in receiving it.

The next day, he was sober and as charming as ever. But Nemesis descended on him in the shape of a South African neighbour who came round to give him a talking-to, bringing with him – unknown to me – a length of rubber hose. At the end of the interview I was horrified to find Timothy with large weals on his neck, where he had been struck.

'Force is the only thing they understand,' said his mentor. 'He won't do it again.'

But I could no longer take the risk of such retribution. I had to admit defeat, and to give Timothy notice. We had a tearful farewell, then William drove him to the station. On the way, he visited the bank, and drew out the savings I had deposited for him there. William and he celebrated this largesse with a few drinks, and the last that was seen of Timothy was a figure leaning from the carriage window, scattering bank-notes to an astonished group of admirers as the train drew out of the station.

The League in Britain was planning a Coronation Display at the Albert Hall in 1953, and we were invited to send a team. This meant finding suitable volunteers, raising funds, and selecting and training the girls: no mean undertaking. However, the idea was greeted with great enthusiasm, and fifty members applied to go to Britain.

While plans were maturing, I visited the Marion Institute in District Six one evening, to watch a nativity play performed by the youngest members of the centre. On the stage, little black angels with large silver wings grouped round the dusky Holy Family, while in the audience their proud relatives looked on. The young Virgin held a live baby in her arms, rocking it gently and gazing into its small dark face. I wondered if it was her own. So many coloured girls already had babies by their mid-teens. My eyes wandered round the hall and came to rest on a group of girls from my Zonnebloem class. They were standing by the wall, watching the performance intently, gazing with that stillness and capacity for complete involvement peculiar to their race, their eyes shining, their thin shoulders drooping, lines of fatigue on their young faces disappearing in the pleasure of the moment.

'How wonderful it would be,' I thought, 'if I could take two of them to England as part of the team.'

I consulted Miss Seth-Smith. 'It will be difficult,' she said. 'We'd have to select two girls that we know well and can trust absolutely. They'd have to get time off from their work. How much would they be financed?'

I explained that we were raising money for the white members of the team and could include the coloured girls in our efforts.

'They'd probably raise money from their own community also,' she said. 'Of course, you may not be able to get passports for them or exit permits to leave the country. But it's worth trying. Let me think about it.'

Meanwhile, I consulted Barbara and Estelle.

'We may have objections from some of the white members,' they said. 'They'd have to rehearse with the coloured girls here, and mix with them on the journey and in England.'

We had now selected twenty-six members from the original fifty who volunteered, and would soon begin rehearsals of the special item we were to perform at the Albert Hall.

We decided to gather all the Cape members together, tell them of our plans for the team, and then put to them the project of including coloured girls.

'In this way,' I explained, 'the team could be truly representative of the League's work in South Africa, and of the Cape community as a whole. What do you think?'

There was a buzz of excited conversation. We waited for objections, but none came. We assumed that the members agreed.

Soon afterwards, the team assembled for their opening rehearsal. Barbara and I were devising a movement item to music by Dohnányi, and it would take six months to rehearse and perfect. For the first time, the two coloured girls whom Miss Seth-Smith had now selected, joined the white group. They stood shyly at the back of the hall, while the others crowded round the platform. They were both young, twenty-three and twenty respectively, both workers in a sweet factory, both members of the Marion Institute since childhood, and the elder of the two was married.

'This is Marjorie Austin and Mary Williams,' I said, introducing them. I gave them the white girls' names and then we all started work, and for the next few hours thought of nothing but the flow of movement and its integration with the demanding music.

After two weeks Barbara came to me with an anxious face.

'The white team members haven't accepted the coloured girls yet,' she said. 'There's an undertone of discontent. Some of them resent having to rehearse all together and say their husbands and parents disapprove. Some of them think the idea of a mixed team will do the League harm in South Africa.'

Several Afrikaaner girls were included in the team, and we guessed that the disaffection came from them. We would have to try to win them over. At the next rehearsal, we assembled the white girls early, before Marjorie Austin and Mary Williams arrived.

We told them that the coloured girls were joining the team as representatives of our large coloured section, and that the gesture of tolerance and generosity needed to accept them might have great value at this time of racial strain.

'We want you to give these two coloured girls – League members like yourselves – the opportunity to serve the same cause as you are going to serve,' I said. 'The decision to take them is in the nature of a test. It is putting into practice what it means to be a member of the League, for the League has no barriers of race or class. It was founded by my mother to serve all women, everywhere. In this country, a mixed performance would not be possible, but you are not being asked to give it in this country, only to prepare here for an event overseas which will take place in a different environment and mental climate. I can't help feeling that if we reject these girls it will be a spiritual defeat for ourselves and for the League.'

So much for idealism! It was hard to read clearly the expressions on the faces before me: some convinced, some uneasy, some enthusiastic, some doubtful. We took a vote, and two-thirds of the team were for including the coloured girls. We felt we had a mandate to continue. But we still had to convince the disapproving one-third.

The next task was to book accommodation on the ship for Marjorie and Mary, and to secure passports and exit permits for them. The Union Castle Line made no difficulties. With relief I heard the reassuring words: 'There's no colour-bar aboard this British ship.' The girls were promised an excellent two-berth cabin. But the Passport Office presented a more formidable hurdle.

'You want to go overseas, heh?' said the brusque official behind the desk. 'What for?'

Marjorie and Mary sat apprehensively on the edge of their chairs, submissive expressions on their faces. I explained that I would look after them overseas, that they were going to friends (League members in England had in fact offered them hospitality) and that I would be responsible for financing them during their stay, and on the return journey.

'You don't like it in South Africa, heh? Why do you want to go away?' I never could get used to the hectoring tone officials adopted when speaking to non-Europeans. We explained the purpose of the journey, saying as little as possible about the girls being members of a mixed team.

'Well, we'll see about it. Exit permits don't hang on trees. We'll let you know.'

Uncertain whether to be elated or depressed, we took our leave.

In the meantime, both the white and coloured sections of the League were working hard to raise money. It would cost £150 to send one girl to England. Each member of the team paid some proportion of her own fare, but we set ourselves a target of £800 to subsidise those who needed it, and to cover costs. In fact, we succeeded in raising £1,000. District Six contributed £150 of this sum in support of half the cost of Marjorie's and Mary's expenses.

At last their passports and exit permits came through, rehearsals ended, and a performance of the item at a farewell party for the team was arranged. Morris Broughton, the editor of the *Cape Argus*, who had given us great support throughout the venture, was the only pressman present. I did not dare to publicise the event, in case at the last moment the coloured girls' passports were withdrawn. Morris gave us a perceptive notice:

The League has ventured into new territory with this team. Ostensibly, the members carry out a series of supple movements to music, but the music happens to be a Dohnányi rhapsody with complicated cross-rhythms, fascinating modulations and variations of both time and key. The whole thing is brief, yet the physical responses are varied, interesting and expressive of the music. At the same time they remain within what previous items showed are the idiom of the League's practical work . . . The pursuit of physical health and well-being is given another dimension; the harmony of movement a new stress, and the individual is merged with the group in a way that even the most disciplined drilling cannot achieve.

There is a quantitative difference between moving together like clockwork and flowing together in something at once responsive to and evocative of music. If it can be adequately seen in the arid wastes of the Albert Hall this movement in music should make a good impression.

The first eighteen members of the team set off in the SS *Zuiderkraus* on the 16th of March. The next batch, which I would accompany and which included the two coloured girls, were due to leave on the SS *Edinburgh Castle* at the end of April.

The day came when we all assembled on the ship. Barbara and Estelle, and a number of our friends, came to see us off, including my mother-in-law, loyal to me, but faintly uncertain of the propriety of the venture. The coloured girls were inundated with baskets of fruit and presents. Their enthusiastic families and well-wishers swarmed all over the deck. 'It looks as though the whole of District Six is here,' said Olly, her eyes blinking with unaccustomed speed.

A press photographer approached me for a photograph of the

team. Yes, now at last, I thought, with only a few moments to go until we sailed, it would be safe to take one. I lined up the members, placing Marjorie and Mary conspicuously near the front. One of the Afrikaaners in the team drew me aside. 'Are the coloured girls going to be in the photograph?' she asked.

'Of course.'

'But my family wouldn't like to see me photographed with non-Europeans.'

'Oh, no!' I thought. 'Even now, even after so many months. And the whole fortnight at sea to go!'

'OK,' I replied. 'Then you stand out of the photograph.' The team appeared next day in the Cape Town papers without her.

The ship's siren blew. Farewells were said, and soon we were leaning over the rail, waving to diminishing figures, as the outline of Table Mountain and Devil's Peak withdrew into the distance. White sea-horses chopped the blue water, the ship gave a little roll, her timbers creaked, and I turned indoors. We were all safely aboard, we were on our way, no passports had been withdrawn.

But now we had to live at close quarters for fourteen days, putting our ideals of integration into practice. The situation could no longer be held at arm's length. This voyage would make or break the team.

CHAPTER 15

Return

I SHARED a cabin with three other League members, and I looked with some envy at Marjorie and Mary, installed in their luxurious two-berth cabin, surrounded by baskets of fruit and boxes of chocolates.

On the first evening, I accompanied them to the lounge, where we met the rest of the team for a drink before dinner, and then placed them firmly beside me at the long table in the dining-saloon reserved for us. A few other non-Europeans were travelling. I guessed that some of the team hoped Marjorie and Mary would eat with passengers of their own race; but I felt it was essential to begin as we meant to go on, and to include the coloured girls in all our activities from the start.

The two moved as though in a dream, hardly believing in what was happening to them. Life in South Africa had conditioned them to an automatic response of self-effacement in every situation. When we were all invited to tea in the Captain's cabin – 'What, us as well?' they said, taking it for granted that they would be excluded. Nothing in their previous experience had prepared them for the luxury and variety of choice on the ship. But as they settled down, they gained confidence and made friends. Their shy charm and sensitivity began to endear them to their fellow-passengers. They could so easily have become spoiled or aggressive, both reactions which were forecast by those who disapproved of the venture. In fact, throughout the trip they remained their own simple selves. Miss Seth-Smith had chosen wisely.

Every morning before breakfast the team rehearsed on the boat deck, and then Marjorie and Mary came into their own. Their grace and expressiveness was inherent, something that was part of them, as natural as breathing, and did not have to be imposed from without. They had the capacity to lose themselves in the music, and to be possessed completely by the movements they were performing. Watching their absorbed faces I realised that in this sphere they need fear no slights or patronage.

'The reaction of fellow-passengers to the coloured girls is rather amusing,' I wrote to a friend in the Cape. 'Slowly they are now coming forward to talk to me, to inquire tentatively what it is all about, or openly to approve (not many have done this). Some, I know, definitely disapprove, but have not told me so directly. The attitude of the team themselves is also revealing. I think at last some – not all – are beginning *really* to accept the coloured girls, with their hearts as well as their minds, and are even starting to be slightly protective towards them.'

The majority of our fellow-passengers were South African. Living in a country where Apartheid is complete, it was extraordinary for them to meet non-Europeans in a social context. Their instinctive reaction was one of patronising superiority, just as Marjorie's and Mary's was one of submission. It was almost impossible for the two sides to meet as people, on equal terms. But as we steamed farther and farther away from South Africa, and the liberating winds of the Atlantic began to blow, the respective attitudes changed.

'I very much disapproved of this mixed team,' said a tough Afrikaaner man to me, at the farewell cocktail party. 'I thought you were making a great mistake in bringing two coloured girls, and that they would become spoiled, and never settle back into their life at home afterwards. But I must say the girls themselves have made me change my mind. They're a fine couple. I wish you all success.'

We were met at Southampton by a barrage of pressmen. There was no question now of any white members of the team refusing to be photographed. Many pictures were taken, the girls wearing their travelling uniform of navy blue suits, with yellow shirts and yellow corduroy hats. Under the heading, 'No Colour Bar Here', the *Evening Standard* reported that night:

The Women's League of Health and Beauty and their leader, Miss Prunella Stack, have won a victory over Dr Malan's colour bar. Among 28 South African girls who will take part in a display at the Albert Hall later this month are two coloured girls – Miss Mary Williams, aged 20, and Mrs Marjorie Austin, 23. The two girls were among a party of nine who arrived at Southampton to-day in the *Edinburgh Castle*. Miss Stack was with them. In Cape Town the coloured and white members of the League have separate classes. On board the ship the nine sat at the same table.

Hospitality from English members had been offered to all the South Africans, and Marjorie and Mary were soon installed in the homes of two London members. The friendships they made proved lasting ones; Marjorie's hostess subsequently became godmother to her first child.

London was *en fête* for the Coronation, and the South Africans were swept into a mood of celebration. A number of them attended a garden party at Buckingham Palace, and most of them fitted in a trip to the Continent at some time during their stay. But their first great event was the Albert Hall display.

We had several intensive rehearsals before it. Labouring to bring our item up to its highest performance pitch, I was consumed with anxiety that even now it might not reach the perfection we sought. We worked hard for several days. And then, at last, we were all assembled at the Albert Hall, the vast auditorium packed with spectators, television cameras poised, and the arena crowded with members, from England, Ireland, Scotland and Wales. A thrill of anticipation ran through the building. The Canadian team took their places to a great ovation, and then it was the turn of the South Africans. Their entrance was like a burst of sunshine. Confident and smiling, their yellow tunics gleaming, they appeared at the head of the stairs below the royal box. The chords of 'Sarie Marais', the old Afrikaans folk-song, rang out, and bearing their flag, the South Africans walked down the broad flight of steps and entered the arena. All strain and conflict had disappeared. They had welded themselves into a composite group, in which the English-speaking, Afrikaans and coloured elements were one, each taking pride in the thrill and achievement of the moment, and bringing to this great London audience a sense of youthful happiness, and an impression of the out-of-doors, and of the sunny open spaces of their homeland.

Applause rippled about them as they appeared and grew to a crescendo as they moved through the arena, and took their places below the platform. We exchanged smiles of excitement and pride, and then I stepped to the microphone, to welcome all the League's large 'family'.

How proud our Founder would have been of the growth of her work, and the inspiration so evident here to-night. Though the League has continued now for eighteen years without her, I think her spirit is still manifest in its activity, and in the hearts and minds of all those teachers and members who worked with her. Particular thanks go to Peggy and Joan St Lo, responsible for so much of our continuity and success.

The League's vitality, it seems to me, is linked with the spirit of youth – a spirit manifest in the events of these days. In a few days' time we shall see our young Queen crowned. Her subjects from all over the world have come to give her their homage. The ties of unity between the mother country and the Commonwealth are thus being strengthened and renewed. In its own way, the same thing is happening within the League. The inspiration, which had its source at the centre, has radiated out to new realms, and now returns bringing with it its own distinctive contribution.

It is my hope that this two-way traffic of vitality and inspiration between the League in Britain and its overseas members, may serve to sustain its spirit of youth, so that from it may stem new growth and development.

A wave of affection and enthusiasm reached me from the massed arena. I felt proud indeed to be part of this great assembly. And then the members rose from their places and the display proceeded, unrolling itself before the attentive audience, item following item in a variety of movement and colour. The BBC televised some of the second half, including an item by small children of the Junior League, and the South African 'Movement in Music'. The team gave an inspired performance, and the BBC cameramen, selecting the coloured girls for many of their shots, relayed the message of the mixed races to millions of viewers throughout the country. The opinion of one of them is worth quoting. He wrote:

I was deeply impressed by the ease, grace and precision of people whom I have been in the habit of regarding only as staid matrons, bridge club addicts or knitting enthusiasts. I never thought they could perform with such grace and freedom. I had the feeling that the whole thing came spontaneously, with a complete lack of discipline, but yet with perfect control. The babies were cute, and the South Africans perfection.

The team had one more group event before the girls dispersed: their visit to Scotland. I met them in Edinburgh, where I had spent the previous few days as a guest at the Palace of Holyroodhouse. David's eldest brother Douglo was Lord High Commissioner at the Church of Scotland's General Assembly that year, and he invited me to join his house-party at Holyrood for this event.

The day started with morning prayers in one of the palatial Holyrood drawing-rooms; continued with attendances at the Assembly, where ministers drawn from parishes throughout Scotland debated matters of concern to the Scottish kirk, and sang resounding hymns; and ended with a formal banquet in the great dining-hall, under the vigilant eyes of a row of bearded kings of Scotland, whose portraits decorated the walls.

As always, Scottish tradition and romance kindled my heart, and I was in a euphoric frame of mind when I welcomed the South Africans. They were entertained in Edinburgh by the Lord Provost, Sir James Miller, who invited them to a luncheon at the City Chambers, where each girl was escorted to the dining-room on the arm of one of the City Councillors; Marjorie and Mary, by now completely at home, chatting vivaciously with their hosts. Complimentary speeches were exchanged amid the solid splendour of the civic luncheon table, and the team fortified themselves against an appearance that evening in Princes Street Gardens, where they were to perform their item on a wooden stage below the Castle Rock.

The Scottish climate lived up to its reputation, and the South Africans shivered in their thin yellow tunics. But the warmth of their welcome from the audience, and subsequently from the Scottish League members, at a rally organised in Glasgow the next day, made up for inclement weather. They responded wholeheartedly to the romance of Scotland, made friends with their hospitable Scottish hostesses, and regarded the visit as one of the highlights of the trip.

With this event over, my responsibility for the team ended. Most of them returned to South Africa soon afterwards. The venture had been an unqualified success, and had lived up to my most ardent hopes. Its end brought a sense of anti-climax, but also a feeling of great relief. After a few weeks' rest in England I too returned to the Cape, where my sons and my life there awaited me.

The boys were growing up. Diarmaid had recently gone to his public school – the Diocesan College in Cape Town, where Ally had been head prefect. Diarmaid's interest in science (manifest since early boyhood when I had been misguided enough to give him a book entitled *The Young Chemist*) now had increasing sustenance. School instruction was supplemented by weekend experiments carried out with illicit chemicals stored in a little shed at the top of the garden. On Sundays the Constantia valley reverberated with a series of explosions, assuring our friends that Diarmaid was home again; while Iain, a willing if inexperienced accomplice, would subsequently emerge somewhat shakily from a dustbin nearby. He had been placed there by Diarmaid, and armed with a periscope so that he could watch the explosion as well as test how close he could get to it without being blown up.

Iain's tastes were less lethal, consisting chiefly in befriending birds or animals; but both boys still loved the Cape and we all three made the most of the outdoor opportunities which it offered, climbing in the mountains and going for expeditions into the countryside. Many of these were shared with our close friends Biddy and Jim McGregor. They were a Scottish couple who had emigrated to the Cape soon after the war. Jim had built up a practice as one of the leading neurologists in South Africa, and their hospitable house became a second home to us. With them, and their two young daughters, we explored the Cedarburg and the Hottentots Holland Mountains, camped out under the stars, and swam from the wonderful beaches which extend all round the Peninsula.

I did one more severe climb: Africa Wall, which traverses a section of the vertical cliffs below the summit of Table Mountain. This was carried out with three expert South African mountaineers, and was the hardest piece of rock I ever tackled. After five exhausting pitches, on the final rocks below the summit, I missed a handhold and fell, dangling on the rope 3,500 feet above Cape Town, until I managed to regain my footing on the cliff-face and be hauled thankfully up to safety.

The easy enjoyment of life in the Cape tended to seem complete in itself. I had made a niche for myself and was happy, with a circle of congenial friends, work which I found most rewarding, and a setting of unrivalled natural beauty. But I knew that the environment was too confined and the racial pressures too distressing to stay permanently. Soon I would have to bring Diarmaid and Iain back to Britain to complete their education, and to renew their ties with their family.

The Nationalists had now been in power for five years, and their policies showed no sign of changing or weakening. They had the support of most of the country; in April 1953 they had won the elections with a considerably increased majority. Although in 1952 the Supreme Court had invalidated the race legislation of the Prime Minister, Dr Malan, thus gaining a significant victory for the forces of law, two months afterwards Parliament had approved a Government-sponsored bill to restrict the Supreme Court's powers. A non-white campaign began to defy 'unjust laws'. But in spite of demonstrations and deliberate violations of the law, leading to wide-scale arrests, the non-Europeans had little hope of changing conditions. All the power lay in the hands of the Government.

Some whites felt the danger and the injustice of the position. They became dissatisfied with the cautious line followed by the official opposition, the United Party, and in May 1953 two new 'anti-Malanism' parties were launched: Alan Paton's Liberal Party, which favoured full rights of citizenship for all civilised people; and the Federal Union Party, which advocated a federal state. My sympathies were with the Liberal Party, although I realised it could never command wide support.

In July, shortly after my return from England, the United Party decided to block the Prime Minister's plans to segregate the coloured voters. This deprived Malan of the opposition votes he needed to amend the constitution, and was a victory for the anti-Apartheid forces. And the following year, in June 1954, for the second time the legislature rejected legislation sponsored by the

Prime Minister to separate Cape coloured voters from the rolls.
But the writing was on the wall. It was only a matter of time before
the will of the more extreme whites prevailed. Early in 1956
J. G. Strydom, who had followed Dr Malan as Prime Minister,
and who was an uncompromising leader of Afrikaaner nationalism, revealed plans to remove 60,000 coloureds from the common
roll of voters in the Cape Province, and to establish Parliament as
the supreme governing body in the country, thus denying the
right of the courts to pass judgment on the validity of parliamentary acts.

A spontaneous women's movement had arisen to protest
against this legislation: the Black Sash. During 1955 mass marches
and meetings were organised in Johannesburg and other cities.
Women, wearing black sashes, mounted all-night vigils outside
Parliament. Embarrassed Cabinet Ministers were forced to pass
between their ranks, as they stood with bowed heads, demonstrating their silent mourning for the threatened South African
constitution.

In Cape Town a Black Sash protest meeting and march was
held in November 1955. Hundreds of housewives and professional
women, and many of my South African friends took part. I too
joined in, and was much impressed by the seriousness and
determination of the marchers. But in spite of brave efforts the
Black Sash movement proved powerless to alter the Government's
policy. The most it could do, during the ensuing years, was to
develop into a social service which tried to right some of the
individual wrongs suffered by the coloured and African communities.

To live in a country which is dominated by a belief alien to
one's own is a claustrophobic experience. I could be very happy
in the Cape, provided I looked no farther than my own intimate
circle of friends. And indeed I had leisure there as never before to
read, to listen to music, and to discuss books, poems and ideas.
There were opportunities for play readings and musical evenings
in friends' houses; and when cultural events such as concerts
by visiting virtuosi or a season of the Royal Ballet came to Cape
Town, they were eagerly shared. But, no matter how much
enjoyed, these activities were surface events. Below the surface
lay the dark tide of suffering and injustice which one knew was

always flowing. Unless it could be effectively resisted, it would in the end contaminate one's life.

For some time, I hoped that the League might play a positive part. In 1954 we mounted a display at the City Hall, which Peggy St Lo came over from England to attend; and once again we included items by coloured members as well as white. Once again, also, there was opposition from some of the white League members, who did not wish to be associated with the coloured girls, or to perform before a mixed audience. Some of these dissidents felt strongly enough to drop out of the display altogether.

In fact, the League had succeeded in extending its work among the coloureds to a significant degree, and in 1954 four centres were in operation for them in various parts of Cape Town. This was encouraging. But I realised that this small achievement was of little significance beside the magnitude of the problems which existed.

I had grown to love the Cape, with its leisurely traditions, its informal life, and its breath-taking beauty. And I knew that the Cape had given me much: friends, a home, constructive work, time to think and read and meditate, above all a faith which I felt would remain with me wherever I went.

It had taken much, also. Ally's loss grew no less. On two occasions I climbed back to the ledge where he had fallen, and placed wild flowers on the little cairn there, built to commemorate his death.

I wrote after one of these visits:

> The living cannot reach the dead,
> For hard as rock and grey as stone
> The path, returning, climbs alone.

I had to face life now without Ally. Yet, while I was still in South Africa, in the home we had made together, many memories of his presence remained. The decision to leave his country was as difficult as the decision had been to come to it five and a half years ago.

It was the thought of my sons' future which finally impelled me. I entered them for Gordonstoun School in Scotland, for January 1956, and we spent a last poignant Christmas in the Cape.

We said goodbye to all our favourite places, packed our belongings and sold our house. The boys were deeply excited by the prospect of their new life in Britain, and another sea voyage as its preliminary; I was as deeply sorrowful to go. I knew it would be very hard to replace the work and friends which I was leaving behind, and that our departure would leave a gap in my mother-in-law's life which nothing could fill.

The League gave a farewell party for me, and many members, both white and coloured, came to see me off. The League's future in South Africa under Barbara Keys was assured. It had developed on sound foundations, had a steadily increasing membership, and recently we had sent two South African girls to train as teachers in London. They would return in due course to help Barbara and to extend the work. But the knowledge of the League's continued success scarcely mitigated my sadness. I was heart-broken to go.

Once again the ship pulled out of the harbour and I watched Table Mountain fade away into the distance. How long it seemed since my first sight of it from my porthole window six years ago! And how much had happened: such extremes of joy, sadness and effort. The great humps of the Apostles heaved into view, rising from the shore in a frieze along the horizon, as the ship changed course for the open sea. The sinking sun clothed them with golden fire. On one of them stood Ally's little cairn, all that was left of our life together in the Cape.

We landed at Southampton in a thick fog. David's sister Jean, and Elizabeth Mallett, one of the League's foremost teachers and an old friend, met us. Elizabeth bore telegrams of welcome from the League Council and the Executive Committee. These served to encourage me, as we drove through the wintry landscape, freezing rain beating on the car's windscreen. We had left the Cape at the height of summer. Now we shivered in January winds, our blood thinned by six years of African sun, trying to adjust ourselves to the British climate.

Creative gain often comes out of a period of flux and change, but this is impossible to gauge at the time. All that can be done then is to endure. My first months in England called for all my powers of endurance.

Jean welcomed us hospitably into her Sussex home; but, in

spite of her kindness, I felt that I had no roots, no home, no work, and I missed the Cape intensely. The first step was to get the boys established at Gordonstoun. Kurt Hahn, an old friend and the founder of the school, was no longer headmaster, but he had arranged places for Diarmaid and Iain. I knew the aims of Gordonstoun well, having been in close contact with them when David ran his Highland Fitness Schools before the war, and having seen them develop in the work of Outward Bound.

I felt that Gordonstoun, with its unorthodox methods, its accent on adventure, and its situation on the wild and beautiful east coast of Morayshire, would preserve the freedom of life which the boys had known in the Cape, and at the same time acclimatise them to Scotland.

We travelled to Morayshire overnight, and parted on a bleak and windswept platform the next day. Black clouds loomed over-head, threatening hail. The boys, now aged fifteen and thirteen, were at once excited and apprehensive at the prospect before them. Their six years in South Africa had given them confidence and independence, but had made them feel like strangers in Britain.

I left them with some misgivings, and returned to Sussex, where I set about finding a house which would become our new home.

Now I had time to contact my League colleagues, and to catch up with events since my last visit to England. Lord Sempill had been chairman of the League Council for some years. His colour-ful character endeared itself to the members (particularly his habit of departing for Scotland in the middle of chairing the Annual General Meeting, having first kissed a fond farewell to all the ladies present on the platform).

Under his aegis, the League had recently launched into a most important development: the opening in October 1955 of a new training college for teachers, at Morley College in London. The Principal of Morley College, Denis Richards, a man of vision and enterprise, showed himself ready to welcome new experiments under his wing, and he agreed to lease daytime accommodation to the League. Morley had been partially destroyed during the war, and rebuilding was soon to begin. By the time this was completed, the League enjoyed the use of a large hall, two classrooms, the refectory and well-equipped dressing-rooms. But as well as this material advantage, the League students could also share in Morley's cultural life. It had a tradition longer than the League's, stretching back to the 1880s, when its classes had started in the spare dressing-rooms of the Old Vic theatre. One of London's most important centres of adult education, it specialised in the arts. Its evening programme of activities comprised subjects as widely varied as painting and philosophy, languages and dance, science and literature, drama and psychology. And its music was renowned. Gustav Holst and Michael Tippett had been former Directors of Music, and its student orchestras and choirs had achieved almost a national reputation. Frequent concerts were given in the rebuilt large hall – named the Emma Cons Hall after the redoubtable founder of the Old Vic and the College – and the London Philharmonic and the other great London orchestras often rehearsed there. This milieu, with its wide artistic interests, was an ideal one for the League students; and before long they were joined by students of the Opera School run by Anne Wood and Joan Cross, and by the Jooss-Leeder School of Modern Dance, both of which organisations also rented daytime accommodation at Morley.

The League's new training college followed in the traditions of the original Bagot Stack Health School and had much the same curriculum. It was called the Bagot Stack College, and its first Principal, Joan Wilder, one of the League's senior teachers, had been trained by my mother. Her contribution was of great value in establishing the first two-year diploma course, setting the syllabus, and laying secure foundations for future development.

The students, two South African girls among them, were keen and interested, and worked hard to achieve the high standard demanded. I visited them soon after my arrival in England, and was most impressed by their spirit, and by this significant new venture. It seemed that at last the League teacher-training, vital for its future, was being established on a sound basis, and might receive the recognition and status which it had so long sought.

After establishing the first course, and acting as Principal for two years, Joan Wilder resigned, and I took over the direction of the Bagot Stack College in 1957. I had good reason then to be grateful for her excellent ground work and preparation. A viable course had been created, which was to continue, with only slight

modifications, for the next fifteen years. I continued as Principal
for four years, and then handed over to Anne Lillis in 1961, who
in turn, brought her own distinctive contribution to the life of
the College. Throughout the years, Denis Richards supported the
venture with unfailing encouragement and wise advice. He became a member of the League Council, and, on Lord Sempill's
death, took over its chairmanship, a position which he holds
to-day.

The other organisation with which I soon became re-connected
was Outward Bound.

At that time four Outward Bound Schools were operating: two
sea schools, one at Aberdovey and one on the Morayshire coast,
and two Mountain Schools, both in the Lakes, at Eskdale and
Ullswater. Courses for girls had been held at the Eskdale Mountain School and at the Central Council of Physical Recreation
Centres at Bisham Abbey, in the Thames valley, and Plas y
Brenin, in Snowdonia. Girls came to these courses from every
kind of background and occupation. Many of them had never
before walked on anything but pavements, and the majority had
never been away from home.

The experience of community life for a consecutive month
presented as great a challenge to them as the climbing, canoeing,
expeditions and camping which were the course's main activities.

The benefit to girls of Outward Bound training had been amply
proved. Now the task was to extend their opportunities. With this
end in view I took my place once more on the Outward Bound
Management Committee, under the expert chairmanship of Sir
Spencer Summers. I much enjoyed this reunion with old colleagues, but I soon realised that I would have to press hard to get
a full-time school for the girls established. There were many prior
calls on Outward Bound funds, and a certain measure of prejudice
still existed against extending its work to girls. A first step had
been taken in the appointing of a Girls' Principal, who was in
charge of the three or four *ad hoc* courses run each year. The next
development was the inclusion of some permanent girls' courses
in the next new Outward Bound School, one in Devon which was
opened in 1959. This gave the opportunity to include more
training in drama, movement, public speaking and other indoor
pursuits which helped to counter the criticism that Outward

Bound training for girls was likely to produce only tough Amazons.

Finally, in 1963, the girls secured their own school, at Rhowniar, Aberdovey, where they have remained ever since. After extensive rebuilding and alterations, a beautiful home for Girls' Outward Bound has been created. Sandy Henderson, who helped David to run the Fitness Training Schools in the Highlands before the war, is chairman of the Board of Governors, and ten courses are run there each year, under the guidance of the warden, Anne Cordiner and her staff. Approximately 900 girls pass through the school each year. In addition, the experiment of several mixed courses, of men and women, has been tried at Rhowniar with success; and women staff have been seconded to a number of the City Challenge Courses now run by Outward Bound in cities: a development which provides an opportunity for boys and girls to experience together the problems of a crowded urban environment at first hand.

Girls' Outward Bound training is now firmly established in Britain, and has spread to many of the other Outward Bound Schools which have extended throughout the world.

In 1956 these achievements lay in the future. I could not then foresee them, nor could I know that I would once more find constructive and rewarding work, renew family ties and old friendships, and even again experience love and marriage. For me, at that moment, all happiness seemed to be in the past. Alone in the house we had bought in Sussex, and which I was trying to make into a home for my sons, I felt desolate indeed.

Where, I wondered, was the key to the riddle of life's disparate events? What thread ran through all experience which could be a guide to truth? Did absolute truth, in fact, exist, or was truth relative, changing with changing circumstances?

I thought of my mother's life, so brave and poignant, ending in the fire of endeavour which consumed her. I thought of the League: the inspiration with which it began, the struggle to carry it on, the difficulties which it must surmount if it was to survive. I thought of my own life, its happiness and its loss; the gift of my sons, my responsibility for their future.

How could these things be reconciled? I longed to make a

synthesis which would embrace them, and bring with it some pattern and continuity to which I could cling. But in the course of events there seemed to be no abiding reality. The certainty of faith which I had known in the Cape was with me still, but it gave me no clue as to the next right step – here and now.

Then I remembered a saying of my mother's: 'Action is the prayer that is answered.' Solitary brooding would bring me no solution. I must put aside the temptation to withdraw into dreams and nostalgia, and be prepared to enter the arena of life once more. There must be something I could do: some challenge I could answer, some test for the mind and spirit which I could meet.

> Who dares not put it to the touch
> To win or lose it all
> He either fears his fate too much
> Or his deserts are small.

The poem that had been David's yardstick flashed into my mind.

'Look outwards,' I said to myself. 'Forget yourself.' In spite of present loneliness, I must remember that life still had much to offer. And I must believe that I still had something to give. So I closed the door on my South African era and opened it to a new life in Britain.

CHAPTER 16

Hebridean Haven

IF life is a spiral, as some believe, then similar situations and circumstances are bound to recur during its course. They may or may not be welcomed 'at the next turn of the stair', but they will wear an air of familiarity which is unmistakable. I recognised my period of lonely adjustment as something that had happened before and must be lived through again. In the same way, it was probably inevitable that sooner or later I would migrate back to Skye.

This did not occur until 1960 when my son Diarmaid, who had already left Gordonstoun, was up at Oxford reading physics at Balliol College. At his instigation, I rented a house near Portree for the Easter vacation. A year later Iain also went to Oxford to read zoology at Oriel College. I took a three-year lease on the house and from then on we visited Skye every vacation until Iain's Oxford days were over.

But our Skye home was only rented. It did not belong to us. We all three wished for a more permanent Highland abode. And it was with this thought in mind that we sailed out of Portree harbour one Easter morning in 1962. We were bound for the island of Raasay which lies between Skye and the mainland: an oblong strip of an island, fifteen miles long and about five miles wide. The lure which drew us there was four small crofters' houses situated in a remote part of the island. They had been discovered some years before by Peter Zinovieff, related to us through his father Leo's marriage to David's sister Jean. Peter, exploring Raasay for material for his Oxford geology thesis, had come upon the houses and had always remembered their remote charm. He now suggested we should visit them.

It was a fresh spring morning, with the sun just risen. The MacBrayne's steamer slipped out of the harbour, past hills dusted with snow, and headed into the Sound of Raasay. Soon the island lay spread before us. Dun Caan, the highest point, with its flat-topped rocky summit like an extinct volcano, reared above layers of grass, heather and stone. Raasay House, standing amid its mantle of woods, slowly came into view: a noble seventeenth-century mansion, once the home of the Macleods of Raasay, but now empty and falling into decay. Its green pastures swept down to the sea-loch, where Boswell and Johnson had landed on their tour of the Hebrides in 1773.

A group of white houses appeared: the village of Inverarish. We sailed on past them, and past a rocky bay, until a long ugly pier jutted out into the loch. The steamer stopped. We mounted the gangway and stepped ashore.

The first impression, I must admit, was one of neglect and gloom. On the hillside beyond the pier stood several large stone buildings, roofless and windowless, relics of the iron-ore mines which were worked on the island during the First World War. Below them was a disused quarry where a broken-down old Land-Rover had come to rest. The corrugated iron roofs of some stone huts rattled in the wind. Nothing else could be seen, except a road winding away beside the sea-shore, down which were disappearing the red post-van and the car of the harbour-master. Both had come to meet the steamer. Now, the one great event of the day over, they were returning to Inverarish. The steamer, already a speck in the distance, continued on its way to Kyle. We were left alone with our quest.

An hour or so later, we found our four houses. They were standing on a steep slope of hillside on the south-east corner of the island, about two hundred feet above the sea. There was quarter of a mile or so between each of them, and they faced one of the finest views in the Hebrides. To the west, the Cuillins of Skye thrust up their spectacular peaks. To the south, the white Kyle lighthouse and the cottages of Kyleakin gleamed across a six-mile stretch of water. Beyond soared the Five Sisters of Kintail, while to the east lay the mainland mountains of Apple-cross and Torridon, dappled with cloud and changing light.

The houses belonged to crofters who now lived elsewhere. No one had occupied them for from twelve to twenty years, and they were in a state of extreme dilapidation. Floors were rotten, roofs leaked, window-panes were broken, doors hung drunkenly.

Wallpaper peeled off the walls, and sheep dung spattered the floors. But their situation was superb. A trance of silence surrounded them, broken only by the rush of a burn. Sheep browsed on the short-cropped grass, and a tranquil movement of waves and tides passed across the shining sea. We turned to one another.

'What a place!'

For me, it was love at first sight, love which was also recognition: a strange feeling of belonging more closely and feeling more at home here than anywhere else on earth.

We decided to try to buy.

Months of negotiation followed. Raasay is owned by the Scottish Department of Agriculture. Before the Department could sell the houses to us, permission had to be gained from the crofters who owned them. They also had to be publicly advertised, and all tenders for sale considered. At last in the summer of 1963, when we had almost given up hope, we were told that they were ours. Two of them were bought by my sons, the other two by Peter Zinovieff and his wife Victoria.

So now we possessed our dream dwelling in the Hebrides, but the work of renovation was formidable. We decided to concentrate on one house at a time, and to tackle the one highest on the hillside and nearest to the rough road first. Peter and Victoria started work on their houses immediately, but it was the autumn of 1965 before our plans were passed by the Inverness County Council and we were ready to begin. By then, both my sons were abroad: Diarmaid working in the Department of Astronomy at Harvard University, and Iain, having gained his degree in zoology at Oxford, conducting research on elephants in the Lake Manyara National Park, Tanzania. Responsibility for the croft was handed over to me. But fortunately, I was not alone. The previous year, I had re-married. My husband, Brian St Quentin Power, an Irishman, shared my love for the Highlands, and my enthusiasm for Raasay. Together we supervised the two Raasay men who had taken over the task of renovation.

It was a daunting assignment. Not only did all building materials have to come from Skye – dumped by the steamer at the pierhead, from whence they were conveyed four miles along a rough road, and finally manhandled down a steep slope to the level of the house – but deliveries were spasmodic, and essential commodities

Prunella with her sons
and 'Pirate' before
leaving for South
Africa, 1950

With Ally in South
Africa

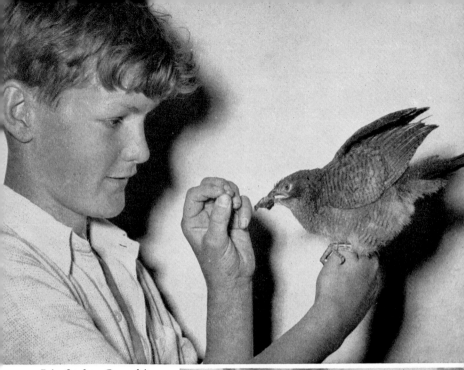

Iain feeds a Coucal in
the Cape

Iain in Manyara, 1969

Diarmaid and Margaret
at their wedding, 1967

Iain and Oria with their
daughter Saba

Prunella with her grandchild Saba, the latest League member

often unavailable. When the south-west gales roared sheets of gyp-rock, for wall-covering, blew away. Sheep wandered in and out of gaping doors rubbing themselves against drainpipes. The ground froze hard, and the eighty feet of trenches which we needed for water-pipes had to be hewed out of icy turf.

All winter, while snow covered the Cuillins, and bitter winds blew off the sea, Jock Rutherford and Callum Macrae, our builders, walked the six miles to the house and back again each day. My weekly telephone call to Jock often ended in a mixture of mirth, frustration and despair. It seemed the house would never be finished. But at last, in the summer of 1966, it was ready for occupation. Water, a sewage system, a bathroom and a Rayburn cooker had been installed. New boards covered the ground floor, with good foundations and a damp course beneath them. The roof was creosoted, the walls freshly painted, new windows shone, even a puff of smoke appeared from one of the chimneys, and a kettle boiled on the kitchen stove.

Shining white outside, and welcoming within, our Hebridean home awaited our arrival; and at the end of July, with a van-load of furniture, thirty-nine packages, a bull-terrier and a Siamese cat, we moved triumphantly in.

Now began six weeks of bliss. Nothing disturbed our solitude but the deliberate procession of sheep, each ewe followed by her lamb, which passed before the door morning and evening; or the friendly visits of Highland cattle who wandered round the house in a somnambulistic fashion, leaving large liquid puddles to show us they had called. We set our watches by the steamer plying once a day up the loch to Portree or down again to Kyle. Telephones, cars and electricity belonged to another existence.

During that magical first summer on Raasay we felt a strange kinship with the birds and beasts around us, for we were living an almost identical life. We had returned to a child's awareness of the minutiae of nature, and a child's absorption in the animal kingdom. The sun, rising from the eastern sea, awoke us. As it described its arc across the sky we fulfilled the simple pattern of the day. When it sank behind the Cuillins in the west, we were ready to sleep. The chaffinch which sang each morning in the rowan tree, the gannets plunging like thunderbolts into the sea, the buzzard family whose wild mew tore the sky: all these became our familiars, looked for and recognised each day.

We walked seven miles up the east coast of the island to Brochel Castle, ancient home of the Macleods of Raasay. In the seaweed below the ruin a golden otter played, his tawny belly rolling towards the sun. The round heads of seals popped out of the water, whiskers bristling, domes shining. They surveyed the landscape, then quietly withdrew below the surface to flash like mermaids through the green swell.

One evening, for an hour at twilight, I watched a basking shark circle slowly round and round a small bay. Its tail, swishing from side to side, threw rivulets against the beach; its large dark triangular fin rose with infinite menace from the sea.

The place and the life encouraged reflection. Wandering along the pebbled shore, where fossils lay half-hidden between the rocks, I felt myself to be living in a different world. The pressures of civilisation dropped away, and the rhythms of nature replaced them.

Here there was no need to divide oneself into fragments in order to meet the many demands which life forced upon one. Here one could be self-sufficient and complete, gathering together emotions which had become scattered over too wide a range, resting a mind tired with the complexity of the global picture, releasing a spirit exhausted by the clamour and superficiality of much of modern life.

I thought of a phrase of Dante's: the opening sentence of the *Inferno*, which I had recently re-read.

In the middle of the journey of our life I came to myself in a dark wood where the straight way was lost.

How exact an image this was for the mental state of middle age! Now that I was half-way – more than half-way – through life, I recognised it. The experiences of youth, and the attitude which they engendered had passed, but their integration in new modes of thought and being had not yet taken place. So the straight way was lost.

In youth, I had occupied the centre of the stage. Now I realised that no experience is unique, and that most of what had happened to me was part of the common lot. 'No man is an island.' The desire to share, to communicate, to love and to be loved was as strong as ever. But perhaps now it could be felt in a less personal context, embracing more of humanity than one's own immediate circle. I began to realise something of the process that had caused my mother to found the League: her burning desire to expand her work to all.

The second half of life, I thought, should consist in harvesting one's knowledge and experience and then giving it freely back to others, without making demands or casting accounts. But this was only possible if one could achieve some kind of inner balance. Only by being free oneself could one give others space to grow.

Here in Raasay one had the opportunity to be still, awaiting enlightenment, rather than continually on the move, trying to shape events and circumstances. Perhaps that was the best way to 'come to oneself', to know oneself and to prepare for the second half of life.

I watched the water lapping on the stones. Its touch was gentle and mysterious, scarcely palpable. The stones appeared to be unmoved, yet over the years they had been changed, eroded to a different shape. 'So life tempers us,' I thought, 'forming a new structure.'

Day was ending. I rose from the rock on which I had been sitting, and stretched myself in the evening air. Pebbles gleamed in the receding tide, seaweed lifted and fell. Two oyster-catchers, flying past with companionable chatter, banked and turned, their wings illuminated in the last rays of the sun.

My mind ceased questioning. The first star, rising above the mountains, reminded me of the stars that had shone on Dante, bringing him evidence of the glory of the universe, its permanence and inviolability. This star drew to itself the last of the light. My feet turned reluctantly homewards.

'Beauty is truth, truth beauty,' I remembered, as I mounted the path to the croft.

Perhaps, like Keats, that was all one needed to know.

Every three or four days we walked into the village for supplies. The Co-op shop stocked most necessities. Gaelic conversations flowed across the counter, while Raasay inhabitants ordered their groceries in a confidential whisper. Loaded up, we would return along a road whose every twist and hump we now knew well. Sometimes we were greeted by a cheerful hail from the three Macleod shepherds busy at the sheep-fank half-way home. Sometimes the small red post-van, driven by Norman-the-Post, would labour towards us down the steep hill with letters from the outside world.

But the magic had to cease. This existence, which seemed more real than any we had known before, had to end. The summer passed, and with the early autumn days we boarded the steamer bound for Kyle, on the first stage of the long journey south. As we drew away from the island, I gazed intently at the four white houses. Poised on the hillside, each with its guardian rowan tree, they faded gently into the landscape like a dream.

It was small consolation that next holidays we would return, and that our Hebridean home would await us. When one has fallen in love, to leave the beloved even for a moment is a physical pain.

I was still working for the League, teaching students at the Bagot Stack College, and visiting a number of League centres throughout the country. The following March, in 1967, I was invited to be present at the first African Reunion of the League to celebrate the Johannesburg centre's tenth birthday. This centre had been opened in 1957, by Betty Bingham, one of the South African students who had attended the first course at the Bagot Stack College. I accepted gladly, the more so because I could combine it with a visit to my son Iain in Tanzania.

I had been back to South Africa a number of times, principally to see Ally's mother. But she had died in 1965, so now my chief link with the Cape was severed. Nevertheless, I had kept in close touch with Barbara Keys and was looking forward to seeing her and the Cape Town members who would travel to Johannesburg for the display.

The impact of the South African sunshine was immediate as I stepped out of the plane at Jan Smuts aerodrome. No low cloud ceiling, only a high wide sky with puffballs of white cloud floating far up in the intense blue. I was met by the Johannesburg and Pretoria League teachers, one English, two South African, and told that teams from Cape Town and from Salisbury, Southern Rhodesia – both 1,000 miles away – would soon converge on Johannesburg. Three days of rehearsals and preparation followed. Then came the display. It was held in Johannesburg's City Hall, which was completely filled, but alas! there were no dark faces among the audience as in my Cape Town days. Johannesburg lacked the Cape's more liberal tradition, and the climate of opinion there had not allowed any extension of the League work beyond the white population. Members of the English-speaking and the Afrikaans communities had joined, but there were no classes for Africans. It was clear where the sympathies of the audience lay, when they gave the ovation of the evening to the girls from Southern Rhodesia, who entered the hall carrying the Southern Rhodesian flag.

An excellent programme followed, containing much original and imaginative work composed by the teachers concerned. It was inspiring to know that the League had become a viable means of communication on this vast continent, and that it was developing in a creative way, as well as bringing together members from places so far distant from one another as Johannesburg, Cape Town and Salisbury.

I was sorry that on this occasion its work was confined to the white community. But later, in 1970, an Indian girl, Leila Jaffer, who had completed her training as a teacher at the Bagot Stack College that year, returned to her home in Kenya and opened classes for Africans and Asians at Mombasa, thus extending the League work in Africa once again to all races.

After a visit to the Pretoria centre, and a birthday party in Johannesburg at which a cake of mammoth proportions was cut, I regretfully left my League friends and boarded a plane for Nairobi, on the next stage of my African safari.

My son Iain had been in the Lake Manyara National Park for eighteen months, engaged in elephant research for which he had received a grant from the Royal Society. He had by now fully explored the Park and was in the process of building up a photographic file of the elephants who lived there, so that he could learn to recognise each one and study their family behaviour. It was an ideal place for such a task, as the elephant population in

Manyara was denser than anywhere else in Africa. In an area of thirty-three square miles, over four hundred elephants had their home.

Iain met me at Arusha, and then drove me in his battered Land-Rover (twice dented by charging rhinos) through the Park gates. For the first three miles or so the rough road ran through forest with large acacia, fig and tamarind trees growing from thick undergrowth. Then an open plain emerged, studded with scrub and walled on the right side by a high wooded escarpment. On the left shimmered the lake, an expanse of shining water stretching to the horizon on which rose smoky blue hills. Animals appeared: zebras tossing their fat rumps; giraffe with long-lashed eyes and rippling gait; impala, graceful as dancers. Flamingoes and pelicans fringed the lake like a line of breaking surf, and buffaloes browsed on the shore. In this Eden, owned by the animals, man seemed redundant, the Land-Rover his cage.

Iain was looking out for his elephants, and soon we glimpsed the vast shapes moving deliberately among the trees. We turned off the road to drive among them, Iain recognising the matriarch of each cow-calf herd. 'There's Boadicea,' or, 'This is Queen Victoria,' he observed, introducing them to me, as he recorded the composition and movements of their families.

The Land-Rover came to a halt beside a tree. 'Look up,' said Iain. Two lion cubs sprawled among the branches. They descended with effortless grace to join their mother prowling watchfully below. Then all three rolled and played together, growling to each other, and occasionally sending us a warning flash from their tawny eyes.

The sun was slanting low when we reached a fork in the road and a sign saying 'Elephant Research Camp. No Entry.' Another half-mile and we were at Iain's camp. It consisted of two *rondavels* built of stone with thatched roofs, standing twenty feet or so above the Ndala river gorge. A waterfall cascaded down steep yellow rocks above the camp. On a ledge just below the rushing water stood one more rondavel, shaded by a large flat-topped acacia tree: my sleeping quarters. The whole camp had been carved by Iain out of the bush, and here he had lived alone for many months. Elephant skulls, collected for his research, gleamed a bizarre welcome in the gathering dusk. His African ranger and cook greeted us: '*Jambo, bwana. Jambo, mamma.*' Then the swift tropical night fell, and its strange noises besieged the little human clearing. Round us the animals prowled, each perfectly attuned to this primitive world. Only man, with his gift of conscious thought, needed to evoke an ancient past to feel at ease.

Next day I woke with the dawn, announced by the honking of two Egyptian geese flying from the Lake to a pool below the waterfall. A huge yellow sun rose from the hills beyond the water and peered into my *rondavel*. Innumerable awakening bird noises followed. The harsh piping, whistling and clicking of the African bush dwellers mingled with the coo-ing of doves.

To the sound of this chorus I ran down the track to Iain's rondavel for breakfast – steaming coffee and bowls of paw-paw, melon, and pineapple – produced by his cook, Suleiman.

The days at Ndala followed a leisurely pattern. I spent much time bird-watching. March was the mating and nesting season, and many of the birds were in their brightest plumage. Colours were exotic with a brilliance seldom achieved in our more temperate zone. Azure-blue and chestnut European rollers; malachite kingfishers with ultramarine breasts; graceful sacred ibis, with white plumage and dark purple tail-tufts; crested cranes, with straw-coloured tufts growing out of their sleek black heads, like feathers on a smart woman's hat – all these were new to me. The marabou storks looked like birds of doom, perching on the stumps of dead trees. In the air their huge wing-span glided amongst the pelicans and flamingoes which flew up from the Lake shore. One day I saw a young Martial eagle. His eyes were deep and gentle like an owl's, but when he turned his flexible neck his profile displayed an authentic majesty.

Most afternoons the elephants congregated in the river-bed below the camp. Emerging from the forest they wandered up and down the river in family parties, splashing water over themselves, drinking and giving the *totos* dust-baths. Iain would recognise the herd, and when they ambled off again we would follow in the Land-Rover, for further identification. To observe them at close quarters, Iain would drive straight into the bush, and often we were surrounded by elephants. Trumpeting, and aggressive display by some elderly matriarch, would be airily explained away by Iain with – 'She's only preparing for a dummy charge. Don't worry!'

A week after my arrival Iain decided we would climb a hill in the southernmost section of the Park – called, appropriately enough, Enderbash – where the animals tended to be wilder, owing to poaching and hunting activities just beyond the Park boundary.

We left his Land-Rover beside the shallow Enderbash River, waded across it, and soon were walking in single file – Iain, myself and Kiprono, his game ranger – along an elephant track surrounded by dense bush about seven feet high.

The fierce African sun filtered through interlaced leaves. All was silent, yet intently aware. Occasionally a bird flew out of the bushes with a clatter of wings, or a butterfly flitted from side to side of the path. A rustle in the undergrowth might be a mongoose, a lizard, or a snake. We passed a rhino-scrape, and the powerful acrid smell of rhino faeces filled the air. I heard a faint snort some distance away and the unease which I was beginning to feel accelerated. However, soon afterwards we emerged on to the grassy lower slopes of the hill and began to climb it. Iain and Kiprono turned and scanned the bush with Iain's binoculars. They could see nothing. Rhinos might or might not be there. We continued our climb to the top of the escarpment, and then gazed for some time at a magnificent view; layer upon layer of wooded undulating country, the only mark of man some small clusters of flat-topped African dwellings, just discernible between the trees.

At midday we started to descend. The strip of thick bush looked very dense from above, the sunlight glittering on its dark green leaves, no movement discernible. We entered it silently, Iain leading, I following, and Kiprono, carrying the gun, at the rear.

We passed the rhino-scrape, and I thought, 'Thank goodness! Not much more to go,' when suddenly, directly beside the path, not five yards away, came a deep snort. It was short, sharp and unmistakable. An electrifying silence followed, then the snort was repeated, louder and closer. The word 'Rhino' was forming on my tongue, when Iain called, 'Run for it!' and dashed into the bush on the right of the path. I turned and ran back along the path, while Kiprono sped away to the left.

I ran wildly, through thorn and scrub, over roots and across fallen branches, scratched, bruised, panting, driven by primeval fear and by the terrifying noise of the rhino charge, which sounded like several large tanks in action. My mind emptied of every thought except to get away. Time elongates on such an occasion. I ran only for a minute at the most, but it seemed endless.

At last silence fell. I stopped. The leaves of the bushes quivered. Each one seemed to mask a deadly peril. I felt blood running down my nose: a scratch from a thorn-tree. I stood waiting, shivering, afraid to move, and then I heard Iain's voice call, 'Kiprono.' Together we followed the sound, and found Iain lying in a small clearing. It was at once apparent that he was seriously injured. The rhinos – there were two – had chased him, gaining on him, until finally he had tripped, fallen, and been kicked by one of them as they charged past.

Three hours later Kiprono carried Iain into his house. Together we had helped him to the Land-Rover, which I had driven to within half a mile of where he lay. The journey home had then been accomplished at snail's pace, down the elephant track, over the river, through the bush and finally along an agonisingly bumpy road back to his camp.

It was now imperative to find a doctor. I drove to the Park gates, and thence by steeply winding road up the hillside to the Lake Manyara Hotel, 1,000 feet above on the escarpment. I was told that a doctor was out in the Park viewing the animals, and immediately I set out in search of him.

As my Land-Rover churned round one of the hairpin bends of the descent I saw the zebra-camouflaged bus climbing slowly upwards. I leapt out, and signalled it to a halt. The camera-laden tourists gazed at me through their sun glasses, noting, I suppose, my scratched legs, torn shirt, and dishevelled hair. 'Is there a doctor here?' I asked. A deeply-tanned man, standing at the back of the bus, his head out of the sunshine roof, binoculars slung round his neck, answered, 'Ja.'

I explained my predicament. He hesitated, consulted his watch, consulted the tour leader, then shook his head. He spoke in German to the tour leader, who translated:

'He says he cannot come. It would upset his schedule. We are due to leave for Ngorongoro in half an hour.'

I reiterated my plea, offered to drive him back to the hotel, after he had seen my son. He was adamant. He could not come.

Suddenly I felt immensely tired. The whole weight of the extraordinary day descended on my shoulders. Speechless, I climbed back into the Land-Rover, and drove on, in search of aid in the African village.

Mahunga, the African Park Warden, at once offered to drive Iain to the hospital at Arusha, seventy miles away; and at 7.30 p.m. we set off, Iain bedded down in the back of Mahunga's station-wagon, having had a shot of morphia from the local African medical assistant. We sped through the night, off the dirt road on to the tarmac, and I thought our troubles were nearly over. But after about an hour's drive, the near-side front wheel of Mahunga's Cortina began to wobble. Mahunga stopped, then started again. The wobble improved slightly, and we continued at a reduced speed. 'We'll go on till the wheel drops off!' he said. And that was exactly what we did. Before long there was a frightful heave and lurch and the car tipped sideways. The wheel was off.

It was now 10.30 p.m.; we were forty miles from Arusha, in the midst of the wide star-filled African night, jackals and crickets the only sound. Mahunga walked up and down the road in the moonlight, looking for the nuts and bolts which had fallen out of his wheel, and Iain and I prepared for a night-long vigil. However, our guardian angels had not quite deserted us.

An hour later we were rescued by a Land-Rover containing John Owen, the Director of the Tanzania National Parks, who had come in search of us, bringing with him a nurse, morphia, blankets and food. We reached the Arusha hospital at 1.30 a.m.

An X-ray later disclosed that Iain had suffered a compressed fracture of a lumbar vertebra, but that with rest and care he should recover completely. In fact, a month later, he was back in the Park, viewing his elephants with undiminished enthusiasm.

As for me, I had sought to evoke the feelings of primitive man, and been taken at my word. No experience could go further back in human memory than that of being chased by a wild beast. But the primeval fear which had engulfed me left no lasting trace. It was so intense at the time that it had a cathartic effect. I was haunted by no subsequent nightmares, nor was my nerve broken for future forays in the bush. When later we flew over the

Ngorongoro crater and dipped to salute three rhinos grazing there with armour-plated indifference, I certainly viewed them with respect. But my predominant impression of the whole wonderful safari was summed up in the notice on the landing-strip at Seronera, in the Serengeti Park, which says: 'Here the world is still young and fragile, held in trust for your sons and ours.'

The following October, 1967, my son Diarmaid was married in the United States. His bride was Margaret Hambrecht, an American girl who had just completed a law degree at the Boston University Law School, having previously gained a BA in English at Wellesley College, and an MA in literature at Syracuse University. The couple were married in Lakeville, Connecticut, where Margaret's parents lived. My husband and I flew over for the wedding, joined by Iain who came from Africa to be best man. The New England countryside, with its white high-steepled churches, and green-shuttered clapboard houses, its birch woods, and broad highways, flamed with autumn colours. They glowed too, around the old red-brick buildings of Beacon Hill, where Diarmaid and Margaret had decided to live. This district, one of the earliest residential areas of Boston, has been preserved intact since the turn of the nineteenth century, and its paved sidewalks, period lamps, and graceful façades hold echoes of citizens whose ancestors arrived on the *Mayflower* and whose strict standards helped to shape Boston's image.

Diarmaid bought a house on Beacon Hill, very reminiscent of Campden Hill Square, David's and my first home. In this old-fashioned setting he and Margaret live busy contemporary lives, Margaret practising as a lawyer, Diarmaid working first in the Department of Astronomy at Harvard and later undertaking research in physics for a large industrial complex in Boston.

I stay with them from time to time, and have formed a strong attachment to Beacon Hill and to their delightful home.

With one son in the States and the other in Africa, I possess a footing in two very different worlds, and welcome the opportunity to visit both.

And what of the League during these years? It embarked on two new ventures. The first was a series of Overseas Conventions held in League centres abroad. These were conceived and organised by Elizabeth Mallett, one of the League's senior teachers, a member of the Council and Executive Committee, who trained before the war, and taught in Canada as one of her first League assignments.

Under her enthusiastic guidance, members from Britain flew by charter plane to League centres overseas. There they were met and entertained by their fellow-League members who gave them hospitality, ending in a large rally and display in each place.

Starting with three plane-loads of over a hundred each to Toronto, in 1968, this new development continued with visits to Vancouver in 1969, Johannesburg and Cape Town in 1970, Southern Rhodesia in 1971 and New Zealand in 1972.

The excitement and enthusiasm of the British members was intense. For many of them it was their first trip overseas, but one which took place in the familiar ambience of the League, with the certainty of a warm welcome at the other end. For the overseas members the scheme provided a link with Britain and the stimulation of new contacts; and for all a fresh realisation of the League's aim of international friendship.

The mantle of my mother's visionary ideals seemed to have descended on Elizabeth Mallett's shoulders, particularly as she organised each venture with exceptional tact, verve and determination.

The second new development was the decision to widen the field of League teacher-training and to enrol students for part-time courses in other areas besides London. This training took the place of that which had been given at the Bagot Stack College, which closed in 1970.

The first of these courses was held in the Midlands and South-West during 1969 and 1970, followed by a second of two years' duration in Yorkshire and Lancashire, starting in 1971, and a third in London and the Home Counties, starting in 1972.

This new policy enabled a larger number of teachers to be trained – something essential for the future of the League – and also gave more scope to regional development, uncovering hidden talents at both teacher and member level.

The League still lived largely on its own resources. From 1964 onwards it received a small grant from the Government for administration, and in 1969, this was increased to include teacher-training. But for the most part the 'darling human capital' which my mother had believed to be its most valuable asset still generated the means for its existence. In an age of subsidies the League is exceptional in, to a large extent, still paying its own way. Torquil Macleod, who had done so much to establish the League on a financially sound basis, died in 1970. He was succeeded as League Secretary by Herbert Mussen, his close friend and colleague.

In 1970, the League became forty years old. Its birthday party, organised by the London centre and Peggy and Joan St Lo, took the form of a rally attended by fifteen hundred members, which was held in Brighton, where the participants spent a luxury week-end, joined together in massive classes, and toasted the League's health at three great banquets, presided over by Denis Richards, chairman of the League Council, and its staunch friend and supporter for many years. Brighton, invaded by so many women, produced sparkling May weather for their enjoyment, and turned an indulgent eye on the black-and-white uniforms parading up and down the esplanade. Godfrey Winn was a guest of honour and made a stirring speech to the members.

Those who assembled for this anniversary came from all parts of the country, and were representative of an active League membership of 26,000 in Britain and overseas. In spite of – or perhaps because of – its forty years, the League could still attract to itself a large measure of appreciation, good humour and affection.

And there my chronicle of the League must end. Has it lived up to all that its founder hoped? Those who have worked for it since the early days – and there are a number of teachers who have given more than thirty years of service to the League – can point to concrete results in the increased health and happiness of the women who have passed through their hands, including those in specialist classes held in mental hospitals and institutions for the handicapped. Three generations have belonged to the League, and now it is the task of the third generation to carry it on, for the continuation of the League beyond its half-century will be the next test of its vitality.

In an age of shifting values and ever-accelerating problems, the old-fashioned virtues of idealism, loyalty, balance and health may seem to have no place. *Mens sana in corpore sano* may appear too limited a concept for the space-age, when so much that is artificial is accepted as a way of life. Yet the fundamental needs of the body and the mind do not change. Human beings are happiest when the two work in harmony, when the body becomes a means of expression for the mind's insights, and each part of the personality develops to make a balanced whole.

This was the basic truth which my mother perceived. The means which she created to foster it, if they are as valid as the years seem to have proved, will have relevance for the future as well as the past.

I end my book in Raasay, the place which more than any other has become a haven for me.

Both houses are now finished and complete; my sons own the first, and my husband and I the second, which we renovated in 1967, and moved into a year later. These two Hebridean homes have proved a compelling magnet, drawing together our scattered family from time to time in a place we all love.

In the summer of 1971 Iain brought his wife Oria, whom he had met in Kenya two years before, to Raasay, and introduced her and their year-old daughter to the joys of Fearns. Oria, half-Italian, half-French, the youngest child of Mario and Giselle Rocco, pioneer Kenya settlers, had shared Iain's life of adventure in the bush. Kenya born and bred, she understands his dedication to his elephants, and has helped to make a fine photographic record of his research. A second daughter was born to them in November 1971.

As I write now, it is the beginning of a new year in Raasay. The January sea has an opaque depth of colour which reflects a snow-laden sky. I hear the crunch of pebbles, as the tide recedes from the shore, and the rush of the burn pouring over the waterfall in full spate. Through bare red-tipped branches of silver birch the mountains loom white, each with a mantle of snow which softens their noble shapes. To-night they will gleam in the light of a full moon, mysterious guardians of our solitude. A pattern of waves moves across the wide stretch of sea, and now the little steamer comes into view, chugging forward on her way up to Portree, the low throb of her engine reverberating like conversation from the outside world.

How I wish that time could stand still, and that none of this need ever change. I would like to wave a wand and enfold Raasay in an enchanted sleep. But alas! change it will. A car ferry will come, tourists will arrive, the island will be opened up to visitors. Its solitary magic will fade.

This is inevitable. All outer life consists of flux and change.

But I believe there is an inner region of the heart and spirit which can remain inviolate. Experiences cherished there need never change. In this deepest, most secret core of the personality resides a familiar, whom we recognise as having been with us from the earliest days, and who will continue with us until the end, guardian of all that has been most precious in our lives.

In these pages, I have tried to describe some of the experiences which for me have reached this deepest level, and which remain there. I cannot tell them all, some can never be put into words, but I carry them all with me as pledges to love, to faith and to beauty.

Because of this, after all that has happened – the loss, the gain, the effort, the failure, the hope, the despair – I can still feel, as I did long ago climbing Ben Nevis, that life must be answered with an affirmation.

The dark and the light threads weave together into a pattern beyond our making. When the time comes to see not 'through a glass darkly' but indeed 'face to face', we shall know that every arc is completed in a rounded whole, and that no fragment has been lost.

Index